OPINION WRITING

OPINION WRITING

By

A. Dash

DISCOVERY PUBLISHING HOUSE PVT. LTD.
NEW DELHI-110002

Reprinted - 2019

First Published - 2009

ISBN: 978-81-8356-432-8

Opinion Writing

Published by:

DISCOVERY PUBLISHING HOUSE PVT. LTD.
4383/4B, Ansari Road, Darya Ganj
New Delhi-110 002 (India)
Phone: +91-11-23279245, 23253475; 43596065
E-mail: discoverybooksindia@gmail.com
discoverypublishinghouse@gmail.com
web: www.discoverypublishinggroup.com

Printed at:
Infinity Imaging Systems
Delhi

Contents

Preface

Opinion writing is an important and interesting job in our day-to-day life. In periodicals, particularly, weeklies, fortnightlies and monthlies, there is a column under the head of 'Letters to the Editor', or 'Editor's Mail' or 'Letters', or 'Readers' Views', etc. The columns are specifically set for readers, to which they send their views about the contents of the concerned magazine or newspaper. Not only this, readers also contribute their thoughtful and insightful writings to the periodicals, concerning current and significant issues of national and international importance.

The articles, dispatched to the editor, contain sometimes appreciatory matter; sometimes critical and analytical and sometimes appreciatory-cum-critical. Also, they may contain some very useful suggestions for the improvement.

While writing some opinion piece; certain points have to be taken into consideration. First and foremost thing is that one should be unprejudiced and the intent behind writing must be honest and not degrading. Before writing, the topic under consideration, should be well read and analysed. Points of suggestion or analysis should be in a well-knit, clear and easy style, so that the intended purpose may be served.

Though, there are lot of books on this subject, demand for more enhanced and comprehensive work keeps arising, from the concerned quarters. Hence, this endeavour.

For further improvement, readers are invited to send their just opinion.

Pattern of Expression

Shakespeare knew the value of a name. In *Othello* he says, "But he that filches from me my good name/Robs me of that which not enriches him/And makes me poor indeed." A name misspelled in a person misidentified. Of all the errors a newspaper is capable of making, one of the most serious is a misspelled or a misused name. In radio and television it is the mispronounced name.

Extraordinary Factors

Reporters and copy-editors have no business playing doctor, If a child is injured in an accident, the seriousness of the injury should be determined by medical authorities. To say that a person who was not even admitted to the hospital was "Seriously injured" is editorialising.

Hospitals may report that a patient is in a "guarded condition," but the term has no meaning for the reader and should be spiked. The same goes for "he is resting comfortably."

No one can sustain a "fractured leg." He may suffer a *fracture of the leg* or a *leg fracture* or *better still,* simply a *broken leg. Injuries are suffered, not received.*

A story described a murder suspect as "a diabetic of the worst type who must have 15 units of insulin daily." The quotes were attributed to the FBI. An editor commented, "In my book, that is a mild diabetic, unless the story means that the suspect is a diabetic who requires 15 units of regular insulin before each meal. A wire service should not rely on the FBI for diagnosis of diabetes and the severity of the case."

The name of the doctor can be used in a medical news story under these circumstances:

1. If he is the attending physician to a prominent person, such as a governor.
2. If he is the officially designated spokesman for his medical society.
3. If his medical society has furnished his name as one from whom authoritative information may be obtained in his speciality and he has consented to the use of his name.
4. If he is an official, such as a state epidemiologist, the doctor is treated the same as any other individual in the news.

Doctor and Scientist are vague words to many readers. *Doctor* may be a medical doctor, a dentist, a veterinarian, an osteopath, a minister or a professor. The story would be clearer if it named the doctor's speciality or the scientist's specific activity, whether biology, physics, electronics or astronautics.

Medical doctors diagnose the illness, not the patient. The proper term to use in determining the remedy or in forecasting the probable course and termination of a disease is *prognosis.*

Mothers *delivery;* babies are born.

Everyone has a heart condition. It is news only if someone's heart is in bad condition.

"The wife of the governor underwent major surgery and physicians reported she apparently had been cured of a malignant tumour." It is unlikely that any doctor said she was *cured* of a malignant tumour. They avoid that word with malignant growths.

> "A team of five surgeons performed a hysterectomy, appendectomy and complete abdominal exploration." Why the unnecessary details? It would have been enough to say, "Five surgeons performed the abdominal operation."

Unless they are essential to the story, trade names of narcotics or poisons should be avoided. If a person dies of an overdose of sleeping pills, the story should not specify the number of pills

Also, *use Caesarean section or Caesarean operation.*

Usually, no sane person has his leg broken or his pockets picked. Use the passive tense: "His leg was broken;" "His pockets were picked."

Use the expression *physicians and dentists,* not *doctors and dentists.* The second suggests that dentist are not doctors.

A doctor who specialises in anaesthesia is an anaesthesiologist, not an anaesthetist.

A person may wear a sling on his right arm. He doesn't wear his right arm in a sling.

"He suffered a severed tendon in his right Achilles' heel last winter". It was the Achilles' tendon in his right heel or his right Achilles' tendon.

"A jaundice epidemic also was spreading in Gaya, Indian health officials said. The second disease claimed 30 lives." Jaundice is not a disease but a sign of the existence of one or another of a great many diseases.

Technical terms should be translated.

Term	*Translation*	*Term*	*Translation*
Abrasions	Scrapes	Suturing	Sewing
Contusions	Bruises	Haemorrhaging	Bleeding
Lacerations	Cuts	Obese	Fat
Fracture	Break	Respire	Breathe

An editor said, "Ever since the National Weather Service started naming hurricanes alter females, reporters can't resist the temptation to be cute." He then cited the lead, "Hilda — never a lady and now no longer a hurricane — spent the weekend in Louisiana, leaving behind death, destruction and misery." Thai, the editor said, is giddy treatment for a disaster causing thirty-five deaths and millions in property damage.

Another editor noted that a story referred to "the turbulent eye of giant storm." He remonstrated that the eye of the hurricane is the dead-calm centre.

A story predicted that a hurricane was headed for Farmington and was expected to cause millions of dollars in damages. So the Farmington merchants boarded their windows, the tourists cancelled their reservations – and the hurricane went around Farmington. This is the trouble when an editor lets a reporter expand a prediction into a warning.

The headline *Freeze tonight expected/ to make driving hazardous* was based on this lead: "Freezing temperatures forecast for tonight may lead to a continuation of hazardous driving conditions as a result of last night's snow and freezing rain." The story made no mention of anyone's saying there would still be dampness on the ground when freezing temperatures arrived. There wasn't and driving was unimpeded.

A lead said, "One word, 'miserable,' was the US weatherman's description today of the first day of spring." The head was *Snow predicted/It's spring, miserable.* It was the weatherman's prediction, not his description. The sun stayed out all day, the clouds stayed away, and readers of the paper must have wondered where this US weatherman was located.

Temperatures can become higher or lower, not "cooler" or "warmer."

On flood stories, the copy should tell where the flood water came from and where it will run off. The expression *flash flood* is either a special term for a rush of water let down a weir to permit passage of a boat or a sudden destructive rush of water down a narrow gully or over a sloping in surface in desert regions, caused by heavy rains in the mountains or foothills. It is often used loosely for any sudden gush of water.

Weather stories, more than most other, have an affinity for the cliche, the fuzzy image, overwriting, mixed metaphors, contrived similes and sundry other absurdities.

> "A Houdini snow did some tricks yesterday that left most of the state shivering from a spine-tingling

storm." Houdini gained fame as an escape artist, not as an ordinary magician. Did the snow escape, or was it just a tricky snow? After the lead, the twenty-two-inch story never mentioned the angle again, Spine-tingling means full suspense or uncertainty or even terror. Sports writers are fond of using it to describe a close game, called a heart stopper by more ecstatic writers, often in conjunction with a gusty performance. If a cliche must-be used, a very cold' storm is spine-chilling; not "spine-tingling."

"Old Man Winter yesterday stretched his icy fingers and dumped a blanket of snow on the state." How would reporters ever write about the weather without Old Man Winter, Jack Frost, Ice Fingers and Old Sol? Why do rain and show never fall? They are always "dumped."

"Atleast two persons were killed in yesterday's snowstorm, marked at times by blizzard-like gales of wind." By Weather Service standards, this is an exaggeration and a contradiction. By any standard, it is a redundancy. A blizzard is one thing. Gales are something else. Gales of wind? What else, unless may be it was gales of laughter from discerning readers.

An editor's moral: Good colourful writing is to be encouraged. But a simply written story with no gimmicks is better than circus writing that goes awry. To quote a champion image-maker, Shakespeare, in *Sonnet 94,* "Lilies that fester smell far worse than weeds." The writer who plants the festering lilies is only a little more guilty than the copy-editor who lets' them grow. They have a way of reproducing.

Blizzard are hard to define because wind and temperatures may vary. The safe way is to avoid calling a snowstorm a *blizzard* unless the Weather Service describes it as sudi Generally, a blizzard occurs when there are winds of 35 m.p.h. or more that whip falling snow or snow already on the ground and when the temperatures are 20 degrees above zero Fahrenheit, or lower.

A severe blizzard has winds than: are 45 m.p.h. or more, temperatures 10 degrees above zero or lower,, and great density of snow either falling or whipped from the ground.

The Weather Service insists that ice storms are not sleet. Sleet is frozen raindrops. The service uses the terms ire *storm, freezing, rain and freezing drizzle* to warm the public when a coating of ice is expected on the ground.

A cyclone is a storm with heavy rain and winds rotating about a moving centre of low atmospheric pressure.

A hurricane has winds above 75 m.p.h.

A typhoon is a violent cyclonic storm or a hurricane occurring in the China Seas and adjacent regions, chiefly from July to October.

The word *Chinook* should not be used unless so designated by the Weather Service.

Temperatures are measured by various scales. Zero degree centigrade is freezing, and 100 degree centigrade is boiling. On the Fahrenheit scale, 32 degrees is freezing, and 212 degrees (at sea level) is boiling. On the Kelvin scale, 273 degrees is freezing, and 373 degrees is boiling. To convert degrees centigrade to Fahrenheit, multiply the centigrade measurement by nine-fifths and add 32. To convert degrees Fahrenheit to centigrade, subtract 32 from the Fahrenheit measurement and multiply by five-ninths. Thus, 10 degrees centigrade is 50 degrees Fahrenheit. To convert degrees Kelvin to centigrade degrees, subtract 273 from the Kelvin reading.

Weather Cliches

Fog rolled (crept or crawled) in	Mercury dropped
Jupiter Pluvius	(dipped, zoomed, plummeted)
Fog-shrouded city	Rain failed to dampen
Winds aloft	Hurricane howled
Biting (bitter) cold	Storm-tossed
Hail-splattered	

Conjecturing about possible damage to settlements from forest fires is as needless as conjectures on weather damage. The story should concentrate on the definite loss. Stories of forest fires should give the specific area burned, the area threatened and the type of timber.

Most stories of earthquake attempts to describe the magnitude of the tremor. One measurement is the Richter scale, which show relative magnitude. It starts with magnitude 1 and progresses in units with each unit ten times stronger than the previous-unit. Thus, magnitude 3 is ten times stronger than magnitude 2, which, in turn, is ten times stronger than magnitude 1. On this scale the strongest earthquakes recorded were the South American earthquake of 1906 and the Japanese earthquake of 1933, both at a magnitude of 8.9. Intensity generally refers to the duration or to the damage caused by the shock.

In train and plane Crashes the story should include train or flight number, the place of departure, the destination and times of departure and expected arrival, "Passenger train" is adequate, "Crack passenger train" is a cliche. Airplanes may collide on the ground or in the air (not "midair"). Let investigators *search* the wreckage not "comb" or "sift" it.

In fire stories, the sad truth is that in nine of ten cases when somebody is "led to safety," they're not. Except for an occasional small child, they simply have the common sense to beat it without waiting for a fireman to "lead them to safety."

In both fire and flood stories the residents of the area are rarely taken from their homes or asked to leave. Instead, they're always told to "evacuate" or they're "evacuated." What's wrong with *vacate?*

Eliminate terms such as *three-alarmfire* and *second-degree burns.* "An estimated $ 40,000 worth of damage was done Jan. 29... Damage isn't worth anything. Quite the contrary."

"The full tragedy of Hurricane Betsy unfolded today as the death toll rose past 50 and damages soared into many millions." *Damage* was the correct word here. You collect *damages* in court.

Disaster Cliches

Rampaging Rivers

Weary firefighters

Fiery holocaust

Flames licked (leaped, swept)

Searing heat

Tinder-dry forest

Raging brush fire

Traffic fatals or triple fatals (police station jargon)

Labour Disputes: Stories of labour controversies should give the reasons for the dispute, how long the strike has been in progress and the claims by both the union and the company.

Copy-editors should be on guard against wrong or loaded terms. Examples: In a closed shop the employer may hire only men already members of the union. In a union shop, the employer may select his employees but the workers are required to join the union within a specified time after starting work. A conciliator or mediator in a labour dispute merely recommends terms of a settlement. The decision of an arbitrator is binding. There is a tendency in labour stories to refer to management proposals as "offers " and to labour proposals as "demands." The correct word should be used for the correct connotation.

Strikebreaker and *scab* have no place in the report if used to describe men or women who act as individuals in accepting positions vacated by strikers. The expression "honoured the picket line" frequently appears in the report even though a more accurate expression is "refused (or declined) to cross a picket line."

Union leader is usually preferred to *labour leader. A* longshore man is a waterfront leader. A stevedore usually is considered an employee.

On estimates of wages or production lost, the story should have authoritative sources, not street-corner guesses. An individual, however voluble, does not speak for the majority unless he has been authorised to do so. Statements by workers or by minor officials should be played down until they are documented.

If a workers gets a 10 cent an hour increase effective immediately, an additional 10 cents a year hence and another 10 cents the third year, he does not receive a 30 cent an hour increase. His increase at the time of settlement is still 10 cents an hour. "The company has been on strike for the last 25 days." No. The employees are on strike. The company has been struck.

Criminal court terms should not be applied to labour findings unless the dispute has been taken to a criminal court. The National Labour Relations Board is not a court, and its findings or recommendations should not be expressed in criminal court terminology. In most settlements, neither side is "found guilty" or "fined." A finding or a determination may be made or a penalty may be assessed.

Financial News: A news release from a bank included the following: "The book value of each share outstanding will approximate $ 21.87 on Dec. 31, and if the current yield of 4.27 per cent continues to bear the same relationship to the market price it should rise to $ 32 or $ 33, according to..." The copy-editor changed the ambiguous *it to the book value.* Actually, the release intended *it* to refer to the market price, which shows what can happen when copy-editors change copy without knowing what they are doing.

Another story quoted an oil company official as saying that "the refinery would mean $ 7,000,000 in additional real estate taxes." It should have been obvious that this was a wholly unrealistic figure, but for good measure there was an ad in the same paper that placed the total tax figure at around $ 200,000 and said "The initial installation will add about $ 7,000,000 a year to the economy of the state, not including taxes."

A story and headline said the interest on the state debt accounted for 21 per cent of the state government's spending. An accompanying graph showed, however, that the figure was for debt service, which includes both interest and amortisation.

All who edit copy for financial pages should have atleast some elementary knowledge of business terms. If they can't distinguish between a balance sheet and a profit and loss statement, between earnings and gross operating income, and between' a net profit and net cash income, they have some homework to do.

This was brought home by a syndicated financial columnist who cautioned business news desks against using misleading headlines such as *Stocks plummet – Dow Jones average off 12 points.* It may be a loss, the columnist noted, but hardly a calamity. Dow Jones may indicate that the market is up, whereas it is actually sinking. Freak gains by a few of the thirty stocks in the Dow may have pushed up that particular indicator. Nor does a slight market drop call for a headline such as a *Inventors loss millions in market value of stocks.* They lost nothing of the sort. On that day, countless investors the nation over had substantial paper profits on their stocks. If they sold, they were gainers on the buying price in real terms; if they held, they had neither gains nor losses.

The Dow Jones Industrial Average is one of several indexes used to gauge the stock market. Each uses its own statistical technique to show market changes. The Dow Jones bases its index on thirty stock. It is an index number change, not a percentage change.

Reports of dividends should use the designation given by the firm (regular, special, extra, increases, interim) and show what was paid previously if there is no specified designation such as regular or quarterly.

The story should say if there is a special, or extra, dividend paid with the regular dividend and include the amount of previous added payments. When the usual dividend is passed, or reduced, some firms issue an explanatory statement, the gist of which should be included in the story.

Newswire stylebooks recommend that news of corporate activities and business and financial news should be stripped of technical terms. There should be some explanation of the firm's business (plastics, rubber, electronics) if there is no indication of the nature of the business in the firms's name. The location of the firm should be carried.

Savings and loan firms object to being called banks. Some commercial banks likewise object when savings and loan firms are called banks. There need be no confusion if the institution is identified by its proper name. In subsequent references the words *firm or institution* are used. Some newspapers permit *S & L Firm* in tight headlines. Actually a *firm* is a partnership or unincorporated group. It should not be used for an incorporated company. *Concern* is a better word for the latter.

Jargon has no place in the business story, "Near-term question marks in the national economy – either of which could put a damper on the business expansion – are residential housing and foreign bade, the Northern Trust company said in its December issue of *Business Comments.*" Are near-term question marks economy question marks? If so, can they put a damper on anything? Isn't all housing residential?

Major producers scrambled today to adjust steel prices to newly-emerging industrywide patterns... . The welter of price changes was in marked contrast with the old time industry practice of posting across-the-board hikes.

This approach apparently breathed its last in April, 1962 when it ran into a Kennedy administration buzzsaw, and a general price boost initiated then by United States Steel Corporation, the industry giant collapsed under White House Fire.

Readers of financial pages read for information. False colour is not needed to retain these readers. The following story should have freely butchered on die desk:

> Stock of the Communications Satellite Corporation went into : an assigned orbit yesterday on three major stock exchanges, rocketing to an apogee of $ 46 a share and a perigee of $ 42 '.' and closing at $ 42.37, unchanged.

It was the first day of listed trading on the exchanges. The stock previously was traded over the counter.

The countdown on the first transaction on the New York stock exchange was delayed 12 minutes by an initial jam of buy and sell orders...

Percentages: Two types of errors appear frequently in stories dealing with percentages. One is the failure to distinguish between percentage., and percentage points; the other lies in comparing the change with the new figure rather than the original one. For example, when a: tax rate is increased from $5 per $ 100 assessed valuation to $ 5.50, the increase is 10 per cent, New figure less old figure, divided by

$$\$5.50 - \$5; = \frac{50}{\$5} = .10 \text{ or } 10 \text{ per cent.}$$

"Jones pointed out that the retail markup for most other brands is approximately 33 per cent, whereas the markup on Brand is 50 per cent, or 17 per cent higher/" No. It is 17 percentage points higher but 51.5 per cent higher,. Divide 17 by 33.

"Dover's metropolitan population jumped from 16,000 ten years ago to more than 23,000 last year, an increase of better than 70 per cent." Wrong again. It's a little less than 44 per cent.

Is the figure misleading or inaccurate? The story said, "A total of $6,274 was raised at each of the four downtown stations." This adds up to $ 25,096. What was meant was that "A total of $ 6,274 was raised at four stations." A not-so-sharp copy-editor let this one get by: "Almost 500,000 slaves were shipped in this interstate trade. When one considers the average price of $800, the trade accounted for almost $20 million."

Are terms representing figures vague? In inheritance stories, it is better to name the amount and let the reader decide whether the amount is a "fortune." One of the wire service editors noted, "Fifteen thousand might be a fortune to a bootblack, but $200,000 would not be a fortune to a Rockefeller."

For some reason, many stories contain gambling odds, chances and probabilities. When a princess gave birth to a son, reporters quickly snatched on to the odds on his name. Anthony was 1:2, George was even money and Albert was 3:1. One headline played up the third in the betting. The name chosen was David, an 18:1 shot. All of this shows the foolishness of newsmen who play into the hands of gamblers. If odds must be included in the story, they should be accurate. The story said that because weather records showed that in the last eighty-six years it had rained only nineteen times on May 27, the odds were 8:1 against rain for the big relay event. The odds mean nothing to readers except to those who like to point out that in the story just mentioned the odds actually were:

"Dr. Frank Rubovits said the children came from a single egg He said the chance of this occurring 'probably is about 3 million to 1," He meant the odds against this occurring. The chance of this occurring is 1 in 3 million.

"The Tarapur plant will be the world's second largest atomic generator of electricity. The largest will be the 500-ton mega watt plant at Hinkley Point in Britain." A 500-ton megawatt plant makes no sense. What the writer meant was a 500-mega watt plant.

Some readers may rely on the idiom and insist that "five times as much as" means the same as "five times higher than" or "five times more than." If so, five times as much as $50 is $ 250 and five times higher than $50 is still $250. Others contend that the second should be $300. If earnings this year are 3½ times as large as last year's, they are actually 2½ times larger than last year's.

Insist on this style: 40,000 to 50,000 miles, not 40 to 50,000 miles; $3 million to $5 million, not $3 to $5 million.

"The committee recommended that a bid of $ 26,386.60 be accepted. After recommending the higher bid, the committee also had to recommended that an additional $326.60 be appropriated for the fire truck, since only $26,000 was included in the budget." The sum is still $60 short of a bid.

Equivalents should be included in stories that contain large sums. Most readers cannot visualise $20 billion, but they can understand it if there is an indication as to how much the amount would mean to each individual.

Here is an editor's advice to the staff:

> We can do a service for those important people out there if we use terms they are most acquainted with. For example, to most of our readers a ton of come is more easily visualised if; it is reported as bushels, about 36 in this case. We normally report yields and prices in bushels and that is the measurement most readers know. The same goes for petroleum; barrels is probably more recognisable than tons. When the opportunity presents itself, translate the figures into the best-known measurement.

Nothing is duller or more unreadable than a numbers story. If figures are the important part of the story, they should be related to something – or atleast presented as comparisons.

Two of the most common mathematical errors in news copy are the use of millions for billions and vice-versa and a construction such as "Five were injured... " with only four persons listed.

Ships and Boats: Belay using nautical terms unless they're used properly, "Capt. Alberts Kolly, the 75-year-old pilot, who manned lite Delia JueenX tiller yesterday...". What he manned was her *helm or her wheel.* Few vessels except sailboats are guided with a tiler.

A story referred to a 27-foot ship. Nothing as small as 27 feet is a *ship. Ship* refers to big seagoing vessels such as tankers, freighters and ocean liners. Sailors insist that if it can be hoisted onto another craft it is a boat and that if it is too large for that it is a ship. Specific terms such as *cabin cruiser, sloop, schooner, barge and dredge* are appropriate.

"A rescue fleet ranging from primitive by you pirogues to helicopters prowled through the night," That should send the copy editor to a dictionary so he can explain to readers that a pirogue is a canoe or a dugout.

"The youths got to the pier just before the gangplank was lowered." When a ship sails, the gangplan is *raised.*

Commercial ships are measured by volume, the measurement of all enclosed space on the ship being expressed in units of 100 cubic feet to the ton. Fuller description gives passenger capacity, length, age, and so on. Naval vessels are expressed in tonnage, the weight in long tons of a ship and all its contents (called displacement). A long ton is 2,240 pounds. All this is "Greek" to many readers. Copy-editors should translate into terms recognised by readers, who can visualise length, age and firing power more readily than tonnage: "The 615-foot Bradley, longer than two football fields..."

A knot is a measure of speed, not distance (nautical miles an hour). A nautical mile is about 1 – land miles. "Knots per hour" is redundant.

Some readers may understand when the story says, "The limestone carrier was enroute home in ballast," All will understand if the story says simply that the ship was enroute home empty.

Some of the best writings in American newspapers appears in the sports pages. So does some of the worst.

Many of the weaknesses could be minimised if sports copy were submitted to a universal desk for editing or if the sports copydesk were permitted to edit for all readers – the women, the teenagers and those with only a lukewarm interest in sports, as well as the sports experts. Too often, the sports copydesk permits the abuses of sports copy and magnifies the excesses.

Sports pages should be, and are, the liveliest in the paper. They have action photos, a melange of spectator and participant sports and an array of personalities. Sports writers have more latitude than do other reporters. The good ones are among the best in the business; the undisciplined ones are among the worst.

Attractive pages and free expression meant little if the sports section is unintelligible to half the paper's readers. Too often, the editing reflects the attitude that if readers don't understand the lingo they should seek elsewhere in the paper for information and entertainment.

The potential for readers of the sports section is greater than ever because of the growing number of participants in golf, bowling, fishing, boating and tennis. The spectator sports, especially automobile racing, football, golf, basketball, baseball and hockey, attract great audiences, thanks to the vast number of television viewers. Thus the sports pages, if edited intelligently, can become the most appealing section in the paper; But first, writers and copy-editors must improve their manners.

A report of a contest or struggle should appeal to readers if, it is composed in straightforward, clear, honest English. The style can be vigorous without being forced, honest without being awesome. Sports fans do not need the fillips to keep their awesome. Sports fans do not need the fillips to keep their interest whetted. Those who are only mildly interested won't become sports page regulars if the stories are not understandable.

Know the Game: One of the elementary rules in sports writing is to tell the reader the name of the game. Yet many stories talk about the Cubs and Pirates but never say specifically that the contest is a baseball *per cent>:* game. Some writers assume that if the story refers to the contest a "dribble derby " all sports page readers must understand that the story concerns a basketball game.

The story may contain references to parts of the game yet never mention the specific game.

Here is an example.

Three teams tied for low at 59 in the sweepstakes division as the 11 to annual Sliceroo got under way Thursday at Lakewood County Club

Deadlocked at 59 were the team of...

In the driving contest, it was...

In the putting and chipping contest...

A best ball is set for Friday and a low net for Saturday, final day of the Sliceroo. A $5,000 hole-in-one competition on the 124-yard 11th hole is set for both final days.

Golfers will understand this story. But non-golfers, even many who enjoy watching golf matches on television, should be told outright that the story concerns a golf tournament. The added information would not offend the golfers. It might encourage a non-golfer to read on.

Some stories fail to state categorically who played whom. Again, the writer assumes that if he names the opponents managers, all hard-core sports readers will recognise the contestants. Perhaps so, but the general reader might like to know too. The legend under a two-column cut read, "They cant' believe their eyes. Coach Andy S — , left, and Manager May S — , right, showed disbelief and disgruntlement as the Braves belt Pitcher Don C — for five runs in the eighth inning of their exhibition baseball game. Wednesday at Clearwater, Fla. The Braves won, 10-2." Now, whom did the Braves play?

Not all readers understand the technical terms used to describe a sports contest. It might be necessary to explain that a seeded team gets a favoured placement in the first round, and that if Smith beats Jones 2-1 in match play it means that golfer Smith is two holes ahead of golfer Jones with only one hole left to play and is, therefore, the winner. The name of the sport should be used in reference to the various cups. The Davis Cup is an international trophy for men tennis players. The Heisman Trophy is an award presented annually to the most outstanding college football player in the nation. America's Cup refers to yachting, and Americas Cup to golfing. Technically, it is *All America,* not "All-American."

Unanswered Questions: Answering more questions is one way to win more readers for the sports department. The key questions frequently overlooked are how and why. Why did the coach decide to punt on fourth down instead of trying to make one foot for a first down? How does a tournament get the funds to award $200,000 in prizes?

"The shadow of tragedy drew a black edge around a golden day at Sportsman's park yesterday, bringing home the danger of horse racing with an impact that cut through the $68,950 Illinois Derby like a spotlight in darkness," So, what happened?

The best training for copy-editors or the sports desk is a stint on the news copydesk. But before they go on the sports desk they should become familiar with the intricacies of all sports so they can catch the technical errors in sports copy. Here are examples:

> "Centre fielder Tony Cafar, whose fine relay after chasing the ball 'a country mile', held Ripley to a triple." Unless Tony also made a throw of "a country mile," another player, the shortstop , or second baseman, made the relay throw after taking a good throw from Tony.

When a writer covering a basketball game refers to a "foul shot," his reference should be nailed on the sports desk rim. The fouled player gets a free throw from the free-throw line, not the foul line or the charity lane.

The copy-editors also has to be alert for some of the wild flights' of imagination used by sports, writers. "The Tar Heels hurdled their last major obstacle on the way to an unbeaten season but still had a long row to hoe." Is this a track meet or a country fair?

The following passage is a sure way to discourage sports page reader:

> Kanicki's troubles in yesterday's 27-c factory over the Dallas Cowboys before 72,062, largest crowd ever to see the Texans, was the reason. Gain was in the trenches to receive a shattering kick with 6:24 left in the game.,

This example suggests another tendency in sports copy — turning the story into a numbers game. Box scores, league standings and records have a place in the sports story, but generally they should have a subordinate rather' than a dominant role. It i questionable whether gambling odds or the role of gambles shoul be used in either the story or the headline. Such intrusion often comes in races with their extra special payoffs.

Abbreviated Sports: The addiction for abbreviation is strong in both sports copy and headlines. *Broncos get first AFL win over NFL* announces a headline. It means that Denver's professional football team scored the first victory of an American Football League team over a National Football League team.

The seventh paragraph of a story referred to NPSA. The reader, if he was interested, had to reread the lead to know that the initials stand for National Professional Soccer League.

An editor told his colleagues, "There is nothing more exciting than a good contest. There is nothing duller than reading about it the next day." Yet many spectators who watch a Saturday contest can't wait to read about it the next morning. What were the coach's and player's reaction to the game? What was the turning point? How long was the pass that won the game? What's the reporter's comment on the crowd's behaviour?

This should argue that if there is an audience for the report of a contest, the story needs no special flourishes. Loaded terms such as "wily mentor," genial bossman, "vaunted running game," "dazzling run" and "astute field general" add little or nothing to the report. Adjectives lend false colour. The Associated Press reported a "vise-tight race," "the red-hot Cardinals" and the "torrid 13-4 pace" as if these modifies were needed to lure readers.

If all copy-editors were permitted to aim their pencils at copy submitted by the prima dogmas of the sports world, there would be no sentence structures like the following ones: "Benny (Kid) Paret showed 'very slight improvement' in his battle for life today while his embittered manager branded the New York State Athletic Commission's report absolving Referee Ruby Goldstein of blame for the boxer's condition as a whitewash."

"Maris, who has been bothered by a sore rib this spring, played eight innings yesterday, collected two singles and drove in a run." He didn't collect them; he hit them.

"Oritiz threw his first bomb in the second round when he nailed Laguna with a left and right to the jaw." How can you nail something with a bomb?

"Left-hander Norman, who started on the mound for Chicago, recovered from a shaky start and pitched six-hit ball for eight innings before a walk and a botched-up double play caused Manager Bob Kennedy to protect a 4 to 1 lead, as a result of a three-run homer by Ernie Banks in the seventh." The sentence is hard to understand because it is overstuffed and because the facts are not told in chronological order. Revised: "Left-hander Norman started on the mound for Chicago. He recovered from shaky start and pitched six-hit ball for eight innings. Then a walk and a missed double play caused Manager Bob Kennedy to bring in a new pitcher. Chicago was leading, 4 to 1 as a result of a three-run homer by Ernie Banks in the seventh."

Here is how to tell a story upside down: "Waldrop's 17 yard explosions for high eighth touchdown of the season punctuated a 65 yard march from Army's reception of the kickoff by a courageous Falcon team which had gone ahead for the second time in the game, 10 to 7, in the ninth minute of final period."

An overstuffed sentence of any sort will be just as damaging and harder to repair, than compound sentence leads. Note this one: 'The heaviest betting non-holiday Monday crowd in the Balmoral Jockey club's eight years at Washington Park poured $ 1,066,919 into the machines yesterday on a nine-race programme headed by the $ 7,500 Harvey purse, a six-furlong dash which drew six starters and was won by Mighty Fenriec, piloted by Bill Hartack" Revised: "Horse-race fans put $1,066,919 into the Washington Park machines yesterday on arrhae-race programme.

It was the heaviest betting non-holiday Monday crowd in the Balmoral Jockey club's eight years at the park. The $7,500 Harvey purse for the six-furlong race drew six starters. It was won by Mighty Fennec, ridden by Bill Hartack."

"Statistics don't tell the story," he explained, "looking many straight in the eye." If he looked more than one person straight in the eyes while he said that, he must have been a long time between words.

It takes some editing to convert sports writers into Homers and Hemingways. At least, though, copy-editors can try to help writers improve their way of telling a story.

Copy-editors can excise cliches such as "pay dirt," "turned the tables," "hammered (or slammed) a homerun," "big eight hardwoods," "circuit clout," "gridder," "hoopster," "thin dads," "tanksters," "sweet revenge," "rocky road," "free loads" (foul shots), "droughts" (losing streaks), "standing-room-only crowds," "put a cap on the basket," "as the seconds ticked off the clock," "unblemished records," "paced the team," "outclassed but game," "roared from behind," "sea of mud," "vaunted defence," "coveted trophy" and "last-ditch effort."

They can insist on the correct word. Boxers may have *altercations* (oral) with their managers. They have *fights* with other boxers.

They can tone down exaggerated expressions like "mighty atom of the ring," "destiny's distance man" or "Northwestern comes off tremendous effort Monday" (Northwestern tried hard). They can cut out redundancy in phrases like "with 30,000 spectators looking on."

They can resist the temptation to use synonyms for the verbs *win, beats and defeats:* annihilates, atomises, bayyers, belts, bests, blanks, blasts, boots home, clips, clobbers, cops, crushes, downs, drops, dumps, edges, ekes out, gallops over, gangs up on gouges, gets past, H-bombs, halts, humiliates, impales, laces, lashes, lassoes, licks, murders, outslugs, outscraps, orbits, over comes, paces, pastes, pins, racks up, rallies, rolls over, ramps over, routs, scores, sets back, shades, shaves, sinks, slows, snares, spanks, squeaks by, squeezes by, stampedes, stomps, stops, subdues, surges, sweeps, tops, topples, triggers, trips, trounces, troubles, turns back, vanquishes, wallops, whips, whomps and wrecks.

They will let the ball be *hit,* not always banged, bashed, belted, blooped, bombed, boomed, bumped, chopped, clunked, clouted, conked, cracked, dribbled, drilled, dropped, driven, hacked, knifed lashed, lined, plastered, plunked, poked, pooped, pumped, punched, pummeled, pushed, rapped, ripped, rocked, slapped, sliced, slugged, smashed, spilled, spanked, stubbed, swatted, tagged, tapped, tipped, topped, trickled, whipped, whistled, whomped and whooped.

They will let a bill be *thrown* and only occasionally tossed, twirled, fired and hurled.

They will let a ball be *kicked,* occasionally punted and never toed or booted.

They will resist the shopworn puns; Birds (Eagles, Orioles, Cardinals) soar or claw; Lions (Tigers, Bears, Cubs) roar, claw or lick: Braves (Tribesmen, Indians) scalp or tomhawk; Mustangs (Colts, Broncos) buck, gallop, throw or kick.

They will insist on neutrality in all sports copy, avoiding "home policy" slanting.

They will not make verbs out of nouns: "AP – Chicago manager Eddie Stanky non-chalanted the White Sox strike-breaker, saying, *My food's going to taste the same...*".

They will not string modifiers endlessly: "UPI – The Pistons won 29 and lost 40 under the guidance of the then only 24 years old Dubusschere."

Society: One of the brighter changes in newspapers has been the transformation of the society pages, with their emphasis on club and cupid items, to the Women's section or the family section with a broader-based appeal. The philosophy of the new approach has-been well expressed by two editors:

Pages of the Women's Section are edited not for the ladies who write the stories, not for the ladies who are the source of the stories and not for gruff voice of the advertising department. They're edited for the people who buy the paper. Women's pages were formerly edited for the few. Now the pages appeal to the woman as mother and working girl and as an intelligent human being involved in the total society. Such sections still carry engagement announcement and wedding stories, but their added fare is foods, fashions, finance, health, education, books and other cultural affairs. They are edited for active women in all ranks, not solely for those in the top rank of society. They also are edited for the increasing number of men readers.

The better editors regard readers of the women's section as alert individuals who are concerned with problems such as prostitution, racism, civil disorders, women's prisons, alcoholism among housewives and educational reforms. Such editors strive to make their pages informative as well as entertaining.

Improvements are likely to continue. Some executives argue that newspapers should not segregate women, that material of special interests to the family should be scattered throughout the paper. Some maintain the club and social news should be held to a minimum because of low reader appeal. Others argue that the pre-occupation with foods, fashions and furnishings squeezes out important items of women's activity. A quarter of a page devoted to a picture of a cherry pie might be trimmed a bit to accommodate a good story.

Some papers now handle engagements, weddings and births as court of record items. And a few charge for engagements and wedding stories and pictures unless the event is obviously news, such as the wedding of the President's daughter.

To add some spice to its pages devoted to wedding accounts, the Gannett Rochester Newspapers started a "Wedding Scrapbook" page to its Saturday section, "Brides Book for Greater Rochester."

Included are features on how the couple met, amusing incidents of the participants on the way to the ceremony, pictures of the couple in faraway places.

In many daily newspapers, especially the medium-sized and smaller ones, reports of engagement and wedding will perish slowly, if they will die at all. Still, some conventions may change — such as giving the bridegroom a break for a change. The point was delightfully argued by Paul Brookshire in his column in the South Dade (Homestead, Fla.) *New Leader,* and reprinted in *The Quill* (October, 1967). Here are some excerpts:

> In these days when the world is quaking in its boots and news of great significance is daily swept into newspaper trash cans for lack of space, it is sickening to read paragraph after paragraph about some little girl changing HER name to HIS. The groom? He apparently wasn't dressed at all...if he was even there. But Mother and Mother-in-law? Yes. They were fashion plates in beige ensembles and matching accessories or something. I ask you. Is it a wedding or a fashion show? If it is a fashion show, why isn't

it held in a hotel ballroom and why isn't the groom given a tiny bit of credit for the showing up with his clothes on?

The blackout of the bridegroom in wedding accounts is an unpardonable sin. If the groom is mentioned at all he is afforded as much space as an atheist gets on the church page. And pictures. Did you ever see a photograph of a bridegroom? May be in the Post Office but not in the newspaper. I'm going on record right now in favour of wedding announcements being run as legal notices – payable in advance by the father of the bride.

Better still, if the bride insists on giving a minute, detailed description of every inch of clothing she happens to have on her person, I suggest she take out a paid display advertisement. In this manner, trade names may be used and shops that sold the girl all her glorious gear could get equal space on the same page.

Newspapers would reap untold profits from this arrangement and readers might be able to get some world news for a change instead of bouffant skirts highlighted with tiers of lace and aqua frocks with aqua tipped orchids and maize silk linen; ensembles with... whatever you wear with maize silk linen ensembles.

Even though many newspapers have refined the society section, some retain a static style, especially on engagement and wedding stories. Wedding story leads usually read like these: First Methodist Church in Littleton was the setting for the double-ring wedding rites of blank and blank.

Miss Blank has become the bride of Blank, it was announced by her parents, etc.

After a wedding trip to Las Vegas, Nevada, Mr. and Mrs. Blank will live in...

All Saints Roman Catholic Church was the setting for the single-ring rites.

Newspapers continue to use the following:. Stock words and phrases – holy matrimony, high noon, Benedict's, exchanged nuptial vows.

Descriptive adjectives – attractive, pretty, beautiful, charming, lovely.

Non sequiturs – "Given in marriage by her parents, the bride wore a white silk organza gown with a sabrina neckline and short sleeves." "Wearing a gown of white lace cotton over taffeta with empire waistline, square neckline and short sleeves, the bride was given in marriage by her father."

Confusing collectives – "The couple is on a trip to Northwestern and will live at blank Fairmount Ave., Whitefish Bay, when they return." Generally a collective noun takes a singular verb when the noun indicates a group acting as a unit and a plural verb when it means individuals performing individual actions: "The Board of Park Commissioners gave its blessings..." "The platoon fought its way up the hill" "Their headquarter is in the Bennett building..." "The crew have returned to their homes." Therefore, make it couple *are,* not is.

Details – gown and flower descriptions and social affiliations that reflect status.

Euphemistic headlines – *Betrothal told, Holy voivs exchanged, Wedding ceremonies solemnised.*

Excerpts from an error-tilled account of a wedding (2½ pages of copy) reveal the unbelievable triteness of such stories:

> A petite white United Methodist Church nestled below the towering Rocky Mountains in Lyons. Colorado was the setting for the marriage of Shirley Ann M – and Wesley William B – on August 4. A happy sun brought windows at precisely 3 pm when Gloria L.... played The Wedding March, and guests stood from hand carved oak seats, curved into an intimate half-circle to witness the double-ring ceremony.

The Rev D.L.N. – officiated at the afternoon ceremony amid arrangements of mint-green carnations, white gladiolas, and white daisies with giant white satin bows which adorned the alter. Pews were delightfully enhanced with waterfall baskets of fresh greenery and wild mountain flowers plucked early that morning from beside that St. Vrain River and tied with lime and powder blue satin ribbons.

The Bride tossed her bouquet from the stairway and "went away" all dressed in white and yellow.

Copy-editors who handle news and features for the women's section will not allow writers to single out women's achievements by sex, such as housewife and woman doctor. They will delete phrases like "is affiliated with," "refreshments will be served,"' "featured speaker," "special guests," "noon luncheon," "dinner meeting." They will refuse to let a person "host (or hostess) a party," "gravel a meeting" or "chair a committee."

They will not let reporters go out of their way to use *female, feminine* and *ladies* in all manner of sentences where the word *women* would be proper and more appropriate.

They will catch slips such as "Mrs. Richard Roe, nee Jane Doe," *Nee* means "born" and people are born only with their surnames. The first (not Christian) name is given later.

They will remain on guard for awkward sentences:

Do you keep track of your weight and lose the first five or ten pounds too much?

Seniors realise the importance of proper dress more than younger students, but after a while they catch on.

All copy for this section, as well as for the other sections of the paper, should be edited for its news value. This should apply to the syndicated features as well as to the locally produced copy.

The copy-editors should not allow any story aimed at younger readers to contain anything that patronises these readers. Even terms like *teen, teenager* and *Youth* can be avoided, or at least can be held to a minimum. Copy-editors should make sure that both copy and headline talk up, not down to these readers.

The Instructions

Persons die of heart *illness,* not "failure"; after a *long* illness, not an "extended" illness; *unexpectedly,* not "suddenly"; *outright,* not "instantly"; *following* or after an operation, not "as a result of" an operation; *apparently of a heart attack,* not of an "apparent heart attack." A person dies of a disease, not *from* a disease!

The age of the person who died is important to the reader. The copy-editor should check the age given; with the year of birth. Generally, the person's profession or occupation, the extent of the illness and the cause of the death are recorded, but without details. The length of the story is dictated by the fame of the person. Winston Churchill's obit ran eighteen pages in the *New York Times.*

A person *leaves* an estate; he is *survived* by his family. Usage: varies as to whether he is survived by his wife or his widow. He is survived by his children if they are children and by sons and daughters if they are adults.

If the family requests that the story include the statement that donations may be made to such-and-such organisation, the statement should be used. Whether such a statement should contain the phrase "in lieu of flowers" is a matter of policy. Some papers, in deference to flourists, do not carry, the phrase.

A straightforward account of a death is better than one told euphemistically. The plain terms are *died,* not "passed away" or "sticcumbed"; *body,* not "remains" or "corpse"; coffin, not "casket"; *funeral* or *services,* not "obsequies" "interment," unless interred in a tomb above the ground. Flowery expressions such as "two of whom reside in St. Louis" and "became associated' with the blank company shortly after college" show no more' respect for the dead than do the plain expressions "live in St. Louis" or went to work for the blank company."

Few stories in a newspaper are more addicted to formula writing than the obituary. Here is a lead from an Associated Press story: *New York – If you area movie fan, you will remember Mary Roland as the fluttery matron, the foolishly fond mother, the ladylike scatterbrain. The character actress who died yesterday at the age of 80 was none of these in real life.*

The Copy-editor should be on guard for the correct spelling of all names used in the death story and for slips such as "cemetery" for cemetery and "cremation" for cremation. Errors are inexcusable.

A postmortem failed to disclose the cause of death because the girls body was too badly decomposed.

Thousands followed the cortege. The thousands must have been *in,* not "following," the cortege (the funeral procession). Even after death, a medal won by serviceman is awarded to him. It may be presented to his widow, but it is not awarded to his widow.

If the service is at a funeral establishment, the name of the funeral establishment should be included for the convenience of mourners. It is not a "funeral home" A funeral service is *at* a place, not *from* it. A mass is *offered;* a funeral service is *held.* Even so, "held" usually is redundant, "The service will be at 2 pm on Thursday..."

The passage should leave on doubt for whom the service was held. This one did leave doubt: "Services for 7-year old Michael L......., son of a Genoa Intermediate School District official who was struck and killed by a car Monday in Bay City, will be held..."

People are *people,* not "assaults" or "traffic deaths" or "fatals" or "dead on arrival":

A youth stabbed at a downtown intersection and a woman pedestrian run down by a car were among assaults on six persons reported to police during the night.

Hugo Woman/among nine/traffic deaths.

Dead on arrival at Hurley after the crash was Oscar W-who was decapitated.

The events in a person's life that should be included in his obituary pose a problem for the desk. One story recited the death of a former school administrator who died at the age of 87. It said he had been the first principal of blank high school and had served in that capacity for seventeen years. Then the story recalled that he resigned two months before he was found guilty of taking $ 150 from the school yearbook fund and was fined $500. Should an account of a minor crime committed a quarter of a century ago be included in the obituary? To those who knew the former principal intimately the old theft was not news. Those who didn't know him so intimately could hardly care about the single flaw in a otherwise distinguished career.

The following death story illustrates several errors overlooked by the copy-editor:

Two Jefferson children were killed when the automobile in which they were riding was struck by another auto Saturday night at the intersection of Eastern Boulevard and Brooks Avenue in Clarksville.

They were killed instantly due to skull fractures sustained in the accident, "according to Clark County Coroner Edwin M.." Coots. Their father George M. Gilbert Sr., Morris Ave., was driving the car in which the children were riding.

"Three other Gilbert children were hospitalised. Lori and Brian are in satisfactory condition and Karen is in intensive care at Clark County Memorial Hospital".

Michael was an eighth grade student at Parkview Junior High School and Christine attended Eastlawn Elementary School.

In addition to their father, survivors include their mother, Mrs. George M. Gilbert Sr., a brother George M. Gilbert Jr.: and grandparents. Mrs. Emma Cannon, and Mr. and Mrs. Gobel Gilbert, all of Jeffersonville.

The funeral for Michael and Christine" will be at 2 pm tomorrow at Coots Funeral Home here, with burial in Walnut Ridge Cemetery.

The Headlines

Few editors have escaped letters that begin something like this: "Dear Sir: the attached clipping from your paper of July 14th contains a mention of our product and we very much appreciate this unsolicited publicity. However, the name of our product was used with a lower case 'c' As you know...."

Makers of trade-name products want to protect their rights under the Lanham Trademark Act of 1947 and insist that in any reference to the product name the manufacturer's spelling and capitalisation be used. This is to protect the trade name from becoming generic, as happened to aspirin, cellophane, escalator, milk of magnesia, zipper, linoleum and shredded wheat.

Much of the confusion and protest can be eliminated simply by using a generic term rather than the specific trade name — petroleum jelly for Vaseline, freezer for Deepfreeze, fibre glass for Fibreglass, tranquilliser for Miltown.

Where the product is trade-named and there is no substitute, the trade name should be used, especially if it is pertinent to the story. The withholding of such information on the ground of free publicity is niggardly.

Institutions should be labelled correctly – Bell Telephone System, not Bell Telephone Company; Lloyd's, not Lloyd's of London; D'Oyly Carte: J. C. Penney Co. (Penneys in ads. Penney's in other usages); American Geographical Society; National Geographic Society.

It is the Tomb of the unknowns, not the Tomb of the Unknown Soldier.

Jewish congregations should be identified in news stories as Orthodox, Conservative or Reform, and the terminology of the congregation concerned should be followed in naming the place of worship as a temple or a synagogue. When grouping, the generic term is "Jewish houses of worship."

To help readers, the copy-editor should insert "Branch of Judaism" or whatever other phrase might be necessary to convey the proper meaning.

Most Orthodox congregations use *synagogue*. Reform groups use *temple* and Conservative congregations use one word or the other, but *synagogue* is preferred. It is never *Church,* which applied to Christian bodies.

Sect has a derogatory connotation. Generally it means a church group espousing Christianity without the traditional liturgical forms. *Religion* is an all-inclusive word for Judaism, Islam, Christianity and so on. *Faith* generally is associated with Protestants. *Denomination* should be used only when referring to the church bodies within the Protestant community.

Religious labels can be misleading. *Jews* and *Judaism* are general terms. *Israelis* refer to nationals of the state of Israel and *Jews* to those who profess Judaism. The state of Israel is not the centre of or the spokesman for Judaism. Some Jews are Zionists; some are not.

Not all denominations use *Church* in the organisation's title. It is the First Baptist Church but the American Baptist Convention. It is the Church of Jesus Christ of Latter-day Saints (not Mormon Church); its units are Missions, Stakes and Wards. It is the Episcopal Church, not the Episcopalian Church. Its members are Episcopalians, but the adjective is *Episcopal:* Episcopal clergymen.

Mass may be *offered or celebrated.* High mass is *any;* low mass is said. The rosary is *recited* or *said.* If mass is sung, the "high" should be omitted. The copy-editor can avoid confusion by letting the statement read something like this: "The mass (or rosary) will be at 7 pm" An official presides at solemn high mass. Requiem mass is not necessarily high, but it usually is. It is *offered,* never "celebrated" or "sung". The Benediction of the Blessed Sacrament is neither "held" nor "given", services close with it.

The order of the commandments varies depending on the version of the Bible used. Confusion can be spared if the commandment number is omitted. Also to be deleted are references to the burning of a church mortgage unless there actually is a burning ceremony. It is an elegant but ridiculous way of saying the mortgage has been paid off.

The usual style in identifying ministers is the *Rev.,* followed by his full name on first reference and *the Rev. Mr.* on second reference. If he holds a doctorate, the style is *the Rev. Dr.,* or simply *Dr.* on subsequent references. *Reverend* should not be used standing alone, nor should plural forms be used, such as the Revs. John Jones and Richard Smith. Churches of Christ do not use the term *reverend* in reference to ministers. They are called *brothers.*

Rabbis take *Rabbi* throughout.

Catholic priests who are members of orders take the initials of their order after their surnames: S. J., S. S., etc. Priests who are rectors, heads of religious houses or presidents of institutions and provinces of religious orders take *Very Rev.* and are addressed as *Father.* Priests who have doctorates in divinity or philosophy are identified as *the Rev., Dr.* and are addressed either as "Dr." or "Father."

The Church of Christ is not the same as the United Church of Christ. It is Seventh day Adventist, but Seventh Day Baptists. When used as an objective, Bahai is spelled *Ba-hai.*

The words *Catholic* and *parochial* are not synonymous. There are parochial schools other than Catholic schools. The writer should not assume that a person is a Roman Catholic simply because he is a priest or a bishop. Other religions also have priests and bishops.

Not all old churches merit the designation of *shrine.* Some are just old churches. *Shrine* denotes some special distinction, historic or ecclesiastical. Usually, shrines are structures or places that have religious connections or that are hallowed by their associations with events or persons of historic significance, such as Mt. Vernon.

Use *nun* when appropriate for women in religious orders. The word sister is confusing except with the person's name (Sister Mary Edward).

Significant Assignments

One of the important functions of the copy-editor is to make sure that all names in the copy are double-checked. The proper form is the form the person uses. He may be Alex rather than Alexander, Jim rather than James, Will rather than William. He may or may not have a middle initial, with or without a period (Harry S. Truman). No one has yet explained why today's newspapers are so insistent on using middle names or initials of well-known men. After seeing Richard Nixon's name in the news hundreds of times, most readers didn't have to be reminded that the story concerned President Richard M. Nixon instead of plain Richard Nixon. Men's first names are seldom used alone, except in sports copy. The same should be true for first names of women.

Anyone resents an attempt at cleverness where his name is concerned. Such "cuteness" should be felled on sight:

Orange County will have a lemon as district attorney. Jack Lemon was elected to the job yesterday.

Of the five patrolmen on the staff, two are crock

The last name was Crook.

A title generally precedes a name unless it is a long title. It is Harley F. Taylor, principal of Philip C. Showell School, rather than Philip C. Showell School Principal Harley F. Taylor.

Nor should the story make the reader guess at the identification. Here is an example.

Albert A. Ballew took issue with Mayor Locher today for announcing in advance that the post of administrative assistant in the Safety Department will be filled by a black. The president of the Collinwood Improvement Council commended the mayor for creating the post, but added... Now then, who is the president of the Collinwood Improvement Council? Will readers assume it is Ballew? The solution is so simpler "Ballew, president of the Collinwood Improvement Council, commended the mayor...."

The first reference to any person is by full name and professional, scholastic or religious title, if appropriate. Titles may be used on second reference to aid the reader.

Newspapers traditionally have used Mrs. on first reference only with the husband's given name: *Mrs. John Smith* and *Mr. Smith* thereafter; or, if it is her preference, *Gladys Smith* and *Mr. Smith thereafter.*

Women on second reference are identified by Miss, Mrs. or Ms., according to the women's preference. It is the responsibility of the reporter to determine which the woman prefers.

Editors may determine which women are sufficiently well-known in their professions to be referred to on second reference by last name only. Billie Jean King and Joan Sutherland, for example, could be identified as King and Sutherland, but the mother of a high school swimmer or the lead in a civic theatre production probably could not be, unless that was their stated preference.

It may be Mrs. Richard Harris Jr., but not Mrs. Dorothy Harris Jr. Her husband may be Jr., but she is not.

Newspaper style may dictate that certain positions be neutralised (chairperson for chairman) but even this rule could lead to the absurd *(person kind for mankind).*

Editor's can be fair to both sexed by eliminating purely sexist adjectives before women of accomplishment and by using plural forms when possible and substituting the relative pronouns *they* or *them* instead of *he* or *him.*

All males on second reference are identified by surname only although some newspapers use Mr. on second reference in obituaries of prominent persons.

Newspapers have no firm rule about when to identify a person as a girl or a woman, or as a boy, youth or man. Generally, a girl becomes a woman at 18; a male is a boy until he is 13, a youth from 13 to 18 and a man from 18 on.

Appropriateness should determine whether males and females 18 and older or even those under 18 should be referred to by the familiar given name.

A surname alone is used in half-column cutlines except when two or more half-column photographs of persons with the same last name are used with an article. In that case, first names or initials are needed.

Pupil describes a person attending grade school; *student* applies to those attending junior high school, high school, college or university.

A maiden name can cause trouble: "He married the former Constance Coleman in 1931." This is incorrect; Constance Coleman was Constance Coleman when he married her. He married Constance Coleman. His wife is the former Constance Coleman.

Woman is used as a general descriptive possessive – woman's rights. *Women's* is used as a specific – women's club (but Woman's Christian Temperance Union). It is women fliers. Young Women's Christian Association, women workers, but woman suffrage. It is never the Smith woman.

Foreign names are tricky. In Spanish-speaking countries, individuals usually have two last names, the father's and the mother's – Adolfo Lopez Mateos. On second reference, Lopez Mateos should be used. In headlines, Lopez Mateos is preferred, but Lopezs will do.

A Chinese family name is usually given first, and the second part of the hyphenated name is given in lower case – Chiang Kai-shek, Lee Su-kun. On second reference, use Chiang, not Kai-shek.

In Arab names, *al* generally is hyphen, Al-Azhar. Some Arabs drop the article – Mamoun Kuzbari, not al-Kuzbari. Compound names should be left intact – Abdullah, Abdel, Abdur Pasha and Bey titles have been abolished. Royal titles are used with first names – Emir Faisel, Sheik Abdullah. *Haj* is used with the first name in both first and subsequent references – Haj Amin al-Hussain, Haj Amin.

The U in Burmese names means uncle, our equivalent of *Mr. Thakin* means master. *Daw* means Mrs. or Miss. Many Burmese have only one name — U Thant. If a Burmese has two names, both should be used — U tin Maung, Tin Maung.

Some Koreans put the family name first — Park Chung Hee. The second reference should be Park, not Chung Hee, the given name.

Many Indonesians have only one name — Sukarno, not Ahmed Sukarno.

Swedish surnames usually end in *son,* and Danish names usually end in *sen.*

Critical Writing

Journalism is by nature a subjective process. It can no more help producing and projecting views of the world than a cow can help making milk. Be it intentional or unintentional, overt or covert, comment comes with the territory. To deny this is to deny that ink makes a mark on paper.

As far as intentional comment is concerned (columnists, leading articles) no one would want to deny it. After all, a newspaper without such opinion would be like someone who has had a personality by-pass operation. The problem comes with comment that goes in disguise, dressed up as straight reporting, speaking in its voice and aping its mannerisms. The problem, too, is with comment that creeps in under cover of a paragraph in a news story and has infiltrated before either the reader, and sometimes the writer, realises.

Comment, then, is only a problem when it does not advertise itself. We can never eliminate this, but we can hope to minimise it by searching for it, studying it, thinking about it and trying to recognise it for what it is. This, plus the more up-front types of comment, is what this chapter is about.

Deep Comments: There are three types of comment in news stories: overt, covert and inadvertent. Overt comment is where the reporter passes judgement or states an opinion in a direct and open way. This type of comment is simply banned on news pages in many papers around the world. Indeed in Britain and the United States, it is thought to be so obviously wrong that many journalism textbooks do not even give it more than a passing mention. The authors take it for granted that none of their readers would contest the view that news pages are for information given as straight as it can be, and comment is for columnists and opinion pages.

In most circumstances (the exceptions are dealt with later) this is right. Readers will know where they are and can read stories assuming that what they are getting is an attempt to present facts, even if it is not always successful. As noted earliar, everyone has a comment, relatively few have fresh information. The one is commonplace, the other scarce. That is why news is invariably more interesting than comment and it is certainly why there is a real risk of devaluation when the two are mixed. For when they are, hard information becomes tainted and so loses its worth.

But there are exceptions. The highly experienced reporter writing a background piece on a subject which he has followed for a long time should be allowed to let his judgements inform a story, and hence the readers. The same latitude should also be given to specialists or foreign correspondents who have been resident in their posts for a long time. Their comment should not appear in the form of drum-banging opinions of the 'Well he may say that, but here's what I think...' variety, but appear as asides, little nudging remarks which give the story, or aspects of it, context. They work best as little notes of scepticism, forecasts of the likeliest scenarios, views about which policy might be adopted, etc., preferably displayed in a different way from hard news reports.

Such comment should be used sparingly but perhaps deployed more often than it is. Conventional facts-only reporting must be the mainstay of the paper's news coverage but other, broader forms should be used more often, especially in longer, overview-type pieces. As television news channels and websites proliferate, such comment is an important part of newspaper content. And it is plainly hypocritical for newspapers to spurn any idea of overt comment when other forms are unavoidably part of news stories. The only stipulation is that overt comment should be honest and immediately apparent for what it is and not try to hide itself or masquerade as something else.

Surreptitiousness is what is wrong with covert and inadvertent comment. The difference between the two is that covert is intentional, inadvertent is not. But they both deliver the same thing and by the same routes: in the language, material and sources they use, or omit. In news writing the chief vehicle for covert and inadvertent comment is loaded words. These are words with pejorative meaning and there are many examples in every language. Here are two situations which produce many examples in almost every language.

Attribution of Speech: The words 'said' and 'told' are neutral verbs. They merely inform us that the words quoted were spoken. Reporters often look for alternatives, but the problem is that many of those alternatives are not neutral. The words 'confessed' and `admitted' do not merely tell us that words have been spoken, they communicate more than that. They mean that someone has either been pressured into revealing some hitherto unknown, perhaps shameful, act; or that they have decided, after wrestling with their conscience, to tell all. Both cases are rather different from 'said'.

'Concede' also implies an admission (or concession) of guilt, while `alleged', 'claimed' and 'maintained' can also carry the implication that you do not believe what is being said. Meanwhile, 'emphasised', 'stressed' and 'pointed out' all imply that you support the speaker. Similarly, if someone is explaining some of their actions or decisions, do not write without reasons that they 'tried to justify' their actions or 'defended' them. That would only be appropriate if they had been criticised or were under some other pressure to explain.

Another rich source of unintentional comment is the story that begins, 'Fears that...' or 'Hopes that...' and omits to mention who it is that is doing the fearing and hoping. There is no harm when the fears or hopes are ones that every person would share, as in: 'Fears are growing for the safety of three children who failed to arrive home yesterday after attending an after-school party.' But when the story is: 'Hopes rose yesterday that a lower price for gold is coming...', you really have to say whose hopes. Gold producers, and those whose economies benefit from higher gold prices, will presumably be fearing rather than hoping.

Politics: Describing briefly someone's views and political position throws up all kinds of problems. Terms like 'reformer', 'radical', 'hard-liner', 'reactionary', 'moderate' and 'extremist' are used all the time as if they were fixed reference points in the same way that party labels are. But they are not. They are frequently on the move, and most depend on the position from which you are describing them. And they are all used pejoratively. Someone who disagrees with you, or the mainstream, is an 'extremist', which carries all the implications of 'excess' that are so obviously in the word's antecedents. Never lose sight of that old adage that one person's 'freedom fighter' is another person's 'terrorist'.

There are many more loaded words where these came from. Their use often depends on your prejudice, conscious or otherwise. Action by the authorities against a particular group of people is, depending on your point of view, a 'crusade' or a 'witch hunt'. People you approve of make 'mistakes' or 'errors', people you don't care for 'bungle' or 'blunder'. Demonstrators you disapprove of are a 'mob', others constitute a 'crowd'. And people can be 'refuseniks' or 'rebels' and so on.

The moral is that you should choose words with great care and always be aware of their connotations. The most innocent choice of phrase can convey the wrong impression. In the United States and elsewhere, for example, abortion rights have been a highly contentious issue for many years. Call what is growing inside a woman an 'unborn baby', however early in its gestation, and you are unwittingly lining up with those who would restrict abortions. Call their protagonists 'pro-abortion campaigners' and you double the offence. 'Aborted foetus' and 'pro-choice campaigners' are the more neutral descriptions.

The Big I: The personal pronoun is one of the most contentious words in any language. Some journalists will go to great lengths to avoid ever typing it, writing such variants as 'this reporter', 'your correspondent', or 'this paper's representative'. Others will use it at the slightest excuse, making almost every story they write an exercise in informative vanity. There has to be a middle way and preferably one that is a lot closer to the modesty option.

Yet achieving this is not always easy. When President John F. Kennedy was composing his inaugural address, one of the most memorable speeches of this century, he told his advisers that the personal pronoun would be banned. Some of the best brains in America worked on successive drafts, but 'I' still crept in four times.

Reporters covering 'big stories' are particularly vulnerable to the temptations of the first person, perhaps feeling that some of the importance of the story has rubbed off on them. Then there are those journalists who believe that their reactions to a story, their emotions, their doings, are so fascinating that they should be frequently included. As a character in British dramatist Tom Stoppard's play, *Night and Day,* says, 'A foreign correspondent is someone who flies around from hotel to hotel and thinks that the most interesting thing about any story is the fact that he has arrived to cover it.'

Of course, as a reporter, you are seeing things, meeting people, having experiences that are, by definition, interesting - after all, you would not be there if they were not news. But what the reader wants to know is *what you* saw and *what you* discovered, and not *how you* saw it or found it, and certainly not what you ate, drank, or felt while finding it. In as much as anything in reporting is a rule, this is one, unless you are a big name journalist whose stock-in-trade is personal reporting.

On the assumption that you are not, you should save highly personalised writing for when you have a personal experience to relate which is utterly fascinating (to the readers, not to you and your family). In any normal career, such occasions will be few and far between. As an example, here is a piece George Orwell wrote while covering the Spanish Civil War. The personal approach is justified here because Orwell had an experience considerably out of the ordinary and one that many people wonder about - being shot. It is a model of understatement:

> I had been about ten days at the front when it happened. The whole experience of being hit by a bullet is very interesting and I think it is worth describing in detail.
>
> ... Roughly speaking it was the sensation of being at the centre of an explosion. There seemed to be a loud bang and a blinding flash of light all round me, and I felt a tremendous shock - no pain, only a violent shock, such as you get from an electric terminal; with it a sense' of utter weakness, a feeling of being stricken and shrivelled up to nothing. The sandbags in front of me receded into immense distance. I fancy you would feel much the same if you were struck by lightning. I knew immediately that I was hit, but because of the seeming bang and flash I thought it was a rifle nearby that had gone off accidentally and shot me. All this happened in a space of time much less than a second. The next moment my knees crumpled up and I was falling, my head hitting the ground with a violent bang which, to my relief, did not hurt. I had a numb, dazed feeling, a consciousness of being very badly hurt, but no pain in the ordinary sense.

Accurate Wordings

At opposite ends of a collection of words are two little marks. These indicate that what is inside them is a verbatim record of what was said. Not an edited version of their words, or a tidied up or summarised account. Nor what someone meant to say, or would have said if they had only been sufficiently well educated to speak in such grammatical sentences. But a word for word, syllable by syllable, accurate report of their actual words. If not, what on earth is the point of those little marks at either end?

And if you do not have a verbatim note or tape, or the person you would like to quote does not speak in a way that, when written down, makes sense, then you use reported speech. Unless, of course, their incoherence is part of the story. In which case you quote them, accurately, with every unfinished sentence, every ungrammatical statement, and every misuse of words faithfully preserved.

Ums and Ers: A proper reverence for the sanctity of what you place within quotation marks does not normally extend to solemnly reporting every um, er and strangulated throat-clearing. In most situation, reporters naturally filter out the ums and ers - either when taking notes or writing the story. But sometimes, when writing colour pieces, profiles or news stories, giving warts and all quotes is called for. A story, for instance, where the quoted person's hesitancy or uncertainty is a relevant element would be a case in point. Knowing the difference between such relevance and gratuitous unfairness is, however, a judgement for the experienced.

Lark of Grammar: Some papers, such as the *Philadelphia Enquirer* will allow minor grammatical errors in quotes to be changed, both to avoid confusion and to prevent the speaker looking foolish. I would not even go this far. My aim would be not to save the blushes of the source, but to achieve accuracy and clarity. This means using reported speech to give a clear picture of what is going on or is meant, but using, if it is relevant, quotes to convey the authentic voice of those involved in the story.

After all, if someone's speech is ungrammatical, that's how it is. And if accurate reporting of it makes them look stupid, too bad. Many journalists working in the political field regularly tidy up the language of politicians. They think it is part of their job to take the inarticulate ramblings of politicians and turn them into neat, rounded sentences. It is not. First, cleaning up their quotes gives a false impression. Second, if the politician in question cannot speak his own language properly, it is your job to let readers know. They can then decide if they want to vote for him.

The real problem with allowing reporters to clean up speakers' grammar is that they tend to apply it unevenly; unconsciously tidying the speech of the educated and the official, but leaving other, more humdrum voices with their quotes unimproved. Be aware of this class bias and resist it. Smooth out no one's quotes.

Incoherence and Dissembling: Far beyond poor grammar comes incoherence. There are two issues here and the first is clarity. Your job is to find out what is going on, and if the person your are talking to cannot give a straight or comprehensible answer, then find someone who can. If their words are convoluted and rambling, but their meaning discernible, then use reported speech.

Sometimes, if the source is someone in authority, and their incoherent or dissembling words are a legitimate part of the story, they deserve to be quoted. Consider this, from a White House press conference given by American President Richard Nixon's press secretary Ron Ziegler in 1974. He was asked if certain tapes which may have recorded the President discussing illegal actions were still intact. The question seemed to demand a straight 'yes' or 'no'. Instead, Ziegler gave the following reply:

> I would feel that most of the conversations that took place in those areas of the White House that did have the recording system would in almost their entirety be in existence, but the special prosecutor, the court, and, I think, the American people are sufficiently familiar with the recording system to know where the recording devices existed and to know the situation in terms of the recording process, but I feel, although the process has not been undertaken yet in preparation of the material to abide by the court decision, really, what the answer to that question is.

If the incoherence is habitual, it can become a story in its own right. After all, repeated incoherence is a pretty good indicator of a failure to think straight, having something to hide, substance abuse, or all three.

Dialect: This can be very delicate territory. All social groups, whether they are a self-conscious subculture, a band of enthusiasts for some activity, an ethnic group or people who merely share the same work, have a language and dialect that is their own. Some use this dialect only when speaking to each other, others use it whatever their audience. In many cases, quoting people's actual words poses no great problems. If the footballer says, 'We was robbed blind' on the late night television news, that is authentic and everyone understands it. To render this in next day's paper as 'We were robbed of a deserved victory' is wrong and fools no one.

The problems begin when dialect is not immediately understandable. Do you translate so the meaning is clear, or keep the authentic voice and confuse a lot of readers? It is perhaps the most difficult of the authenticity versus clarity issues, especially where ethnic groups are involved. In recent years Eskimo Indians have objected to an Alaskan paper tidying up their quotes into standard English and so depriving them of their own, stripped-down form of speech. And in Florida, the *St. Petersburg Times* came under fire for verbatim quotes of a black athlete's own argot. The athlete was happy, but black readers thought the paper was holding his speech up to ridicule.

My policy would be to be wary, and where a dialect is not clear to all readers then generally to use reported speech on news pages, but feel more free to use authentic quotes on specialist or feature pages, especially in pieces of greater length. I see nothing patronising about that. And if you are going to quote extensively in dialect, do so only if your ear (and your notes or tapes) are good. This is not an area for the tone deaf.

Expressing Perfectly

Shorten Quotes only by Visible Deletion: There is only one honest, safe way to shorten quotes and that is by omitting phrases and sentences, but making plain by dots that you have done so. For instance, 'I think it is outrageous that we should be asked to do this... We have no intention of giving in. We are going to fight this all the way.' Never just remove the surplus words and join the parts together as if they were said in continuous speech. If you still cannot achieve the brevity you require, use reported speech.

Quoting in Fragments: This is the habit of quoting not sentences, but phrases or even single words. In his *Troublesome Words, Bill* Bryson cites these two examples: He said the profits in the second half would be 'good'.

...loneliness was a 'feature' of Hinckley's life...

The problem here is putting quote marks around a word which is perfectly ordinary and predictable. It suggests either the reporter's notetaking was so poor he only managed to get down one word per sentence or that the writer is trying to signal scepticism about the quoted word. The impression given by the first example above is that there will be something not quite kosher or distinctly qualified about the goodness of the results. The second example conveys irony or even mistrust of the source. The moral is use quotes around single words or phrases only when the words used are particularly emphatic, as in:

He said the profits in the second half would be 'sensational'.

or

He said the profits in the second half 'did not bear thinking about'.

Old Expressions

Said, Claimed or Commented? When it comes to the verb that goes between the name of the quoted and their words, many reporters think that the word 'said' can be regularly replaced by synonyms like commented, claimed, asserted, etc. This is fine so long as the words quoted really are a claim, comment or assertion. To write:

'My dog then hurled himself at the thief,' commented Mr. Black is idiotic, since Mr. Black is not commenting, but stating what he knows to be a fact. Claimed in such a circumstance would be even worse, since it suggests that Mr. Black's words should be treated as a statement which may be challenged or subsequently regarded as a delusion. Unless you have the evidence for this, it is misleading to use 'claimed' when you mean 'said'. Even more unsafe are words which carry a pejorative meaning, like 'admitted', or 'confessed'. Admissions generally involve fresh information which is negative, something the speaker would have preferred to keep to themselves and which has been conceded by them in the face of persistent questioning or under some other duress.

Similarly sloppy is the substitution of words that have a particular meaning and therefore cannot be used as direct synonyms for 'said'. Declared is a frequent delinquent here, as in:

'I am 24,' she declared.

She may have said 'I am 24', but if she declared it, then it suggests she raised her voice several decibels and declaimed the words, as if from a rooftop. This, implying that she is either proud of her age to the point of eccentricity, or that it has recently been in question and she wishes to clear the matter up very publicly, gives an entirely different meaning to merely saying the words.

Said Versus Says: These words are not interchangeable, as many think, but have different functions. 'Said' is for the specific:

'We were astonished when Christmas came twice this year,' said Ms. Brown.

But 'says' is for the general, recurring sentiment, as in: 'Christmas comes but once a year,' says Ms. White.

Inverted Sentences: Some reporters think they can introduce hitherto absent variety into their writing by inverting sentences at will. This is strangely common when approaching a quote, as in:

Said Mr. Smith, 'I am the happiest man in London.'

As Keith Waterhouse points out in *Waterhouse On Newspaper Style,* this became such a disease on *Tune* magazine that the *New Yorker* magazine commented, 'Backward ran sentences until reeled the mind.'

New Expressions

Growing Quotes from One-word Answers: There is one other unsafe practice with quotes and that is the habit some reporters have of putting statements to people, getting a 'yes' or 'no' answer (or even a nod or shake of the head) and then putting that statement in direct quotes as if it was said by the source. For instance, 'Have you ever leaked Cabinet papers to the press?' And when the subject says no, the reporter writes in his story, 'He then said, "I have never leaked Cabinet papers to the press."' Or, even worse, '"Have I ever leaked Cabinet papers to the press? No."' Any such exchanges should be mainly, or all, in reported speech, making clear what the question was and the extent of the reply.

Don't Invent Quotes to Protect a Source: A silly habit adopted by the inexperienced is to try to disguise the identity of the story's source by writing inaccurately that they refused to speak to the paper. Or, even worse, by quoting them as saying, 'No comment'. First, it is not true. Second, if the identity of the source ever comes out, it can be proved that at least part of the story was deceptive.

Overheard in the Street: Making up quotes ought to be as patently ill-advised as sticking a wet hand in a light socket. But some reporters seem to feel that the obvious wrongs of this are somehow suspended when they are doing a story which involves, or would be enlivened by, a few words from the man or woman in the street. Dishonesty is almost the least of reasons for not doing this. First, no words a reporter can invent will be as original or revealing as the public's real ones. Second, the kind of reporters who go in for this, and specialise in filling their pieces with quotes 'overheard on the train', invariably have no more idea of how people actually speak than someone who has been deaf from birth. The normal retort to such 'inventive' reporters is that they should be writing fiction. But, actually, they shouldn't. Ideally they should not be writing anything.

Easy Lining

Some people seem to think that a peer, politician, prizefighter, actress, or other oddity is in the happy position of being wooed by editors, armed with large cheques and lengthy contracts, and that once the name of the fortunate individual has appeared in 30-point Caslon at the top of the page he is relieved from earthly worry for a considerable time. One should like to dispel this illusion.

The Reading: One veteres Western journalist, once observed, with following manners:

I want to tell you how I first came into journalism. I was sitting one day having a Norwegian lesson-I was working for the Diplomatic Service-when an-old Oxford friend rushed unceremoniously into the room-a mannerism learnt possibly during his reporting days-and demanded that I should come and see his editor. The result of that interview was that I agreed to write the *Sunday News* gossip page, under the title "Almost in Confidence" (one of Percy Cudlipp's bright flashes of genius) and under the tuition of my Oxford friend, Patrick Dixon. As I had fully expected, I failed in the Diplomatic Examination, and that – as Sherlock Holmes's clients used to say – is why I am hare today.

I soon discovered in the *Sunday News* office that there was more in gossip-writing than met the eye. Pat Dixon's sighs an he laboriously rewrote my beat paragraphs convinced me of this. Eventually the great day came when Dixon fell ill. His flu meant that, for the first time in my life, I wrote the page, subbed it, saw it made up, and put it to bed. Since that day, ladies and gentlemen — to use a pompous expression favoured by people who take correspondence courses-I have never looked back.

After that preamble and personal publicity, let us get down to business.

Gossip is far older than the news story. The reason for this is, I think, that primitive people can never tell a story without embellishment; and, after all, gossip is a news story, complete with "brass fittings."

Old Fables: As to the actual antiquity of the two, Caesar's dispatches (or possibly those of Xenophone) are about the earliest news stories that I can think of. There was a "sneek-guest" controversy in Roman times. Cicero called the sneakguest one who "sinned against the salt," and (I say this in no way irreverently the Bible is full of excellent gossip stories. In the fifth chapter of Daniel, the story of Belshazzar's feast, in which the writing on the wall appeared, is fail of those touches which delight the gossip-writer. The minute description of who was present, what they (frank and talked about, the King's reactions, the Queen's wise words-the whole thing is a, perfect modern gossip story. We come down through the ages to Pepys and much of Boswell, especially the historic meeting of Wilkes and Johnson at Mr. Dilly's dinner-table. After all, the gap between a biographer and a gossip-writer is very narrow.

In the last century, gossip was much more personal and malicious than it is today. The hostess of that time really had something to complain about, and the gossip of the period was very similar to the type of stuff which appears in Turn Topics today. Here, for instance, is a charming extract from an American paper of this kind.

> "About five years ago, when Lady Donegall brought her only son, the youthful Marquess of Donegall, to New York, it was an open secret that she wished to annex Grace Vanderbilt as a daughter-in-law. The

plan failed and Lady Donegall sailed away disappointed. The Marquess, now 26 years old, has not yet found any girl willing to exchange her millions for his title".

Well, that was the sort of thing that our grandfathers had to put up with. I may say, in explanation of this paragraph, that I met Miss Vanderbilt once and that my mother's health has not been seriously impaired by this great disappointment!

I have tried to show that gossip is nothing new, but there are two sides to everything, and I feel it only fair to say that Mr. Swaffer told me confidentially that he invented it in 1912.

Let us deal with gossip as it is today. The general public classes all gossip together, without discrimination. But there are, of course, many kinds.

We have, first, the serious political gossip, which is a series of comments on events of the day. Each set of paragraphs is really in the nature of a leading article, written in the first person. I should take as an example of this that excellent feature the "Londoner's Diary "in the *Evening Standard*. It is hardly concerned with Society "at all.

Then we have stage gossip. The author of this has the peculiarity of being called a critic instead of a gossip-writer.

Thirdly, there is a woman's gossip, which, to my ignorant male mind, appears always to consist of brides trousseaux and wedding presents, and what people won at a first night... "And then, dearest, there was that lovely man who makes cocktail glasses out of pink tortoiseshell. Too, bogus, don't you think? And Lady X in virgin white. So few women nowadays can wear it. And how slim she is. Divinely clever, considering, don't you think or don't you? "... You know the sort of thing.

Social Aspects: Next we have the social diary. At present there is no signed daily diary, and I have often wondered whether there is any reason for this. It is, of course, obvious that one man cannot do a daily diary without being able, if necessary, to call on contributors. Even daily diaries vary from the serious-minded "Peterborough "in the *Daily Telegraph* to the ever good-natured "Mr. Gossip" in the *Daily Sketch*. The cynicism of the "Dragoman" in the *Daily Express* lends that very well-informed column a cachet of its own. Another feature of the "Dragoman" column is its racing gossip. I stress this last point because, I think that gossip should cover as many facets; of life as possible, and I am fully aware that my own column in the Sunday Graphic falls short where the turf is concerned. However, as I know nothing about wring and I refuse to have my contributors, then is nothing to be done about it.

Lastly, we have the Sunday diarists, whose job, I contend is to give a history of the week, touching on the events mentioned by other gossip-writers during the week, but giving the wader a more personal angle on these events and pointing out aspects of them which had not had time to mature when the daily column went to press. It should be comment, much more than a recital of facts. Whether the comment be humorous, facetious, garrulous, or cynical does not matter. No style can please everyone. It would be the ideal Sunday column to which a man in fifty years' time would go for a pen picture of our age.

Each generation thinks that it is men advanced, more progressive, and naughtier than the last. It is for the Sunday columnist to try to transplant himself into another age and look at 1930 with an unbiased mind. His job is to try to find out what it is really all about and help the reader's mind to sort the hotch-potch of miscellaneous information collected from the week's newspapers.

Let me digress a moment from the ideal Sunday column to note the interesting development that has taken place in gossip since the War. Many people think that gossip is only written by, and for, snobs. Many who are not snobs read gossip, and it is impossible to write it if you are a snob. Before the War, it is true, such gossip as existed was purely social, and, a such, concerned Edwardian society, that small and exclusive coterie round the Court.

But, like everything else, gossip has been influenced by democracy, and almost anyone who is in any way "news" is eligible for mention in a gossip column. A name as a name has no longer the electrifying effect that it had, and a paragraph written after the style of the Court Circular is no longer gossip. In other words, in these days it is no longer any use mentioning a duke if you haw not got a story about him. Of course, if the man who spilled the soup down your neck happened to be a duke, it makes the story doubly worth telling.

In our ideal modern gossip column the writer should have his eye continually on the news and cultivate every kind of acquaintance. You never know when your friend's butter might become news and, consequently, 'gossip' in its new interpretation.

Let us continue with the Constitution of the ideal gossip column. I will take the Sunday column, as my daily colleagues might rightly tell me that I did not know what I was talking about if I encroached on their preserves I have laid down certain broad rules which can be summarised thus:

1. Have as much dialogue as possible.
2. Personal stories about a well-known person are what you want to try to collect. They are always useful and very hard to get to order.
3. Do not write down to the public. It flatters them to be puzzled.
4. Only three paragraphs on each subject.
5. Make the thing read like, a continuous story even your links are far fetched.
6. Never 'reminisce" unless you have a topical news story on which to hang your reminiscences.
7. Make anyone who wants a "boost "give you a good story in exchange.

As to the Constitution of the ideal page, I favour a picture make up such as that used in the *Sunday Dispatch*. It adds a great deal to the value of the feature in the *Sunday News* I used to try to arrange that them should be a story in the matter about every picture in my "frieze." From personal experience I know that it is exceedingly annoying to find no mention of the pictures in the matter.

The introductory paragraphs should either be that big piece of news that you have been sitting on all the week in the hope that some rival would not have "spilled the beans" in a daily, or else about tendencies, new customs, and such like. A good example of this is the increasing popularity of sherry as opposed to cocktails. The fictitious bottle-green bowler hats that led to the undoing of Evelyn Waugh's gossip-writer in "Vile Bodies" is another example.

Next comes the week's entertainments, contrasting parties if possible-a political reception and a "Bright Young People" party, or something of the kind. This introduces stories from personal experience about well-known people who were there.

Exhibitions and charities, in my opinion, make dull reading, but they have to be given a certain amount of space.

A good "grouse" about three-quarter way down the page goes down marvellously, and a talk with a politician once a week is essential. Politics should definitely be covered by the ideal Sunday column.

The page should end in a light vein. "The Glossary," which the Dispatch used to run, was excellent, and I think (though I do not want to blow my own trumpet) that "People Young Mayfair Congratulates" and "My Tame Half Wit" are as good as anything else.

But there is a most important thing I must not forget-"the Stunt," The element of surprise and anticipation which the serial editor relies on can be brought into the gossip page. "What will he do next? "That is the atmosphere you want to create.

Lord Castlerosse's night in Hyde Park and tour of London in a motor coach were both excellent. His experience when he pretended to be his own valet on a journey wag also good.

From the number of letters I received when I worked for a night as a waiter at the Berkeley, nominally for a bet, I gather that little stunt went down quite well, and selling toys as a hawker in Holborn, though it was actually used as an article in the Daily Sketch, would have done equally well for gossip.

Apart from these, I have always found that a little competition, even for trivial prizes, stimulates interest. The number of readers who entered my competition for composing a poem on how to pronounce Dean Inge's mine was a revelation to the competition editor.

Sign of Interrogation: Now we come to the question: "Must gossip be malicious or indiscreet?

There are two schools of thought about this, and Lord Castlerosise would be the first to admit that he has occasionally given it to people straight from the shoulder. So did Lady Eleanor Smith. Lord Castlerosse would say that they deserved it, and I agree with him. Also, it is good journalism. Looking at the question from a purely material point of view, however, I contend that this policy is short-sighted. I am not afraid of making enemies and, if people deserve it, I see no reason why they should not "get it in the neck," But the gossip-writer relies on the goodwill of his friends to get his stuff, and maliciousness, or even severe comment, breeds distrust. No one knows when he will be the next victim and he is careful, in consequence, in front of the gossip-writer. Lord Castlerosse, in the old days, used to think it worth while. I do not, and I do not think that the readers miss it. Ever since I started writing gossip I have been fighting an uphill battle not to lose the trust of my acquaintances. I have been extremely careful, and have tried to balance the scales.

Sometimes, by sitting on a story because someone asked me to do so, I have lost it, but I contend that this policy (I am speaking of gossip, not news) pays in the long run, unit that, in the long run, the page benefits by it. Naturally, I have made mistakes-many of them-and committed unintentional indiscretions. One, as a matter of fact, involved me in hot water in very high circles. Fortunately it was overlooked and I was forgiven.

I explained earlier that the gossip column has become elastic, just as society has. There is no reason to mention these people whom one knows detest publicity. Gossip is concerned with people who "do" things-people who are "news" and most people whose mind have progressed beyond the 'nineties like favourable publicity. This, I may say, includes some of London's meet respected best cases. As to the others, then attitude precludes them from being news, so why make enemies. Naturally, I am generalising, and it is on the exceptions that the gossip writer trips up.

Sometimes we fall into disfavour through no fault of our own. The gossip-public-society is too narrow a term -does not discriminate: gossip-writers are gossip-writers, and that's that! An indiscreet feature that appeared recently is a case in point. We were cold-shouldered and a raging controversy started, causing me to make an incursion into *The Time* on the subject of "sneak-guests".

This controversy afforded an excellent example of the difference between Lord Castlerosse's tactics and, my own. I will not how you with my letter. Suffice it to say, that I tried to point out that many serious and respected journalists were gossip-writers and that the "sneak-guest" was no friend of ours.

Here is what Lord Castlerosse said in the "Londoner's Log": "I don't care a tinker's curse; about the troubles of a society journalist, and leas than half that for the feelings of those who are hurt by what is said about them in the newspapers. I don't care if all the dukes of England go dotty and all the barons become transformed into bloaters."

Well, that was frank, anyway. Magnificent!

I am glad that we had the "sneak-guest" fight. It cleared the air and I think that, if anything, we legitimate gossip-writers have benefited.

I have said enough of our difficulties and he" dwelt rather long on the subject, because many people think that the life of a gossip-writer is one long revel. What are the advantages ? We get the beat of everything. Head waiters, of all men, know on which side their breed is buttered. Free cinemas and theatres come our way.

But there are greater compensations than that, and I will just read a short paragraph of a letter from a place called Mogil; Mogil, in New South Wales. (No, I did make it up!) The letter reads; "This is from an Englishman in a very far-away country. I often wood" what's happening over them, and your page tells me most things I want to know about the younger generation. I'm absolutely fed up with the sight of cattle. Do carry on the good work."

Letters like that make it really worth while.

Another thing that makes me glad I failed in the Diplomatic Examination is that for every friend I may have lost (and I am not aware of any) through writing gossip I have gained ten: people for whom I have been able to do some little service, and, last but not least, the many colleagues who are here with me and helped me when I arrived in a strange world-Fleet Street. Interloper as; I must have seemed to them, they gave me the chance of showing them that I had no intention of being just a Fleet street "stunt," but wanted to be one of them.

Accurate Method

In the last decade or so there has been radical, and overdue, change in the way newspapers write and think about different groups in society: women, blacks, the disabled, homosexuals. All of these have been and often still are patronised and discriminated against. One of the main targets of those trying to correct this has been the language applied to these groups. Although the more extreme advocates of political correctness have provided endless amusement to the mainstream with their excesses, very few of us would want to go back to the days when, for instance, women were called 'ladies' and always with a brief note attached telling the reader whether they were 'pretty', 'vivacious' or 'attractive' and what colour dress they wore.

Political correctness is now an intense pre-occupation to journalism schools in many parts of the world. One recent textbook gave more space to how to write about the disabled than it did to news values. This is silly, because the matter can be resolved into three broad principles, all of which involve applying the sensitivity any educated person would use in normal life:

- Do not refer to someone's race, or disability unless it has a direct bearing on the story.
- Do not apply different standards to writing about one group in society from those you would apply to another. Don't, for instance, describe a woman politician's dress and hairstyle unless it has a bearing on the story or possesses news value in itself. The test is: would you describe a male politician's appearance in the same situation?
- Be precise and do not use euphemisms. The fashion in some countries is now to refer to a blind person as 'visually impaired'. They are not, they are blind. A visually impaired

person is one who can partially see, and is thus better called 'partially-sighted'. Best of all, do not use any vague phrases; be precise. Instead of 'disabled', which many object to, say what the disability actually is - providing it is relevant to the story.

The Evaluation

Any news story or feature of substance should have some measure of analysis in it, whether it is woven in with the main fabric or written as a separate section. But often a story is of such a size or sudden importance that a piece which is nothing but analysis is called for. This will dissect events, themes, issues and developments in an attempt to explain what is happening now or will happen in the future. It should also try to explain the significance of these events and their context.

Such pieces should not merely be a series of assertions. Neither should they be old news stories reheated and served up with a few opinions. They must bring fresh evidence and fresh insights to bear on the story. These can either be yours, or, preferably, those of named authorities and experts. The accent should be on interpretation and explanation. This approach can be applied to other types of stories. Profiles of prominent public figures, for instance, can often be a fairly superficial recycling of well-worn material. But they can also be a serious attempt to set their lives into a context, with some detailed research into their backgrounds and work. The views of those who have encountered them can be collected and added to present a rounded portrait.

Interpretive pieces arc needed by readers even more now that they often receive the first reports of events from television and radio. As well as reporting in depth as the broadcast media cannot, newspapers should also explain what the events and developments mean. This need not be some quiet backwater of the paper, where commentators suck their thumbs, ruminate and, as American journalist A. J. Liebling said, 'write what they construe to be the meaning of what they have not seen.' It should be to report new understandings and insights — a new sense of what things mean.

Editor's Job: Serious comment pieces that read interestingly, and have some pace and authority, are very difficult to write. Too often seriousness comes out as solemnity, authority as pomposity, and the subject is as predictable as tomorrow's date. Such pieces have all the freshness of last week's bread.

It is a near-universal convention that each issue of a paper should have a column that gives the paper's view on some topical issue(s). In countries where basic freedoms are under threat, editorials can be a ringing voice in the defence of people's rights. They send public word to regimes that they are being watched and opposed. They bolster and inspire those who are fighting for freedom and justice.

Elsewhere, in more comfortable circumstances, the value of these daily editorials is more debatable. I have sat in many editorial conferences where for some considerable time the assembled minds rummaged hopefully through recent stories for a subject - any subject - that the paper could sound off about. The clock would tick steadily onwards, until at last some issue was agreed on (invariably one of the ones suggested at the beginning of the meeting). With the problem solved for another day, everyone then heaved a collective sigh of relief. Except the poor devil commissioned to write the thing. A lot of us find it very testing to write a good comment piece unless we have a genuine conviction about an issue. Fabricating one will often produce a piece that is hollow and insincere; trying to write the piece without one leads to inconclusive waffle or, worse, a succession of comments saying it is too early to pass judgement on this matter — a dead give-away that the paper has chosen the wrong subject, or the wrong writer.

Some larger papers have specialists employed to write nothing but editorials. This gave rise, on the *Daily News* of Chicago, to a practical joke from one of the better-class journalists. Groups of readers used to be regularly shown round the paper, which was known for the high moral tone of its editorials. Knowing that such a party was due, a reporter called Eugene Field, later a poet, got together with a member of staff who was the readers' guide and hatched a plan. As the prim matrons of the town reached the door marked 'Editorial Writers', the guide opened it to reveal a figure seated at a desk, composing one of the paper's pious editorials. It was Field, unshaven, snarling, and dressed in the arrowed uniform of a convict, complete with ball and chain. 'He's a trusty from the state pen, up for murder, you know', explained the guide, 'Our editor Mr. Stone is very economy minded, always thinking of the paper's expenses. He used his influence to get this fellow in twice a week. A free editorial writer, get it, Doesn't cost us a dime.'

However, if you are a more conventional member of the paper's staff and have been commissioned to write an editorial on something about which you have no burning convictions, you have two choices. You can either speak to experts inside and outside your paper and collect strong views, or retire to a dark corner and rapidly acquire some. This is not as cynical as it sounds. It is surprising how often a few moments' contemplation suddenly focused by the approaching deadline will give birth to original opinions.

Originality, however, has its limits. Joseph Medill, the ultraconservative owner of the *Chicago Tribune* wrote an editorial in 1884 on the problem of the city's large mobile population of homeless, jobless men. Not for him any plea for work to be found for these unfortunates. Instead, an editorial written in vindictive seriousness and which read in part:

> The simplest plan, probably where one is not a member of the Humane Society, is to put a little strychnine or arsenic in the meat and other supplies furnished to the tramp. This produces death within a comparatively short time, is a warning to other tramps to keep out of the neighbourhood... and saves one's chickens and other portable property from constant depredation.

Passion, too, has its limits which were certainly reached and appreciably exceeded by the *Messenger,* an English-language paper in Cameroon in July 1995. A front-page piece was headed 'Kill This Man', and read in part: 'Such a man is not fit to live and should be wiped out of existence. Such a treatment, however harsh, befits Oben Peter Ashu, Governor of the South West Province.'

Editorials, like all opinion pieces, should not be a series of wilful assertions laid upon each other. As well as a fresh point of view, they should contain sufficient elements of background and analysis to make them understandable to those who have not read the story(ies) they are based upon. They should be arguments constructed as tightly as a well-wound spring.

And if you wish them to have impact, concentrate your creativity on a few memorable phrases. The list of newspaper editorials that have lived beyond the paper's next issue is not long. In fact it is very short. But those that have achieved any kind of immortality owe it not to a brilliantly argued case, but to a memorable phrase. That indeed is all they are remembered for: C. P. Scott's 'Comment is free, facts are sacred' *(Manchester Guardian,* 1921), 'Communism with a human face' *(Rude Pravo,* Prague 1968), 'The smack of firm government' *(Daily Telegraph,* London 1956), 'One picture is worth a thousand words' *(Printers' Ink,* US 1927).

But there is a thin line between presence and pretentiousness. Just as politicians are only politicians, papers are only papers, not players on the world stage. There is nothing more preposterous than a squeaky voice from a newspaper, especially a small provincial one, 'calling on the United Nations to act now'. Witness the *Skibereen Eagle,* a four-page sheet published once a week in the city of Cork, Ireland in late Victorian times. Once, when the Tsar of Russia had done something to displease the *Eagle's* proprietor, one Frederick Peel Eldon Potter, a vehement leading article informed its 4,000 readers: 'The *Skibereen Eagle* has its eye on Russia.'

Individual classified advertisements have done more to change the world than all the billions of words of blustering newspaper editorials in history. The battle of Gettysburg, one of the bloodiest in the American Civil War, for instance, was caused by an ad for footwear. It appeared in the *Gettysburg Compiler* and had been placed by a shoe store announcing fine new boots for sale. It was seen by Confederate General James Pettigrew who at the time was marching his bedraggled army through Pennsylvania. They were in a sorry state, having worn out their boots and many were marching barefoot. Pettigrew ordered his men to change direction and head for Gettysburg. On the way they were spotted by Union forces and so began the bloody, three-day battle of Gettysburg. At the end of it, 5,662 men lay dead and 2 7,203 wounded.

Indeed, it is very hard to find a single case of a newspaper comment actually changing the world. The one usually cited, Emile Zola's famous 'J' accuse' about the Dreyfus case published in the French paper *L'Aurore* in January 1898, was actually an open letter to the government and not an editorial (and had only a limited direct effect). The other case was where the comment was actually made in error.

In April 1888, Ludwig Nobel died. He was the elder brother of the moody yet idealistic inventor of dynamite, Alfred Nobel. A leading French newspaper misread the report and ran an obituary of Alfred, calling him 'a merchant of death'. Reading that obituary and being stung by the idea that he would be remembered as a 'merchant of death', was one of the main reasons why Nobel changed his will and left his fortune to establish the Nobel Prize awards for peace, literature and the sciences.

Columnists: Anyone who has reached the stage of a column either has no need for advice; or has (or will soon acquire) an ego which precludes them from taking any.

Reviews: There are three schools of reviewing and two of them should be closed down. First, there are those professional journalists who are perfectly good reporters when given a story, but when presented with a book, play, film or concert to review are stricken with a sudden desire to prove they are 'writers'.

Then there are those amateurs, often a rival (or, worse, a friend) of those whose work is under review, who grind in-crowd axes in public, to the bewilderment or deceit of readers. In both cases what we often get is a piece where the writer fails to describe the content of the work, so anxious is he or she to discharge opinions, fanciful divinations of meaning, wild guesses at the artist's intent and, of course, what he or she hopes will be the resonating verdict.

Readers should beware these schools of reviewing. So, too, should writers. As Vladimir Nabokov observed of book reviewers: 'Criticism can be instructive in the sense that it gives readers, including the author of the book, some information about the critic's intelligence, or honesty, or both.' The school of reviewing that deserves preservation is that whose prime aim is to give information about the work in question; to describe it as precisely and fully as possible, to scrutinise its style, content and thinking. And remember, it is permissible to write a review that contains no glib opinion. If you feel tempted to ignore this advice, just remember the *Odessa Courier's* anonymous book reviewer who in 1887 wrote of a novel: 'Sentimental rubbish. Show me one page that contains an idea.' The book reviewed was Anna Karenina.

Worth of Quotations

Here, let us reveal a little-known secret of the journalistic trade: you cannot be arrested for writing a story without quotes. I know this runs contrary to what many young journalists are told, but it is true. Most stories benefit from quotes, but it is not illegal to write without them.

I pass this on because quotes have become something of a fetish with many editors. They have come to believe that every story must have quotes dropped into it at regular intervals, like buoys marking the entrance to a port. In mass-market sport reporting, this belief has been taken to extremes, and story after story is little more than a series of quotations laid end to end with odd, linking interjections from the reporter. Spurred, perhaps, by the belief that television has robbed them of the need to relate what happened, they confine themselves instead to reporting reactions to what happened. For their work, the post-event interview has become more important than the event itself.

That is not the only problem with quotes. Some journalists, and a lot of journalism trainers, find the issue of tidying up quotes a terrible ethical dilemma. Others are hugely exercised by how to attribute quotes, or how to use them partially. Time, then, for a few guidelines.

Generally you should always use reported speech to convey information and quotes to add personality, immediacy, authenticity and a change of voice and pace to a story. Quotes can also be used to report verbatim an exchange between interviewee and questioner, especially if you wish to show what built up to some sudden confession, particularly dramatic statement or to show evasiveness. Normally, however, quotes should be reserved for allowing people to comment, or to give an impression of themselves, their opinions or feelings.

They are not to be used as mere padding, and, least of all, as substitutes for reporting. And never forget that you can write a lot more efficiently than most people can speak. For example, instead of 'A United Nations spokesman said, "We utterly deny his claim is or ever was true"', just write, 'A United Nations spokesman denied the claim.'

Compendious Matter

Readability of subject matter is important in written communication.

Clarity of writing and understandability of the subject is the purpose of writing. Lack of the quality of readability in writing leads to not reading the message. So materials should be noted. A number of formulae have been developed for rating materials by measuring their difficulty. Readers do not have the time to read anything involving trouble in understanding. Flesch, Dale and Chall, Farr, Jenkis, Patterson and Gunning have developed readability formulae. Among them Gunning's method of a readability formula is one of the easiest to understand and apply. He advocated seven factors affecting readability. They are:

1. Average sentence length in words
2. Percentage of simple sentences
3. Percentage of verbs expressing forceful action
4. Proportion of familiar words
5. Percentage of personal references
6. Proportion of abstract words
7. Percentage of long words.

Gunning's Fog Index: Gunning used two elements in his formula, the percentage of words of three or more syllables in 100 words and the average sentence length in words. To find the fog index of a passage, take these three simple steps:

Determine the Average Sentence Length: Count the number of words in successive sentences. For long pieces of writing, take samples of 100 words. Divide the total number of words by the number of sentences. Do not count the articles "a", "an" and "the" as words.

Find the Percentage of Hard Words: Count the number of words of three syllables or more per 100 words. Don't count words that are capitalised, that are a combination of short, easy words (like "bookkeeper" and "butterfly"), or that are verb forms made into three syllables by adding -ed or -es (like "created" or "trespasses").

Figure the Fog Index: Add the two factors (steps 1 and 2) and multiply by 0.4.

Educational Impacts

Can the newspaper really teach? Can they improve the literacy rate in the country? Yes, say some professionals in the field who believe that the mainstream media can make an "important contribution" to improve adult education, as well as to fight the adult illiteracy. The world congress of International Press Institute (IPI) was held on 27th January 2001. The congress was addressed by the top world editors, authors and political leaders. Addressing the gathering, president of World Association of Newspapers (WAN) Bengt Braun and Director General, Timothy Balding remarked, "As newspaper executives, we have a duty to help raise educational standards within our societies, whether we live and work in developing countries or in advanced industrialised nations."

World Association of Newspapers (WAN) is a global organisation for the newspapers industry. It represents 17000 newspapers. Its membership includes 66 national newspaper associations, individual newspapers executives in 93 countries. While 17 news agencies and seven regional worldwide press groups are also the members of WAN. It admits that the high levels of education and literacy are essential to ensure the "existence of readers for our newspapers". This shows a projection of the future of the newspaper industry.

Democracy and freedom require that citizens should enjoy access to information, analysis and debate. "Only with this access, provided by education and literacy, can all men and women play their full role in society and share the fruits of the press freedom which underpins our democracies" says the WAN.

It undertook an interesting study of how newspapers can and are playing a role in adult education worldwide. Reading a newspaper is a routine habit of lacs of people which require basic literary skills, yet this readily available and affordable teaching tool is often neglected by the teachers including those who work with adult learners. Following are the successful examples of how the newspaper changed the social and academic life of the student readers.

"Diario Los Andes" of Argentina has an experiment in which children have taught their parents to read with the help of a newspaper. Some assignments given to the children and parents together are:

Look through the paper and identify its major parts. Identify what is advertisement and what is editorial text.

Look at photos and talk about them and the feelings they provoke.

Write captions for a photo.

Learn how to count using numbers in the paper.

"Los Andes" provided newspapers and other material, besides training for teachers. It was the provincial government which paid for the teachers' extra hours. One added benefit was that all the participants' children succeeded better in school.

From Cameroon, the West African country of 13 million that was the birthplace and original homeland of the Bantu ethnic group centuries ago has a news - you-can-use project for rural Africans. "La Vois du Paysan: is a 24 page monthly tabloid (small size newspaper) launched in 1988 by a non-profit organisation. Its editorial committee included farmers and the editorial line was agreed on with selected residents from the three main rural zones in Cameroon. Its goal was to bring useful information to a majority of the rural population in and around Cameroon, Gobon and Chad. Also, to inform non-farmers on "who farmers are and what they do". Finally, to provide a forum for debate on rural issues.

Feedback from readers was in the form of 100 letters a month, which suggested that it is valued both for the practical advice and informed debate in its columns.

Mail, another landlocked western African country that was one of the great cultural and commercial centres of the continent, now has another useful experiment. "Cauris" a weekly economic and social newspaper was founded under dictatorship in 1990, to introduce its citizens to objective news reporting. Publishers learned that distribution in isolated regions is impossible without the full involvement of the rural organisations.

In Mexico, the 'periolibros' experiment offers "a book for the price of a newspaper". This monthly publication features prose and poetry by outstanding Spanish and Latin American writers, and illustrations by well-known artists. It started in 1992 and ran for five years. It aimed to promote the democratisation of reading, the strengthening of regional cultural identity and the process of cultural integration. It did this, by making a low-cost, high quality reading material available to the general public "on a scale seldom seen before". Teriolibros' was a book available at the symbolic cost of a newspaper. It was financed by the Fondo de Cultura Economica, a Mexican publishing house.

Even in the affluent west such initiative are still needed. 'Nieuwsblad van net Noorden' from the Netherlands offered special material for learners to practice reading skills. WAN has observed that in the Netherlands, four per cent of the adults (400000) have difficulties in reading and writing. More than 50 per cent of Dutch illiterates are unemployed. The government developed a programme to strengthen the motivation of learners to read newspapers and develop special reading strategies for neo-literate.

In 1997, the Dutch Ministry of Education set up educational goals for illiterate adults in relations to newspaper reading. So, every illiterate has the right to learn to read a newspaper. Every school for adult education in the Netherlands will include newspaper reading in their curricula.

Norwegian 'Newspaper Chat' sees Newspaper in Education instructors (teachers with special training) get parents to talk about their own media habits and how they could interact with their children in relation to the press.

Suggested activities include:

Look for news from your area.

Find out where these happen.

What news is most interesting today?

Explain "why" to the rest of the family.

Help each other find out what difficult words mean.

Talk together about a photo from today's paper.

Is there a good cartoon in today's paper?

Examine advertisements and prices,

Check out what are the bargains.

Swedish paper '8 Sidor' is written for -not about- people with intellectual disability. It is modelled on a 'normal' newspaper. In 1997, it had 5,500 readers. Seventy per cent of them were teachers. Its goal is to have it in all group homes and day centres where people with intellectual disability live and work. One lesson learnt is that intermediaries are vital. Most of the readers that read '8 Sidor' get it through an intermediary.

'Learn with Echo' is a South African experiment to offer easy reading in English and Zulu. Of its 50,000 copies each week, almost half go free to townships in KwaZulu-Natal, and rest are inserted in the Thursday edition of "the Natal Witness", Pletermaritzburg's daily newspaper, says WAN.

'Help a friend learn English' is a word- a-day column featuring an American idiom or basic vocabulary word. "The beat within' is a writing programme for young prisoners, also from the US.

In late October 2000, WAN announced that the Panama's daily La Prensa has won the 2000 world Young Reader Prize for its efforts on this front. La Prensa worked out a scrapbook that became compulsory reading in many schools and helped offset a lack of quality textbooks about the country and its heritage, the World Association of Newspapers (WAN) said. "The annual award honours the newspaper that devised the year's most innovative project to develop young readership". The Paris-based WAN also awarded a special commendation to 'Vmeste' (together), a Russian newspaper for teenagers in Siberia which held a two-day festival that required student journalists to consider the ethics of their work.

WAN honoured La Prensa for publishing a scrapbook with its Sunday youth section and then encouraging young readership by publishing "stickers" to be used to complete the scrapbook. "The six-week programme required children to access the youth section of the newspaper to create their own quality 'textbooks' for better understanding of the country," said the judges of the annual WAN World" Young Reader Prize. "In the process, the project increased Sunday circulation and generated extra advertising revenue while promoting important educational objectives."

Wendy Tribaldos, the General Coordinator of La Prensa's Newspapers in Education Programme, said textbooks in Panama tend to be out of date and there is a widespread lack of information. This is a situation not usual in any Third World nation. Among other things, the scrapbook and stickers provided an updated political map of the country, which was unavailable from other sources.

Average paid Sunday circulation jumped from 35,000 newspapers to 42,600 during the six weeks the stickers were produced and the newspaper plans to repeat the project annually. "We know from the many calls we received and the visits we make to our NIE schools that many made the album required reading for their students, and added it to the curriculum."

Creatively used, newspapers and magazines can effectively promote learning, critical thinking, creativity and resourcefulness in learners of all ages. Studies have shown that using newspapers in education helps students increase their vocabulary and comprehension, according to the Education for All Forum.

Characteristics of a Newspaper

There are many advantages of newspaper reading. They are the storehouse of the information on various subjects including politics, economy, business, government policies, burning issues of national importance, crime, sports so on and so forth. The list is never ending but the main advantages can be categorised under the following main headings.

1. Students learn to read newspaper at length in which the word usage and the language used by journalist is a perfect piece of "practical writing". As a student takes heavy input of information from the newspaper, directly or indirectly he/she gets conversant with the basic norms of writing. No other medium can teach a person the better way to write other than the newspaper. One learns the style of expression. The newspapers write on the day to day happenings so these fundamentals serves an important function in making a person familiar with process of writing.
2. Newspaper apprises the reader of the latest happenings in the country and abroad. Since general knowledge (GK) is the scale of measurement of a student's awareness as it forms an important ingredient in the career formation of a student. "Knowledge is the power" and this large pool of knowledge can be gathered by reading newspaper. Newspapers are cosmopolitan in nature. They publish stories on virtually very aspect of social life. It means they have something for everybody.
3. Newspapers give wide coverage to the government policies. It is because of these policies that people chalk out their plans and the way of living.
4. Words used in the newspapers are the single most important formative elements as it is assumed that newspapers use those words which are understood by the common people. So these words form the part of active vocabulary of a student. The practice of noting down the difficult words and then looking for its meaning in the dictionary is very common among students which give them more words to use at their disposal.

5. Special category newspapers like Financial Express, Economic Times cater to the needs of businessman. With the growth of media, demassification (separate information sources for the different segment of the audience) has increased and it is predicted that very soon specialised newspapers will be launched for a special audience having special taste.
6. Newspapers are highly subsidised by advertisements. Today's newspapers carry editorial space versus advertisements in the ratio of 40:60 respectively. It is because of advertisements that newspaper industry is running and making profits. A newspaper without ads will cost the reader something between 15 to 20 rupees. Needless to say, nobody can afford to read such newspaper. It is the only and only medium which gives the quality information in plenty and that also at a very cheap, throwaway price. All others sources like Cable TV, Internet, Direct to home (DTH) are very costly sources of information. Newspapers can be sold to the junk dealers for almost the same price at which they were purchased from the hawkers. It means we get the news at not only cheap rates but almost free.
7. Newspaper has a credibility associated with it. A person feels more impressed with the written material. Even today, in the era of computers and digital information, we tend to believe the written word. Thus quality of the news will always keep the newspaper at the top of all other information sources. A written story makes an instant impact on the mind of the reader. While realising this fact, the government of India has not allowed the publication of foreign print media from the Indian soil. As it is feared that the foreign media would mould and change the public opinion. In Cable TV, Internet and other digital media, foreign investment is allowed by the government. But print media is the only field in which government has outrightly rejected the idea of foreign investment. Our freedom fighters made a good use of this quality of the newspaper. Almost every freedom fighter was directly or indirectly associated with the newspaper as they knew that written matter can ignite the

passion of freedom among the masses. Many eminent media persons have argued that due to the arrival of different visual communication technologies, the reading habits of the people are decreasing. Moreover, newspaper gives the previous day's news but many news channels provide instant coverage of the same and that also with impressive visuals. It is feared that the newspaper readership will decrease, as people will shift to these new media of communication. But this assumption proved to be totally wrong as the overall readership has increased, and in that also, the individual readership of the different newspapers has increased of their own, not at the cost of each other's readership. It means overall media is expanding. And the localisation of print media has added on more feather into its cap because with the commencement of the local editions of the national newspapers, the local news has started getting good coverage and the credibility of the newspapers has once again got a fillip.

8. Newspapers are a handy source of information. One can carry it along during travelling thus providing flexibility to the reader. Unlike computers and Cable TV, newspapers don't require electricity to run them.
9. Newspapers can be read by more than one person simultaneously. Within a house or library, it is always read by a number of people thus benefiting multiple readers.
10. Newspapers can be put to another nice use- clippings. Some people collect the news cutting of the important article, news analysis, etc., and preserve them in a file for further use. The database thus prepared can serve useful purpose for further improvement in knowledge. While article writing, the historical background of the subject will add an extra flavour to it and newspapers clippings can readily provide the same. Every newspaper office maintains a good library so as to quickly provide the history of a particular event, calamity, etc.
11. The last but not the least, single most important advantage of the newspaper is its ability to present News Analysis, comments, views, etc., before the readers. We all know that by the time newspaper collects the information and writes

news using great writing skills and prints it in 5 to 10 lacs copies, the news has already become stale and late by 24 hours. We all know what is going to be headline in the tomorrow's newspapers, thanks to the so many news channels. But here role of a newspaper becomes more important by giving in-depth news analysis and comments on the prevalent situation in its editorial page. Editorial is the heart of the newspaper. It helps a reader to know the facts and make an opinion based on them. A very often newspaper present its views on a particular problem and guides its readers to form a healthy opinion. Other media are lacking this quality.

Briefly Speaking

- Newspapers keep students informed about the surroundings.
- Newspapers link students to the real world.
- Newspapers are a common community link.
- Newspapers are a credible source of information which can be referred, quoted and mentioned.
- Newspapers make learning fun which is more easy to learn and remember for long time too.
- Newspapers are very easy to use.
- Newspapers are flexible and adaptable to all curriculum areas and grade levels.
- Newspapers motivate students to read.
- Newspapers help students understand freedom of the press and other rights of a citizen guaranteed by the Constitution.
- Newspapers have ideas for building many educational skills, from critical thinking to analysing information.
- Newspapers can be cut, marked, clipped, pasted, filed.
- Newspapers are a cost-effective way to teach.
- Newspapers build good reading habits.
- Newspapers give everybody something interesting to read.

- Newspapers entertain as they teach.
- Newspaper is living textbooks complete with current information and changes in international boundaries and political leaders.

Importance of the Word

Some writers have compared the words with Brahma (creator of the universe). Since a sentence is composed of different words. These words are like cells. A cell is a basic unit of life and human body is composed of different cells. Similarly, a language is composed of different words. Every word is sacred and holy entity. If we want to learn a language then we have to learn the meaning of the word first. During the course of learning new words, a student should lay stress on the two very important things:

1. Meaning of the word; 2. Exact usage of the word

Many students have vast reserve of English words they also know the meaning of the word but very often; they are not able to use the word in a proper way. Sometimes it happens that we are not able to tell the meaning of the word but we can use the word into an accurate sentence. This is the destination where we have to reach.

It is always advisable to learn a word and use it in many different contexts. Every word carries along with it a sense of expression and degree of understanding. You can call a friend "fool" jokingly but you cannot call him "stupid" as it might offend him. You can call somebody "jolly" in a sense of praise but you cannot call him "joker" as it is likely to hurt him. Hence a philosophy is associated with each and every word. We are supposed to respect this. It is often said that no two synonyms in English have the same meanings. There has to be some difference in the degree of meaning and usage. Diplomats undergo a rigorous training in the usage of "soft words" and avoid using harsh words while communicating between the two nations. Diplomats know that any improper word can harm the friendliness and good relations between the two countries. Hence realising the importance of every individual word, they are given a list of "do's and don't" words. Using a wrong word is like treating a patient by giving wrong medicine.

Sometimes a set of two or three words is often used together for expression. There is no hard and fast rule but the newspapers in writing, and the people in conversation normally use these words. For example, ample evidence (enough evidences) mayhem and murder (extreme violence), fraudulent practices, crass commercialisation, etc.

Evolution of New Words: Language is like running water. If the water stops flowing then it will make mud or marsh. What we have witnessed today in the form of a language is the result of centuries long evolution as the man being has evolved from apes. As the time goes on, many new words are coined and added to the language. Very few of us might be knowing that Times of India coined the word "scam" to publish news stories on the famous stock market scandal allegedly by Harshad Mehta in 1990. Earlier, the word "scam" which means, "a clever and dishonest planning on large scale to make money" was unheard of. Likewise many new strange words have evolved. The quest for creativity and describing the things in a different way, has given birth to many new words, for example:

Fantabulous: This new word is born out of the marriage between fantastic and fabulous.

Infotainment: Infotainment is born out of the web lock between information and entertainment.

Advertorial: Advertorial is the mixture of advertising and editorial.

Webertising: Webertising is an amended form of web advertising.

Prosumer: Alvin Toffler and renowned author of the famous book "third wave" have many times used this word to describe the changing equation between producer and consumer.

Informercials: Evolved with the union of information and commercials.

Hinglish: This word is composed of Hindi and English. Advertising is using hinglish heavily these days. The first example of hinglish advertising was seen in the ad of Zenith in which the copy read "we have said this *hazaar* times."

Talibanisation: This word is coined by the media to describe the religious fanaticism anywhere in the world, outside the Afghanistan also where this word is actually relevant.

Smog: It is coined by the combination of smoke + fog.

The newspapers worldwide covered the story of Princess Diana's accident which was caused when the "paparazzi" were chasing them. The media used this word "paparazzi" extensively but there is no word like "paparazzi" in the dictionary. On deep investigation, it was found that a French novelist has named the photographers as "paparazzi" in his novel who used to chase celebrities and take their photographs anywhere, any time with out their permission. The newspapers lost no time in accepting the word. The same has not been used in any other incident till now.

While English teachers and journalists have always been at the loggerheads. Both accuse each other of using the words and language in an improper way or not writing according to the rules of the grammar. Typical English literature snubs the idea of adding these creative words as there are regarded as "distortion" in the language. But the mass media needs to present its story in the form of catchy words which can entice the reader towards it.

Use of Slang: Slang can be defined as "very common words and expressions that are more common in spoken language, especially used by a particular group of people, (children, criminals, army, etc.). The etymology is the branch of science which deals with the origin of words. The etymology of the word "slang" has not been clearly traced or established. Three categories of slang as defined in the Oxford Dictionary of English corresponding to three stages of its evolution may be mentioned.

In the mid 18th century, slang was a kind of code language. In other words "the special vocabulary used by any set of persons of a low and disreputable character." This was considered to be the language of the 'underworld".

In the late 18th century, slang signified "the special vocabulary or phraseology of a particular calling or profession". Nowadays, the word "jargon" is used to signify "slang", for example, medical jargon, technical jargon, astrologer's jargon, etc.

Since the 19th century, slang, strictly speaking, has been "language of highly colloquial type, considered as below the level of standard, educated speech and consisting either of new words or of current words employed in some special sense". Jargon or slang serves a very good purpose of binding the members of a particular group, fraternity or culture.

Etymology of slang can be traced back to the Norwegian "slengeord". It means "offensive language". The etymology of the word is obscure and uncertain and a matter of guess rather than any scientific explanation.

"Slang" came into use in 1756. In the 18th century the words "slang" and "cant" were considered identical. They referred to the secret language of those engaged in nefarious, anti-social activities like kidnapping, thieving or pickpocketing. While the word "cant" has since got differentiated in meaning and assumed a different sense. H. W. Fowler says "Slang is the diction that results from the favourite game, among the young and the lively, of playing with words and renaming things and actions: some invent new words or mutilate or misapply the old for the pleasure of novelty and others catch up such words for the pleasure of being in the fashion". The use of slang is protest against lack of variety in expression. "The chief use of the slang is to show that your are one of the gang".

Many slang keep on evolving and perishing, a few establish themselves. The tragic part is that they are considered misfit for literary use. Slang are widely employed to convey different moods, expressions, unconventionality, topicality, liveliness of expression, intimacy of communication, innovation, etc. Slang's evolution has evoked mixed response from the people and its reception and adoption was mixed and at no period was its use either universally and totally supported or rejected.

While slang is essentially a part of familiar and colloquial speech. It is not necessarily incorrect or vulgar in its proper place. And it is also not that slang has been the language of lower, disreputable section of the society but many of the slang words have found their way into standard vocabulary. "Slang is a kind of vagabond language, always lying on the outskirts of legitimate speech, but continually straying or forcing its way into the most respectable community".

These days, slang words form an essential part of a writer's vocabulary for example, beef up, idiot box, spill the beans, bet, chap fun, nab, bloody, etc. Slangs are widely used in army, navy, schoolboy, money markets and very commonly in underworld. The "back slang" also originated from the slang. In this, words are spoken with the spelling reversed. Thus "money" would be called "yenom". And "erthewhe si enif yadot" is a back slang for "whether is fine today". It is widely believed that the back slang enabled the London shopkeepers to communicate among themselves without being understood by the customers. North America, Australia, England have contributed a lot to the growth of slang. The breakdown of the strict grammatical rules of language has also contributed widely to increase in the numbers of slang. A. C. Baugh says that slang will be a source from which English will continue to be fed in the future. With the lot of information available these days for the people, the information sources have also started using strange words or "slangs" in order to capture the attention of the audience. Needless to say that English cannot shut its doors to the slang.

Value of the Word

Media of written communication signify tools of written communication. In other words, it means the instrument or instruments applied in communicating any message. Written communication has mostly and primarily been adopted as media for providing information and to get the things done through by achieving the goals of the organisation. Without the aid of written communication it is not possible to make known the organisation' broad objectives, policies, programmes, procedures, etc. To achieve this, no single medium of communication would serve the purpose. There are several media of written communications. It is the responsibility of the executive to select one or two suitable for specific purposes and for particular and peculiar circumstances. Generally executives, by and large, depend on various media.

Magazines (Periodicals): A magazine is a publication issued regularly containing information. The periodicity of a magazine may be a week, fortnight, month, quarterly, half-yearly and annually. A magazine contains articles, opinions, findings of studies, advertisements, etc. A magazine is the most important external communication medium. A magazine is the most important communicating and advertising medium irrespective of its being monthly, bimonthly, semi-monthly, weekly, biweekly, semi-weekly, and tri-weekly. Next to newspapers, magazines are the best form of written communication and offer vast scope for product advertisement.

They appeal to all kinds of people. Each magazine serves a particular section of readers. The life of a message in a magazine is long and continuous. The matter is fresh for a week, month and even longer. No doubt it is a common medium or national medium. But in a country like India where there are several languages, one language magazine is not suitable. Hence many regional magazines have come up. The circulation of some regional magazines has always been restricted to a limited area. Consumer magazines are more useful to advertise product information. Farm publications are meant for rural people. Business publications may be divided into various categories such as industrial publications, merchandising or trade publications and professional publications.

The magazine publishers association, marketing division, USA, suggests the following reasons why magazines sell:

Authority: Magazine authority dates back to man's very acceptance of the printed word as dependable to his own signature which is accepted by a binding pledge.

Colour: Magazine colour spreads before the reader a spectrum of exciting visual pleasure. Colour stimulates interest – creates desire, enhances image, identifies the package. Colour sells.

Believability: Magazine believability builds reader confidence. It influences and affects ideas – opinions – desires. People believe what magazines have to say.

Permanence: Magazines last. People save them aside for future reference – return to them again and again. The permanence of magazines gives your advertising the time it needs for careful consideration – the time that it deserves.

Selectivity: Magazine selectively targets places and people. It reaches your best prospects – wherever they are – while they are most respective to ideas and information.

Flexibility: Magazines offer a full range of prospects – with diverse interests – in one or all of the nation's key markets. The degree to which an advertisement stimulates, dramatises and sells products is entirely at the discretion of the advertiser.

Efficiency: The ability of magazines to offer the widest range of incomparable values which can be translated into dollar sales make magazines the choice of leading advertisers.

Newspapers: A paper, printed daily or weekly, containing news, etc. It is an effective external communication instrument. A newspaper is a daily or weekly publication. It contains news and opinions of current events. Most important as a communication medium in terms of coverage. It represents the most important advertising medium. A newspaper may be a local paper, or at State and National level. There are a number of business publications such as Economic Times, Financial Express, etc. The importance of the newspaper as an effective mass medium of communication is indicated by the amount of money invested in newspaper advertising, and it is also indicated by the coverage. Within the newspaper field there are newspaper supplements, as a part of the main edition. Supplements are issued as a special Sunday section. In recent years colour is also employed in newspaper advertising. In India the great majority of newspaper advertisements appear in black and white. In metropolitan cities shopping newspapers are printed exclusively for advertisement. Newspapers are sold mainly by home delivery, on news stands and by mail subscription, hence cover a wide area. The life of communication in daily newspapers is short, rarely longer than a day. But the cost of using this medium has become prohibitive these days.

Circulars: In order to inform a group of people in the organisation written matter is issued by way of circular. They are mostly used for internal communication to intimate or inform the employees. A notice especially advertising something sent to a number of persons. A number of copies of the same matter circulated among the group. To circulate means to go round. Matters of centralised communication relating to all the people concerned, circulated to the whole department. In other words, circulars' are letters or notices usually printed or cyclostyled and are addressed to a number of persons in the organisation. They are normally issued on some infrequent occasions like change of specimen signature, admission or retirement of a partner, amalgamation, change of address, etc. The head office may issue circulars to its regional or branch offices to inform them of matters for consideration and necessary action. Use of good language, tone, expressing clear intention, are the important principles to be followed by the draftsmen. The other considerations are short matter, simple language, selecting appropriate words, drawing attention to the central theme, etc.

The following are the models of matter written in circulars:

1. A circular notifying holidays.
2. A rumour circulating that he/she is getting married.

House Journal: House journal is also called as 'house magazine', 'in-house' magazine or 'journal' or 'house organs'. These magazines are private journals. The word house indicates to a trading establishment. The term organ means a medium of communicating information or opinion. Internal publications, house magazine or journal is published to keep employees, customers, shareholders, etc., informed. House journal serves as a useful and common platform to convey views of the management.

It ventilates the opinion or voice of the organisation publishing journal. For instance, the " Brooks news", the employee magazine of the Brook-bond of India Limited, "the Youth News" of the YMCA, etc. Big and well established corporations or trading establishments, industrial houses, public, private, Government agencies, educational and social institutions, voluntary associations generally publish house organs or journals. House journal is, therefore, a tool of internal communication.

In-house or corporate organs or house journals are a new kind of promotional medium. In-house is the name by which they are popularly known. In recent years a large number of companies have been publishing in-house journals. It may be mentioned that not only private companies and establishments but some public sector corporations and establishments too produce in-house magazines.

The production of in-house magazines has picked up in recent years with amazing speed. In-house communication plays an important role in disseminating relevant information to the employees working in various levels within the organisation. They contribute not only to staff benefits and welfare but also help in work place and have significant long-term benefits.

From time to time a few large organisations have been attempting to produce in-house journals. The in-house journal may handle only one product or may supplement it, usually with a group of much smaller products.

Nature and Characteristics

Ownership: The basic characteristic of house-organ is a company magazine distributed to employees, shareholders, dealers, customers, etc.

Not Advertising Media: The house-organ is not in true sense an advertising media in the sense that the term has been used for other publications.

Selling Space: Companies may sell magazine space for advertising to collect income which can partially offset costs, make them self-liquidating or actually make the publication a profitable venture.

Sale of Copies: Another method is the sale of copies to the employees to pay for their house journal.

Internal Communication Tool: In-house organs are intended merely to serve as an internal communication tool between the organisation and its internal and external public.

Public Relations: They are primarily public relations vehicles. As such the majority of the house journals are regarded as part of the public relation programme.

Business Publication: Though most of the house organs do not sell space in formal most of the house organs resemble business publications more than any other form of advertising.

Free Circulation: When house organ solicits advertisements from manufacturers to defray the cost of production, in such cases the house journal fulfils some of the characteristics of the free circulation business publication.

Internal and External Relations: House organs are designed primarily to help in promoting and maintaining good employee relations or external public relations.

Dealer Promotion: Sometimes the function of house organ may be largely in the area of dealer promotion.

Variety of House Organs: A company may publish a number of house organs for each group, for each product division or for each manufacturing plant. For instance, general motors in the USA publishes 53 different company magazines, most of which go to separate employee groups.

Publishers: In-house journals the name by which they are popularly known are produced not only by the large-scale private sector but also by public sector corporations, trading establishments, Government agencies, educational and social institutions, voluntary organisations and such other bodies.

Contents: House organs have a specific readership interest. Our modern house organs provide entertainment, information, educational, materials so that the reader may relax, escape from fatigue and promotes friendly relations between the management and managed.

Size of Media: A house journal is both of local medium as well as national medium.

Unit of Selling Space: Selling of advertisement space by house journal or periodicals is in the form of units such as whole page, half page and quarter page and by the column, half column and so forth.

The Classification: There may be different ways for classifying types of house organs. There are various classes of house organs. However, the following is the broad classification of house magazines.

Size: The first basis for grouping is on the basis of size. A house journal may be of: 1) pocket book size, 2) full size or standard size, and 3) large size. In addition there are periodical of various odd sizes. A size of a magazine may be 3-column × 140 line page. There are today a very few represent the older "standard size". Page size may be 2-column × 170 lines (Large size), 3-column × 140 lines (flat size), 2-column × 119 lines (standard size), 2-column × 85 lines (small or pocket size).

Readership: The important component as a basis of classification is the type of readership. A company may publish a number of house organs such as for each group, for each product division, or for each manufacturing point.

Frequency: As usual the other basis of classification is on the basis of the frequency of the publication. They may be daily, weeklies, bi-weeklies, monthlies, fortnightlies, quarterlies, half-yearly, etc. Monthly house organs are by far the largest group. Weeklies occupy second largest group.

On the other hand, bi-weeklies, semi-monthlies, quarterlies, or semi-annualies categories account for a relatively small number of the total.

General and Special: In-house magazines may be broadly classified into special interest magazines.

The Editorial: The Editor is a person who edits and prepares material for house journal by correcting, altering, adding, deletion, etc. He censors the materials received for publication. The word editorial represents a matter or news in a house journal written by an editor or by persons belonging to the editors. In another sense editorial is a leading article in the house journal. It includes comments, opinions, events, feelings, facts of the organisation collected or expressed by the members of the organisation. It is the voice of the sponsor.

The first consideration in a house journal is an editorial policy. The basic question is that, is it necessary to have a separate house journal editorial ? The answer is that it is must. From the standpoint of both contents and writing level designed to appeal to the various kinds of the readers, professionalised editorials is at most important.

Careful observation of several house journals indicate that editorial is indispensable to have. A good house journal formulates a good editorial policy. There must be editorial worth of house journal to its readers, since if the publication is outstanding editorially, it will almost attract a number of readers.

As a matter of fact the editorial policy will of course determine the readers' selection of the in-house journal. Similarly the editorial policy will determine the important of the magazine. If the editorial policy is vigorous and exciting it surrounds the advertising, when space is sold, with this atmosphere. A journal without an editor is a journal without a soul. Usually a separate standing committee or editorial for producing house journal is constituted.

The editor may be responsible for working with the editorial policy. The majority of house journals will be regarded as part of its public relation programme. It is the editor who establishes some sort of rapport between the readers and the editors or as in the case of good house journal the editor and the public relation man.

"The editor should, of course, meet as many of his readers as possible, preferably on their home ground rather than in editorial office, and he will also be in communication with them by telephone and correspondence, but there should also be something in each issue which is seen to spring directly from the editor or the public relations officer".

The Merits: The importance or merits of making in-house magazines are:

1. The magazines depict the progress of the firm to the employees and to the share-holders, dealers, etc.
2. They facilitate them to know about financial position, market potential, foreign collaboration and other activities and future plans.
3. They educate the investors with a view to inviting more capital for existing and diversified products.
4. They show the existing and prospective customers of the company to promote confidence.
5. The magazines probably has the greatest impact on the outside publicity.
6. In-house magazine is owned outright by the organisation and operates under its direct supervision.

7. The in-house committee of the magazine or the editorial performs all of the creative and artistic services as provided by the outside publisher.
8. In-house magazine approach reduces the total cost of advertising. If all the necessary works are done for less money the difference of benefits goes directly to the company.
9. Another advantage claimed by the organisations who own and produce house journal is the prospect of saving money by cutting overhead expenses.
10. Industrial units which run such in-house journals would build good image and goodwill for the organisation and solicits new customers and new business.
11. It serves as a good platform when the management has something interested to communicate. They are circulated at the work and office chit chat.
12. In-house journals promote industrial relations and good mutual understanding between the employees, dealers, share-holders and the management.
13. Another reason in support of publishing house journal is that it provides an objective news service.
14. House journal advertisements are good in quality in terms of printing and colour. They are usually printed on good paper that makes for an excellent reproduction of art and colour work. Such magazines give the advertiser an elegant reproduction.
15. The advantage of house journal is flexibility for the advertiser with a house journal advertisement.
16. Letters written to the editor promote good two-way communication which are invariably motivated by the spirit of organisational service covering suggestions, advice, complaints, public awareness, grievances and fair criticism. Such letters may appear on merely all subjects like cultural, literacy recreational, information, safety, welfare, promotions, organisational image, etc.

The Demerits: In spite of a number of merits emerging from in-house journals, it has its own pitfalls and drawbacks. Critics of the in-house journals offer a number of problems of producing in-house journals. Some of the drawbacks are as follows:

1. Creative personnel are working on only one product line. The talents tend to become stale, or outdated over time.
2. Organisational structure indicates hierarchical relationship. As such a certain independency of the thought and creativity is lost.
3. They may not be effective because outside advertising agencies are more mature, professionals, competitive innovators and see new opportunities, creativity and independence of thought.
4. From the point of view of receivers of journal, the house journal presents the danger that one will be stuck with it, because they are captive of the in-house journal.
5. The in-house journal tend to lack the versatility, experience, and diversity of talents which a large independent outside agency can provide.
6. A house journal may not have effective internal and external readership.
7. In a number of cases the house journals could not conform to the highest standards of Indian Industrial Journalism. They are not national newspapers as far as the freedom of the press is concerned. The overall well-being of the management is paramount. Nevertheless the in-house journals approach appears to be gaining popularity in recent years among the big organisations. Though criticism has been levelled against in-house journal, there apparently have been some successful in-house journals. Although their number in Indian context has not much in relation to number of industrial units, but still there has been an increasing interest in these types of journals in recent years. History has shown, however, that most in-house journals sooner or later benefited the organisations. In recent years there has been some increasing trend leading to the production of in-house journals.

The Suggestions

1. Every house journal should have the guidelines of definite policies and clearly defined objectives.
2. A journal without a policy may face problems of waste of money and manpower.
3. To achieve the objectives of in-house journal the publication should meet the needs of both the organisation and its employees.
4. As to the coverage is concerned the in-house journal should provide useful and meaningful information.
5. To some extent the journal should be distributed externally not only to recover the cost of production by selling space for advertisements but also should go to the group leaders of the community, customers, prospects, researchers, etc.
6. The in-house magazine will be successful only with joint efforts and interest of management and its editorial board.
7. To compensate the cost of production and efforts involved, the journal must accomplish something concrete results for the sponsor.
8. Steps should be taken in this direction of making the publication two-way by inviting questions and making surveys of attitude and accordingly then reporting them in print.
9. The publication should improve good relations not only with one of its principal public, namely, its own employees but also with the other public like customers, authorities, Government, etc.
10. The editors of the journal should try that the magazine should conform to the highest standards of Indian journalism of trade, commerce and industry.
11. A house journal should be informative, instructive, entertaining, stimulating and inspiring occasionally. The employees should consider the journal as the tool of internal communication at all levels as being a medium of

communication upwards, downwards and horizontal within the organisation.

12. There should not be any coverage of matter which is productive and defamatory in nature and to thrive on the exchange of ideas and should give an opportunity to the employees for free expression of their views.

Determinants or Factors

Frequency: The periodicity of in-house organs is an important determinant. The frequency of these organs may also widely vary. These are dailies, weeklies, semi-monthlies, bi-weeklies, monthlies, bi-monthlies, seasonal periodicals, quarterlies, semi-annuals and publications issued at frequent intervals that do not fit any of other patterns. Among them monthly magazines, quarterly magazines and fortnightly are by far the largest group. They are most common intervals at which house journals are published. But annuals are generally rare. The other categories account for a relatively small number. Most other costs will be multiplied by the frequency figure, and the number of issues has, therefore, a big bearing on the total cost. So how often will the periodical be published? Publication frequency may be an important consideration.

Size: Regarding size, house journals may vary in size and shape. Size means size of page or format. It includes factors like columns and columns width, type setting, etc. Generally a house journal is small containing a few printed or cyclostyled pages. Though there is no limit on size actually they run a few pages. There are four standardised periodical sizes. They are:

1. Pocket book size,
2. Full size or standard size,
3. Flat size,
4. Large size.

There are periodicals of various odd sizes.

Selling Advertising Space: Publication of house journals is a costly matter. In a true sense the house organ is not an advertising media in the sense that the term has been used for other publications. Some organisations may sell space for advertisements to have revenue which meets partially or fully the cost of publishing house journals or actually make the publication a profitable. There are two methods to achieve this objective, first being sale of advertisement space, secondly, sale of copies.

Concerns producing large size magazines may have advertisements, while there are no advertisements in small organs. Magazines of educational institutions like colleges and universities we generally find a large number of advertisements from companies and other advertisements from companies and other business establishments. Though such advertisements have no advertising value, but space is sold to collect revenue to offset cost of production.

Pages: The house organ of a small size may have a limited number of pages, say 6 to 12. There are also large house organs. The number of pages reflect the quantity and weight of paper, concerns postage notes. Number of pages is a determining factor to quote printing cost which is usually in multiples of four pages. But the pages have also to be filled and editorial, photographic, art and reproduction costs must be worked out according to the number of pages.

Objectives: House organs are meant to serve as a media of communicating formation or opinion to keep internal and external public to be formed. They communicate in all directions. They are important tools of internal communication to the management, play an important role in communicating the views and desires of the management in various levels within the organisation. They are the media of two-way communication, thereby the employees, subordinates, shareholders, dealers, stock holders, etc., can also communicate with the management as well as others on matters of mutual interest.

Black and White or Colour: Colours are an attraction in a house journal, they shine into the eyes of the readers. Good colour combination is largely a matter of arrangement. If an arrangement is to be pleasing, it should be planned around the principles of emphasis and balance to create interest, which reflect the character of the editor. Each colour beyond the first means an extra printing plate, and an extra working and cost. There are two classes of colours:

1. Chromatic colours,
2. Achromatic colours.

The chromatic colours are yellow, orange, red, purple, blue, green and intermediate colours called *hues*. The achromatic colours include black, white and intermediate series of grey. They are classified as primary, secondary and *tertiary;* yellow, red and blue are primary colours. Orange, purple and green are secondary colours. These colours are obtained by mixing the primary colours. Tertiary colours are mixtures of secondary colours. Full colour requires four colours, yellow, magenta, cyan and black.

Price: The house organs produced and distributed are of two types. They are priced and non-priced, or free copies. The house journals are generally printed and distributed freely without charging anything. They are generally distributed free to all the internal and external public. In colleges and universities, a small magazine fee will be collected from the students. It is also possible for house journals to have income which can partly offset costs, make them self-liquidating or actually make the publication a profitable venture. There are two methods for this. Firstly, sale of advertising space, secondly, to sell the copies to the members.

Method of Distribution: There are two important methods of distribution of house journals. They are:

Handling Out: A very satisfactory and the cheapest method of distribution of house journal is handling out copies to the staff. Under this method copies are taken round from bench to bench or from office to office.

Posting Copies: Sending copies through post is yet another important method, which facilitates the family members to read the journal. Though a better but costlier method. Dealers, stockholders, and other external public generally require posting. A separate mailing list should be maintained adopted from time to time.

There are two methods of posting copies. One flat method. If the journal is mailed then it is more attractive to receive and more inviting to read. A rolled and wrapped magazine can look a mess when unrolled and unwrapped and hence an envelope is usually preferable. The matter of folding should be faced when planning page size and choosing paper.

Editor, Cost, etc.: Generally there may be a separate standing committee or editorial committee to look after its preparation and publication. A chief editor or executive editor or a manager editor is a professional person who is a whole-time editor. An editor should conform to the highest standards of Indian Industrial Journalism. The editorial board may contain other members representing workers; clerical staff, officials, etc. An editor has to devote his full time and professional expertise to the work of producing journals. Allowance has to be made for salary, allowances to the editor, the cost of layout and design.

Get-up: The get-up of house journal is fully attractive because it is printed on art paper, a good quality paper. They are usually printed on good paper that makes for an excellent reproductive of art and colour work. Such journals also give the advertiser an elegant reproduction.

Art and Photography: If a typographical style is decided for text and title the cost can be minimised. The purely photographic materials associated with offset lithography can be both economical and efficient since each character is perfect. As far as possible, obtaining photographs from amateur source should be avoided.

Paid Contribution: Buying contribution is another aspect of a house journal. Cartoons usually have to be bought, reproduction fees have to be paid. Big-name contributors are sought. Authors may be approached through literary agents and fees to be settled.

The Contents

1. Cover photos.
2. Editorial.
3. Feature articles.
4. Board of management and official news. News about programmes and visits of the head of the organisation and other top managerial personnel. For instance, the visit of chairman to foreign countries and the programme and visits of managing director, etc.

5. Photographs. Includes photos of various activities taking place in the organisation like literary activities, cultural programmes, recreational activities of staff, workers, etc.
6. Photos and news about the meetings of various types.
7. Functions organised and management officers attending the functions such as inauguration of a building, plant, flag hoisting, consecration of temple or place of worship, inauguration of family planning unit, school, dispensary, etc.
8. Activities, movements and statements of people who are associated or interested in the organisation like consultants, auditors, business men, entrepreneurs, scientists, etc.
9. News about service and personal matters such as promotion, transfer, retirements, etc. It is usual to have a photo relating to such matters.
10. Accidents, precautions, accident benefits, etc.
11. Photographs and news of marriages, birthdays, deaths and other social and personal matters.
12. Suggestions, complaints, allegations, etc.
13. News of literary activities like adult education.
14. News and social activities of women, children, and their club activities.
15. News and activities of sports and games, participation in competition along with winning prizes and trophies, tournaments conducted, etc.
16. Letters to the editors.
17. Quotations, humour, proverb, jokes, quiz, competition, puzzles, riddles, crosswords, etc.
18. Research and development activities.
19. Results of research as to new method of production and process of production, etc.
20. Speeches, news and messages of chairman, managing director or any occasion like Republic Day, Independence Day, Anniversary, other meetings, etc.

Letters: In a restless world of written communication, letters are business. Letters are used for both internal and external communication. Letters which enable one person to reach another, and thus ensure two-way communication. Writing a lettter is an art. It represents a written message sent by post, sometimes including the envelope, a post card, an inland letter. A letterhead is a printed heading on a paper used for identity, or publicity, etc. Outstation and sometimes local letters are put in a letter box. Through the medium of a letter one person reaches out to another and as such it is still the most important of all media of mass communication.

Total mail load consists of personal, official and commercial correspondence. A letter speaks to a wider cross section like wholesaler, retailer, editor, dealer, pleader, auditor employee, student, foreigner, etc. Friendship, business relations and personal relationships depend to a very large extent on letters. The quality of the letter written promotes the image of the companies. Wide practical writing for different situations results in perfection and quality in letter-writing.

It is easy to write a letter, which is nothing but putting ideas in black and white, but to write an impressive and quality letter is difficult. Like talking everybody can write a letter. The essential of good letter-writing is to put ideas in a clear-cut manner, conveying a message in such a way as is understandable by the recipient. Though the principles of writing a letter are uniform, there is a lot of difference between business, personal and official correspondence. Some views on letters are:

> "A Letter does not Blush" — Cicero
>
> "Carrier of News and Knowledge,
>
> Instrument of Trade and Industry.
>
> Promotion of Mutual Acquaintance,
>
> of Peace and Goodwill,
>
> Among Men and Nations." — Charles W. Elliot
>
> "The Letters are the Soul of Trade."
>
> — James Howell.

A letter may be a descriptive letter, narrative letter, technical, legal, domestic, public, private, foreign, confidential, personal, official, semi-official. The world of letter may be broadly classified as introductory letters, business letters, letters of application, marriage letters, love letters, greeting letters, testimonial letters, resignation letters, thanking and congratulatory letters, letters of condolence and obituary, letter of advice and recommendation. A letter must thus create a first impression, and motivate the reader to respond positively. A good letter must have at least seven main parts like a letterhead, inside address, salutation, body, complimentary close, signature and signature identification.

Pamphlets: Pamphlets which enable the communicator to reach out despite the limitation of time and cost, are among the most common methods of written communication. A pamphlet is a small paper covered book which gives information expressing an opinion on a matter. A small treatise having a fewer pages of sheets, but not in book form, composed and written or printed, unbound with or without paper or hard cover. A pamphlet reports or describes. Pamphleteer is a person who writes a pamphlet. Oxford English Dictionary: More specifically a treatise of size and form described on some subject or question of current or temporary interest, person, social, political, ecclesiastical or controversial, on which the writer desires to appeal to the public. This is merely a consequential specialisation, arising from the fact that works of this kind are those for which the pamphlet form is now mainly employed.

Booklets: The word booklet signifies a small, thin book. Companies publish booklets about the history of the concern or a product. They are issued generally for publicity and information. The prime purpose among these objects is to provide an overall picture of the organisation to visitors, prospective customers, investors, executives, trainees, newly recruited employees and other specialised audiences. Booklets are distributed to tell the story, background and information quickly and effectively to the interested persons. It may be mentioned here that booklets are only supplementary and secondary not primary sources. A personal meeting, handshake, face-to-face communication and informal gatherings are primary media. Also a small book often paper bound.

Prof. K. R. Balan classified booklets and pamphlets into three types. They are:

1. Indoctrination booklets welcome the new soldier, employee, association member, student, supplier, or visitor. (Literature for the customer or product owner usually emanates from the sales or advertising department.) The beginner's booklet helps him to get off on the right foot. It tells him the rules of the game and the benefits of playing according to the rules. It seeks to instil a team spirit – the feeling that he has joined a winning combination.
2. Reference guides are a second type of handbook, one useful to all members. They concern themselves with the group insurance plan, pension plan, suggestion, system, hospitalisation, profit sharing, housekeeping and safety, library content, recreation programme and facilities, contest rules, campus geography, and the like. Handbooks enable members to look up specific information easily. They save time and encourage appreciation of the values of membership. They quickly provide information actually sought by the reader.
3. Institutional booklets, books and brochures have subject matter devoted to an idea or a philosophy, total concept or entity. Typical are messages related to the free enterprise system, national security, educational benefits or charitable aims. In another category are reports of dedications, celebrations, awards, history, success, expansion, and developments in science or the arts.

Memorandum: A written tool of internal communication, a memorandum, is used popularly to inform concerned people about something to be communicated.

It is often abbreviated as memo (singular) or memos (plural). A written note which helps the recipient to remember the matter. In other words, a brief written statement about a particular matter which may be served to one particular individual or meant and passed around between colleagues. In all forms of organisations, whether small or large, private or public, a memo is an effective tool in maintaining internal communication. The managers at different levels generally adopt memoranda to communicate information. The merit of a memorandum is that it provides a record of evidence and proof. Different colours are used for different purposes and sometimes forms are printed and standardised. Memos are a one-way communication generally from top to bottom. It is matter put on black and white to be remembered, placed at the top subject as the head of a note of something that is to be remembered, or a record for future reference.

A note to help the memory. In external legal communication it is a note or document in which the terms of a transaction or contract are embodied. Memorandum of Association is an external informative document required under the Indian Companies Act, 1956, containing certain clauses. A memorandum of a debt between a debtor and creditor. Memorandum of Agreement of a publishing company, containing terms of publication. In an accounting message, it is a brief informal note of a debt in the nature of a due bill. According to the Oxford English Dictionary: "An informal epistolary communication, without signature or formulae of address or subscription, usually written on paper with a printed heading bearing the word 'Memorandum' and the name and address of the sender."

Office Orders: An official document used for internal communication to give instructions to the employees. Office orders may be usually issued to a particular person or persons. Transfers or promotions, increments sanctioned, etc., are normally given effect to by office order. General messages are conveyed by office order by way of distribution of copies to all its employees. The departmental manager and top management are competent to issue an office order.

Written in brief, covering the core of the subject to be informed, it is divided into one or two paragraphs. In a type of office order, a lower executive may issue an office order under the authority and direction of the superior authority. Inter and intra-departmental communications can effectively be passed through office orders. Essentials of good office orders are that they should be simple, brief and easily understandable by the recipient. The respective executives will maintain an effective link in the organisation.

Without the aid of office orders organisations cannot be run effectively. As such executives, by and large, depend on this medium to inform, instruct and to give an introduction.

Official Routine: The language characteristic of an official document. An official order is an authoritative direction, injection, mandate, a command, etc. Models of official orders:

1. A decision of a Board that union meetings should not be conducted during office hours in the premises.
2. A written direction to pay money or deliver property given by a company legally entitled.
3. A direction to make purchases of goods or supply of goods.
4. A written direction to the borrower to make, provide or furnish anything as a good security for a loan.

Thus an office order is a written specific command or notice issued by the commanding authority. It is an authoritative direction of how to proceed or act in a more restrictive application.

Instructions: The ordinary meaning of the word implies to teach or to direct. However, it may be noted in real world situations, the word is used for giving knowledge or information to others in writing. The originator or sender of an instruction or instructions may issue written messages either to an individual, or to a group or employees. Instructions are normally found to be very specific since they aim at achieving a particular purpose. It is, therefore, evident that any such instruction is supposed to move from a higher level of organisation down the ladder.

Thus instructions may be from executives to a lower level, from top levels to the middle level. The basic advantage of instruction is that it helps to educate or enlighten on a particular subject. This medium is also a one-way-communication. It needs to be mentioned that under all circumstances it is the primary responsibility of the originator of the instructions, that they should be well written and brief, instructive and informative. They should be in simple language, concise and understandable by the recipient. The basic objective of such instruction is to help the receiver to grasp, and understand effectively and instantaneously without confusion and in a non-technical manner. The literary and educational background factors should also be taken into consideration by the sender. Some specimen instructions are as under:

1. *Instructions to Individuals:*
   a. Please get ready the agenda and the minutes of the last meeting.
   b. Please pay Rs.... as donations to the flood relief fund and claim deduction.
   c. Please check up the stock position and place orders immediately.
2. *Instructions to a Group:*
   a. Workers or semi-skilled workers are advised to go Unit II the management instructs.
   b. Salesmen of Territory II must please get ready to go to field survey.
3. *Instructions to the Employees of the Company:*
   a. Employees of the company are requested not to hold an election meeting during office hours.
   b. Employees who are desirous of taking a festival advance must intimate to the accounts section at least one week before to facilitate the office make necessary arrangements to disburse.
4. *External Instructions:*
   a. Applicants are advised to write their examination in Hindi or English only.
   b. Inviting tenders.

Manuals: A compilation of directions and instructions in book or booklet form a handbook. Manuals are in popular use both for internal and external communication. They are a medium of exchanging facts and ideas concerning all people in the organisation. They are usually a one-way communication originating from top authority on established principles and rules to be followed in the organisation. A small book which gives information about a particular field of a subject. Manual of law, manual of procedure, manual of duties, responsibilities, handbook of planning, handbook of labour relations, handbook of public relations, etc. They state the rules and benefits following from them. They seek to instil a team spirit. Specific information on a particular subject can be obtained easily.

They serve as guides to discharge one's own duties and responsibilities effectively. Organisational or institutional manuals deal with the subject matter devoted to that particular organisation or institution. A small book for handy use, intended to be kept at hand for reference. A concise treatise, an abridgement. Every office normally has an office manual which contains standard practices, current practices, conventions, instructions and organisational policies based on executive decisions for guidance to the staff.

They are an authoritative guide to office organisation issued for better performance of organisational activities. A manual contains a brief history of the organisation, growth and development, charts, objectives, positions, their functions, the duties and responsibilities of each section, general policies, welfare and working facilities. A manual is useful both for new as well as to existing employees.

Office Notes: Tool of internal communication, hence they are useful in all organisations. A note is a piece of writing to call attention to something. A message written down in short form. A short explanation to the main subject matter. Notes are used in all official communications for getting information passed around or up and down. They are one way of communicating instructions, explanations, clarifications, etc.

It may be mentioned that notes are a widely used technique of communication. They are suitably written communication media in any type of organisation irrespective of the nature and type of business organisation. In restless and busy organisational activities the executives and their subordinates often adopt notes to pass on the necessary information from one person to another person, from one section to another section, etc. It is with the help of the notes that people are kept correctly and properly informed or instructed. It goes without saying that the basic responsibility for official notes rests on the originator or transmitter of the message. So notes help the recipient to understand quickly by catching the central theme. Thus they avoid delay. They should be brief, precise and simple to the receiver.

Explanations: An instrument of internal written communication originating from the authority concerned giving in brief clarifications and explanations, so as to enable the recipient to come to a correct decision. Correct and perfect decision making is possible when the written subject matter is fully clarified and its implication explained. Explanations are communicated to make the main subject matter clear or easy to understand.

A written document or statement of facts, figures, and opinions explaining the matter. Sometimes explanatory notes are added at the end of the matter to avoid delay and to get rid of confusion to the reader. They represent queries, views, opinions and decisions about any particular subject.

It is the duty of the originator to prepare them most carefully pinpointing the central theme or message. Explanations and clarifications are usually sought on subject matter which is written in pompous language, technical jargon and cumbersome approach to the central theme. Explanations should be clear in approach, simple in language and supported with necessary references and information.

Posters: Yet another form of written communication is the poster generally used for external communication. A poster is a large notice or advertisement for sticking on a wall. A written document, a playcard pasted or displayed in public places as an announcement or advertisement. It may include a pictorial or picture poster, a playcard consisting mainly of a picture of an illustration. A poster gives an opportunity to the by-passer to see and read. This form of written communication offers many advantages to the organisation because it draws the attention of many people. A poster is prepared based on planned specialisation and all the activities relating to a poster exhibition are effectively supervised and controlled. A poster in a prominent place attracts a great variety of cross sections of the people. Posters are generally used for product advertisement. The posters are called bill boards. Posters are used widely for outdoor advertising.

Leaflets: A leaflet is a small printed document containing information. A written medium of external communication to inform people outside the organisation. It is used as an instrument to inform the public, well informed about the product, uses, qualities, characters. The main drawback of a leaflet is that it does not serve as a medium of two-way communication. Oxford English Dictionary: A small sized leaf of paper or a sheet folded into two or more leaves but not stitched, and containing printed matter, chiefly for gratuitous distribution.

Thus a leaflet is a printed or written folding circular having several unsewed, unstitched pages in one strip. It is a leaflike part.

Forms: A form is a card or a sheet or a continuous strip of paper used for keeping some record. A form has some fixed data which is generally pre-printed on the form and provides space for variable data or information which the user of the form has to fill in. Thus a form may be defined as a piece of paper containing some information printed or reproduced by any method with blank spaces left for the entry or additional information by the office, staff or/and by outsiders.

Forms save time and energy. A medium by which all messages are supplied and recorded. Forms are generally standardised. Different forms in different colours and sizes facilitate classification and quick reference. Forms are to be controlled. Every organisation must have effective systems of form control to save time and cost. By simplification of work, classification, easy reference and printing, delays can be avoided.

Bulletins: A bulletin is an official written report of news. It is issued to inform about the product, progress results, achievement, etc. It is a printed information sheet. The news given out as a bulletin on a very recent matter of attraction. The news bulletins are broadcast on radio or TV in exact terms in which they are written or sometimes may be amended. A bulletin board is a notice board of news. Bulletins are entirely different from posters. They are an arrangement for outdoor advertisements on printed bulletins. A painted display bulletin is another major type of outdoor communication. It is called as painted display. A bulletin may be a permanent bulletin or rotary bulletin. Painted displays are placed on walls in a prominent place. Embellished painted bulletins are another form, such as cutouts, special illumination and animation. Buying painted bulletins are more durable than poster paper.

Catalogues: Catalogues are mostly used as a written form of external communication. They contain relevant information about products and educate the public about the prospects of making a purchase. Catalogues are a direct medium to draw the attention of the reader. They provide valuable information and can be used as a substitute for the sales information. Catalogues may be issued in loose leaf or folder form and may be released bounded and stitched when there are more pages. Special catalogues may be prepared for certain classes of customers, for certain types of products, and for certain occasions.

Brochures: These are written documents for external communication. They are short booklets containing information about a particular subject. The examples of brochure are brochure of advertisement, brochure of holidays, brochure of product information, etc. A brochure is like a pamphlet on which anything is written or published in pamphlet form.

Union Publications: The place of union publications in communication, particularly in written media, cannot be overemphasised. Unions have equal participation in communication. Union periodicals, or a set of issues, has a channel of communication upon which many employees depend for information.

During periods of insecurity and uncertainty, union literature gives members of the organisation an outlet to ventilate freely or express their fears, attitudes and thoughts. The collective decisions, opinions, ideas, feelings or actions of the members are transmitted through this medium. Management cannot ignore or eliminate the union activities, for it will survive in spite of everything, and the management can make use of the union for effective communication. The union is an informal communication network and can be used to send messages quickly.

The management can transmit some of its communications to the unions with responsibility. Unions' publications in written communication field give confidence to the employees and strengthen the employers. Because of illiteracy among workers trade union literature does not play a very important role in transmitting the message to them. A formal communication with the workers is not effective.

Complaints and Suggestions: In grievance procedure complaints and suggestions are a method. They are one of the instruments of written communication. Employees individually or in a group lodge complaints or offer suggestions in writing. Generally a complaint and suggestion box is installed at a prominent place or places within the premises. The employees who wish to make a complaint on any matter like working conditions, facilities and on general matters and offer suggestions can place them in the complaint and suggestion box. It is a good example of upward communication. The subordinates through this medium can transmit a message to an upward channel. Generally, the suggestion method is not effective. There are many reasons for failure of the suggestions and complaints box:

1. Employees are afraid to lodge complaint,
2. Their inability to express ideas in black and white,
3. Management may ignore the matters,
4. Lack of full knowledge about the issue,
5. There is no interpersonal exchange and
6. The system is impersonal.

House Journals: An internal publication, such as a house magazine or journal is published to keep employees or customers informed. The house journal serves as a useful and common platform to convey the views of the management. For instance, "Brooks News" the employees' magazine of Brooke Bond of India Limited, "The Youth News" of the YMCA, etc.

Handbook: A manual. A small book giving information about something. The most important medium of written external communication.

Handout: A leaflet of information given to concerned people. It is similar to a handbook and meant for external communication.

Handfiles: Like leaflets handfiles are tools of external communication to keep the people outside the organisation well informed about something. They do not serve two-way communication.

Matter Reading

Newspaper is the road on which the locomotive of democracy moves. It is the most important contributor to the philosophy of democracy. A newspaper is like a mirror to the society in which the state of affairs gets reflected and demand attention of the public. It is only through newspapers that general public is informed and guided by. Newspaper has to fulfil its duty of forming healthy opinion of their readers regarding the important issues before a nation and society.

Press gets the honour in terms of fourth pillar of the Constitution apart from Parliament, judiciary and executives. Over the years, editions and the circulation of the newspapers have increased manifold. This has led to increased readership. During independence, country had a literacy rate of 34 per cent and awareness was very low. But due to the passage of time, the editions and circulation of the newspapers began to increase along with the increased literacy rate at present (64%). Highly developed individualistic societies like UK, USA, etc. trace their link of development to the high penetration of the newspapers.

Text Types

Newspapers are cosmopolitan in nature giving information on variety of subjects. This is the easiest and novel way of getting acquainted with knowledge. Newspapers are the best agents of mass communication. They perform the job of communicating the information to the masses at large. The highly professional people, sometimes called "Knowledge Processors" run newspaper industry. At first stage, they perform the task of sifting and segregating the meaningful knowledge components and deliver it to their consumers, i.e. readers. At the second stage, information is processed at the reader's level. Distortions are introduced when information is processed by the human mind. Information processing has two components.

1. Communication of verbal or visual facts.
2. Evaluation of the information.

Distortions can be introduced at one or both levels. These distortions may be semantic (related to meanings of words) or linguistic (language related). The other kinds of distortions can be on the reader's part where he/she fails to understand the meaning of a complete sentence because of less exposure of compatible words which are always used in combinations with other words.

For example: ample evidence, mayhem and murder, fraudulent practices, etc.

But here, the primary concern of the reader is to understand the meaning correctly and use that word in a suitable way. It is often said that no two synonyms in English have the same meaning. There has to be some differences in the degree. E.g. "fool" and "stupid" can't be used alike. Likewise "destruction" and "holocaust" have lot of differences.

Aims and Objectives

Every effort has an objective. While doing the course in mass communication, a student has to read different Hindi and English newspapers. One can find little difficulty in reading Hindi newspaper but this is not true for English ones. A student is supposed to maintain a good deposit in his vocabulary bank. So this effort was made while keep in mind the following objectives.

1. To identify and list down newspaper industry based words since a limited number of words are used interchangeably everyday. If we go on collecting the words for about three months then we would find that only after fifteen days, no new words other than the already listed ones are appearing again and again. Hence it can be assumed that on 16 day,

we may not find new words but we can clearly see the repetition of the old words. If we carefully analyse the conversation of the upper class people then we would find that the words used in their conversation are drawn from the newspapers because there is no other source. So we don't need to remember all the words and get confused in their meaning rather we can learn these 1900 words and find ourselves in the category of English speaking gentlemen.

2. To create a database so as to help the journalism students improve their writing skills while having the large number of core words at their disposal thus making their more acceptable. It is a common problem with the students that they run short of effective words while speaking and writing.
3. To help future students in improving their vocabulary in a right direction. Hardwork is very important but hardwork in the right direction is most important. English language is a big graveyard of dead words which are never used in the practical life. So where to find the practical words from? the answer is "from the newspapers".
4. To identify the often repeated words in English newspapers so as to pay special attention to them.
5. To identify the idioms and phrases commonly used in English newspapers and list them down. Idioms and phrases add flavour to the piece of writing. Sometimes they give a humorous touch to the writing making it interesting to read. Moreover Idioms say the full story in five or six words otherwise a full paragraph would have to be written to describe that story.
6. To help the students to translate the English into Hindi and vice versa. Translation is the most important aspect of any language. Many of our great books like Vedas, Upnishads, Ramayana, Mahabharata, etc., have been translated into the English language to spread their message to the people who don't understand Sanskrit and Hindi. Sometimes the journalist has to translate a piece of writing into English or

Hindi. At that time some basic rules of translation and the exact meaning of the word in other language must be known to the person.

7. To use the word in a correct sentence. Mere knowledge of the meaning of the word would not suffice. The real beauty lies in its exact usage. Many a times, it is seen that some students cram the English dictionary but they are not able to use that word to form a sentence. Why do we learn the new words? Obviously, to make a beautiful sentence out of it.
8. And the last but not the least, to know the exact pronunciation of the word. English is a typical language in which the words are pronounced in an entirely different way. In Hindi and Sanskrit, the words are pronounced in the same way as they should be pronounced.. Any layman can correctly pronounce these words but in English, the words carry a different pronunciation than what it looks on its face. One has to learn to pronounce the word in a proper way otherwise the beauty of the language will be lost. Phonetic symbols used in the dictionary are very difficult to understand for a common man so the pronunciation has been written in Hindi in order to avoid any confusion.

Word Knowledge

The Methodology: First of all, vocabulary of some students was checked by taking a test of 20 words from newspapers. The result was disappointing. So an assumption was made that if the words from different English newspapers are collected by the students themselves along with the author who have undergone the test; then such words and the students will definitely represent the core section of the industry based words and target audience respectively.

A very simple and sensible method was employed to identify and collect the words. First of all the selection of the newspapers was done using the census method. Almost all the freely available English newspapers were selected. These include the national as well as the regional ones, e.g. The Tribune, The Hindustan Times, The Times of India, The Hindu, The Indian Express, The Pioneer,

The Statesman, etc. Out of these, the words commonly used were listed. An assumption was made that the journalists have limited number of words at their disposal which they use frequently to write their stories. The assumption proved to be correct after few days. It so happened that the more new words were not appearing in the newspapers so that they can be listed. It was seen that almost all the words were noted down and newspapers were not using any new word.

The word list so made, was checked time and again. A practical exercise was done. We checked whether the listed words really and regularly appear in the newspapers. Almost one week was spent on checking and tallying these words with the words in newspapers. The result was highly satisfactory.

The Significance: If a student understands the correct meaning of different words used in a particular sentence the he/she can easily comprehend the meaning of the complete sentence but if a single word is incomprehensible the message of the whole sentence gets blurred. Instead of identifying and learning new words daily over two years of his/her duration of the course, a journalism student can consult this ready reckoner and increase his print media vocabulary. Simultaneously, as the official communication taking place between one office and the other, uses the same language and words similarly the students can know the writing styles and learn to follow the same.

Artistic Writing

The role and career of the Third World Journalist has many facts. With limited human resources and economic accessibility, having more than one job, and media cross-overs are facts of life. A young person might aspire to be a journalist, or a writer, and start as a reporter for a newspaper, or for a radio station. Soon the reporter might also work part-time for a magazine, or a researcher or script-writer for a television station.

May be the very same reporter would be promoted to the post of editor, or become an information officer, or even go into politics. The dedicated journalist/writer often realises that he or she has to be flexible and adoptable in her or his creative pursuits, as well as in serving the community; and reporting is only one of the many ways towards the goal of national and economic development.

As press systems in the First World tend to move more and more towards investigative and interpretative reporting, some journalists feel that the scope and craft of journalists should also be expanded. "Literary journalism" is a result of their efforts.

Skill for Writing

Whatever kind of intro you are writing, on whatever kind of story, there are some general points to remember.

Intro should be Direct, Uncluttered and Unambiguous: There should only be one question in readers' minds when they read an intro: 'Do I want to read this story?' The answer is liable to be 'no' if you give them extra questions raised by ambiguity and complication. It is also important to clear out any unwanted clutter, such as needless detail, precise titles, or attribution, that can wait until the second paragraph or later.

Intro should be Self-contained: Except with certain types of features, it should not depend for its sense on what follows, only for its explanation and exposition. Neither should there be any unidentified facts, people, events, organisations or places unless strictly necessary.

Never Start any Story with a Subsidiary Clause: For instance, 'Despite the rising number of murders...' or 'Although murders are increasing almost daily...'. This approach is slow, delays the main point and puts questions in readers' minds. Subsidiary clause beginnings have this effect on any sentence and so should be used sparingly even in the body of the text.

Never Start a Story with Numbers in Digits: Spell out the number or, if it is a large one, find another way to begin the story. Do not just shove in the word about, as in About 47 people died yesterday when....'. This makes precise information sound like a wild guess.

Never Start Stories with Official Names of Official Bodies: Unless you have an exceptional reason or are being ironical, long bureaucratic titles are a bad way to start a story. If you begin: 'The Ministry of Agriculture and Fisheries Pollution Monitoring Unit yesterday announced...', readers will turn away before they have a chance to read that all fish caught in a certain river are contaminated and should not be eaten. Begin instead with either a short form of the name, such as 'Government pollution experts', or, far better, tell people what has happened and attribute it later.

Only Rarely begin with Quotes: Beginning stories with quotes mystifies readers because until you tell them, they do not know who is talking. There are a few isolated occasions when a quote will be a good way to start, but, in these cases, the speaker should be identified immediately.

The bad intro that I most commonly see is the one that begins 'It emerged last night that...'. This immediately begs the question: who or what is it? And `emerged' is a silly word to describe something being announced, revealed, said or published. The only story which would justify an 'It emerged last night' intro would be one revealing the Loch Ness monster's sudden appearance from the depths.

Do not Get too Obsessed with the Length of Intros: Some papers have rules about the maximum length of intros. If yours does, you have little choice but to conform. But otherwise, do not worry too much if an intro's 'length breaches some mythical 'limits'. I have never read a letter from a reader complaining about the length of an intro. So long as an intro is grabbing readers' attention, it is doing its job.

Normally when intros are written about in textbooks, the author will list various types of newspaper story (straight news, human interest, etc.) and set out the intros used in each case. This is unhelpful, stupid and wrong. It gives the impression that writing is a matter of acquiring techniques, that journalists can be provided with a bag of tricks or tools which they open and use according to the circumstances: 'Ah, here is a human interest story, so out comes the delayed intro approach...'. And it produces the formula writing which is such a disease. Far better to set out the different approaches to intros and leave it to the writer to decide how to apply them.

Usage of Words

Papers used to present hard news stories with headlines of many lines, or decks. This gave all the main points of the story and sometimes contained as many words as today's headline and first paragraph combined. Consider this from the *Philadelphia Enquirer* of Monday 17 April 1865 reporting the news of President Lincoln's assassination on the Friday before:

> The Great Tragedy!
>
> A Nation Mourns Its Honoured President
>
> Joy Changed To Mourning!
>
> The Great Martyr To Liberty!

Murder of the President

Full Details of Assassination

Account of a Distinguished Eyewitness

Mr. Lincoln's Deathbed Scene

A Noble Patriot Gone To Rest

Escape of the Dastard Assassin

Mr. Seward Still Alive

His Condition is Favourable

Andrew Johnson Inaugurated as President!

His Inaugural Address

Views of the New President

He Retains The Old Cabinet!

Official Gazette From Secretary Stanton

Our Special Dispatches!

No wonder that after all that there was no need to write what we would now call a hard news intro. There are 80 words in the headlines above, far more than would be in the headline and first two paragraphs of a newspaper story today.

Nearly a hundred years later on the afternoon of 23 November 1963, came the assassination of President Kennedy. Here are the headlines and intro from the following day's *Dallas Morning News:*

Kennedy Slain On Dallas Street

Johnson Becomes President Pro-Communist

Charged With Act

> A sniper shot and killed President John F. Kennedy on the streets of Dallas, Friday. A 21-year-old pro-communist who once tried to defect to Russia was charged with the murder shortly before mid-night.

There are 48 words here for headlines and intro, only a little more than half of the headlines alone for the Lincoln story. Leaving aside the question of the loaded references to 'pro-communist', the intro is identical in form and intent to ones put on hard news stories throughout America, Britain and much of the rest of the world today.

Chronological or leisurely intros on hard news stories began to disappear at the beginning of this century. Headlines became bigger in type size but far smaller in terms of words and so the intro had to do the job that all those headlines did before. Stories shortened as mass literacy spread and so had to be written more crisply, and papers became far bigger, thus increasing competition within the paper for readers' attention. All these pressures within the newspaper industry speeded the evolution of the hard news intro.

Factors outside the press were at work, too. The pervasive impact of advertising with its snappy, catchy language and simple messages has had an enormous effect on popular culture throughout the world. And social changes like mass car-ownership, radio, television and greater general affluence meant people had less time to read papers. Readers wanted, and got, directness.

So much for the theory of the hard news intro. Now the practice. We are talking here about reporting news in the first instance. Stories written on a subject several days after the event may need a different approach and certainly would if they had in the meantime been reported on radio or television.

The aim of all intros is to grab readers and arouse their interest so strongly that they will want to read on. With hard news intros, this means that the most newsworthy aspect(s) of the story should be right up there at the top. This is particularly true if your paper's headline style is cryptic with little detailed information about the story underneath. All the more reason to come to the point as soon as you can. This is not normally difficult on strong or clear-cut stories. If 345 people have been killed in a plane crash, there is not much doubt about the hard news intro: 'At least 345 people were killed when a Global Airlines Boeing 747 crashed into an apartment block in the suburbs of Capital City last night.' But many stories are not as direct as that. They have several angles (aspects) and we cannot get them all into the intro without making it hopelessly cumbersome. You have to decide which is the most newsworthy.

That makes it sound simple, but it isn't. Too many highly experienced journalists have spent too many hours writing, rejecting and then rewriting intros. And the issue of what is the best angle for the intro is probably the part of the job that causes more arguments in more newsrooms around the world than anything else. There is invariably no simple right and wrong, just conflicting opinions.

So if you are in two (or three) minds about how to write the intro for the story, is there any help available? Thankfully there is. It was some advice given to me many years ago by Peter Corrigan and I think it is the single most useful tip anyone has ever given me. It is called the *Parable of The Friend On The Hill* and it goes like this:

> Imagine you have all the story's information in your head and you are walking in the country. Suddenly, on top of a hill, you see a friend who you know will be keen to learn about your story. You run towards him, up and up, and when you get within reach of him you only have enough breath for one sentence before collapsing. What is it that you blurt out? That is your intro.

There are variations on this theme, such as to imagine you are sending a telegram about the story, the charge is £ 10 a word and you are paying. Set yourself a very severe target for the number of words in the telegram: six, or even four. What that will do is force you to think of the key word or words in the story. You can then build the story around that. Geoffrey Murray, an experienced Reuters correspondent, tells an anecdote which perfectly illustrates this. It involves the Reuters correspondent in India covering Mahatma Gandhi at an engagement in 1947. The yarn conflicts with the version in the official history of the news agency, but that does not detract from its therapeutic value to the confused writer of intros.

The Reuters man was at a prayer meeting attended by the Indian leader when an assailant suddenly leapt forward and shot him. Gandhi was badly wounded, but not immediately dead. The reporter ran down the road to the nearest post office to send a cable to London, but found he only had enough money to transmit four words. What should they be? 'Mahatma Gandhi shot here'? – well, you can probably assume your office will know the leader's full name and be aware of his, and your, whereabouts, so 'Mahatma' and 'here' are wasteful. What he filed was: 'Gandhi shot worst feared' – thus conveying an assassination attempt, the victim, method and likely outcome, all in four words. He had also alerted the office to prepare the obituary to run – a vital thing for the agency and all its clients.

(But beware: brevity can breed ambiguity. A message from New York was received at Reuters' London office in September 1901 which read 'McKinley shot Buffalo' and was spiked by a young subeditor with the words, 'These Yanks. They seem to think we're interested in their President's shooting excursion.' The story was rescued by the editor in charge who realised that Buffalo referred not to the animals but to the city in New York State. Thus, did the agency first flash the news of the assassination around the world.)

Another Process

In most cases where you are reporting on news of general interest, and doing so in the first instance, the hard news intro is the best choice. Yet there are, of course, many other ways to begin a story and some of them can be applied to news stories in the right situation. Feature openings are generally a lot more free-form and, for these especially, the only criteria are what works, is that they are fresh and inventive. This point is equally true of intros to analysis, colour, comment and personality pieces.

Every writer should make intros a lifetime's study, taking every available paper or magazine as a potential text. Once you begin to study intros you soon realise that what you thought were about four or five main types soon multiply into scores. The following are some of the main sorts found on news stories and features. Some of them raise the issue, dealt with more fully in the chapter on construction, that intros are often conceived not as one paragraph but as several.

Narrative: This is an intro which deals with the story in a chronological way. Used commonly on features, it is sometimes used on news stories where how it happened is more interesting or important than what happened. Use, and subsequent abuse, of the chronological start in news features by the *Sunday Times* of London gave birth to a now much-derided school of intro writing. For example:

> At 12.47 pm two men in identical blue suits, each carrying a Samsonite attache case, left the Ruritanian Embassy by the rear entrance.
>
> They hailed a taxi, asked the driver to take them to Victoria Station and sat back in its black leather upholstery. In the 25 minutes it took the driver to negotiate the capital's heavy lunch-time traffic, neither let go of his innocent-looking case for one second.
>
> At Victoria Station the taller man took out a brand-new E5 note and paid off the driver, 47-year-old father of three Harry Wingfield. Little could he have known their final destination...

And so it might go on for another few paragraphs. This novel-style approach has its uses, but one warning: tantalising the reader like this means that when you finally get to the point, it had better be a strong one. If, in the example above, they were smuggling secrets or were off to blow up a rival embassy, all well and good. Not so, however, if they had been given a half-day off and were merely on their way home to spend an evening with their stamp collections.

Anecdote: This is an intro which relates a self-contained anecdote to illustrate an aspect of the story's subject, and is often used on lengthy news features either to introduce main players, show their relationships, or relate an unknown vignette from the story's otherwise well-known sequence of events. It is vital to ensure the anecdote is good and makes a point.

Delayed Drop: This is an intro of several, sometimes many, paragraphs where the story's point is saved up, like the punch line of a joke. It is often used on soft news stories and light-hearted articles where ordinary everyday events are described for a few paragraphs, followed by the introduction of the nub of the story in a paragraph that inevitably begins, 'Now...' or, 'And then... Somewhat stylised and hackneyed, it often produces banalities of the 'Little did they know...' variety, as in: 'It was a perfect flight. The weather clear, the wine good and the meal excellent. But little did they know as they fastened their seat belts for the landing that two minutes later the plane would catch fire, fall to the ground in seconds and that only two of them would survive.'

Single Statement Intro: This is the opposite of the story above. Here the whole story is encapsulated in one telling sentence. Economical, evocative and powerful when it works but disastrous when it doesn't; it needs experience, real talent and good judgement. The most appropriate use is on a story which is important, not entirely unexpected and which will be run by virtually all news media. One of the best was on the death of Hitler in May 1945. Imagine that was your story. What could you write on this (already reported on the radio) that would not read as if it were too obvious and unexciting? It is a tall order. But the British *News Chronicle* began its story with the stark sentence: 'The most hated man in the world is dead.' Running it a close second was an intro written by Jack London, author of *White Fang,* for *Collier's Weekly* in April 1906. His assignment was the earthquake and subsequent fire which destroyed most of the buildings in San Francisco and made 225,000 people homeless. London began his report with a paragraph of just four words: 'San Francisco is gone.'

Summary Intro: This surveys the territory into which the reader will be taken by the writer and is used to its best advantage to distil the main elements of a complex chain of events. For instance, a story about a very complicated betting fraud involving horse racing could have begun: 'A betting syndicate yesterday tried to swindle £400,000 from bookmakers across Britain.' But a better alternative might be: 'Joe Martin was a gambler who was so keen to win on the horses that he invented a race course, held a "meeting" there, got his friends to bet on its fictitious results and nearly, very nearly got away with it all.'

This type of intro is used also when the story's interest lies not in one main point but in a number of developments. Although very useful, the danger with the summary intro is that if it is insufficiently comprehensive it only delays the problem of deciding the most important aspect until the second paragraph. Perhaps the best way to avoid this is to think of it as akin to a film trailer, giving highlights of what is to come. Then it is especially valuable on stories surveying a broad range of subjects or people, or on profiles of individuals. For example: 'Farouk is not just the King of Egypt. He is also a road hog, racketeer, womaniser, glutton, pickpocket and, now, an overweight playboy in exile. He is, in fact, the King who never grew up.'

Singular Statement Intro: This is an opening where the writer throws a bizarre or amazing statement at readers in the hope of tantalising them into reading on. A war reporter once began a piece with the line, 'This morning I shaved in vintage red wine...', before going on to write that the unit he was with had just taken one of the more important vineyards from the Germans.

Jolt Intro: This is where you take two pieces of information in the story, most probably the origin and the outcome, and put them together so that they provide a jolt. Deliberate understatement is often essential. For instance, this by an American writer on what might have been a fairly routine accident story: 'Billy Ray Smith lit a cigarette while soaking his feet in petrol. He may survive.'

Scene Setter Intro: This is an intro where the writer paints a word picture of a scene that is unusual or else vital to understanding the subject. Used most commonly on long soft features or on colour pieces, it has to be both well-written and have its significance explained soon afterwards. It is at its best when there is some 'the clock struck thirteen' peculiarity to it. As in:

> Imagine the scene. It is winter and inside an unheated apartment sits an old man wearing nothing but a thin gown. He is bent over a table, examining something through a microscope. A small candle burns by his elbow. All of a sudden, he leans back, smiles, takes a $ 5 note from his pocket, puts it in the candle's flame and uses it to light a small cigar. You are compelled to read on to discover what it is that he is looking at,

why he has no need of heat or warm clothes and what he is doing using dollars to light cigars. He is, the story goes on to explain, a bank note forger fallen on hard times. The trick is to write something where the reader yearns to know what happens next, as in Anthony Powell's intro to his novel, Earthly Powers:

It was the afternoon of my eighty-first birthday, and I was in bed with my catamite when Ali announced that the archbishop had come to see me.

Question Intro: This is a dangerous opening, since readers are apt to give an immediate answer and pass on. So best not ask them direct, easily solved questions. Nor ones to which there is a surprising reply, since this is an infallible indicator that the information given in the answer would be better deployed in the intro. It is often used (ill-advisedly) on soft life-style features, as in, 'How many times did you wash your hands today ?' but is best used on features where the question has a complex solution(s), could not possibly be answered by any reader and you delay answering it completely until the end of the piece. Even then, it should be used very sparingly. Its application to news stories (which are supposed to provide answers, not questions) would be absurd.

Joke Intro: This is one of the most common of all intros, but, humour is attempted more often than it is achieved. Despite this, it is a very effective opening when successful because readers feel they are in the company of an amusing writer and will always read on in anticipation of more humour.

The opening can be a one-liner, like this from P. J. O'Rourke of the American magazine Rolling Stone: 'There are probably more fact-finding tours of Nicaragua right now than there are facts.'

Or it can be a number of sentences that build up to a punch-line, as in this, also by O'Rourke:

> My friend Dorothy and I spent a weekend at Heritage USA, the born again Christian resort and amusement park created by television evangelists Jim and Tammy

Bakker. Dorothy and 1 came to scoff - but went away converted. Unfortunately, we were converted to Satanism.

Philosophical Intro: This consists of making some broad and sweeping, epigrammatical statement that is supposed to sound profound and yet rarely is. Be aware that the thought you conceived about the condition of humanity, which came to you just as the clock ticked towards your deadline, is unlikely to look so rich in meaning the following day.

A variant of this is that old college essay trick of putting up a statement in the intro solely for the purpose of demolishing it in the rest of the piece. The problem with this approach is that it often comes across as a writer's trick rather than an inventive start springing naturally from the material.

Historical Intro: This is when a story begins with a statement about the subject's history, as such: 'In 1948, the Ruritanian government decided that henceforward their borders would be effectively sealed, thus ending their long tradition of automatic hospitality to foreigners.' With this type, either the historical fact itself must be fascinating enough to grab the reader, or the twist (usually provided in a second paragraph that begins: 'But...') must be strong. Otherwise it can appear very flat. It is nearly always better re-worked with the information from the second paragraph in the intro.

False Intros: Finally there is one species of intro which is not a type at all but a widely made mistake. Called a 'false intro' it is an opening which the writer thinks is selling the story to readers but which is entirely disposable. Commonly used on features or light news stories, it has two usual forms. First is the failed joke, as in this on a story about a new sports car: 'Move over girls, here comes a curvy desirable object that's going to replace you in your man's dreams.' Second is the narrative opening which starts one phase too early, as in this on the story of a couple's disastrous holiday: 'Olive and Ian Meredith were really looking forward to two weeks of fun on the sun-soaked beaches of Thailand.' The fact that they arrived to find the hotel only half built and the beach covered in untreated sewage is only revealed in the second paragraph. It should be in the first. After all, most people do look forward to their holidays.

Do you Always Write the Intro First? In both the above cases, the piece would be far better without the annoying, inane intro. Practice intros are like a dancer's warm-up routine - perhaps essential to the performance, but certainly not part of it. They are a private thing and should not reach the public. They are also a reminder that we often need to get something down on paper or screen just to get ourselves going. There is nothing wrong with that; any behind-the-scenes routine that delivers the goods in the paper is worth following. Just don't let anyone else see it.

Some feature writers, if they have the time, prefer to write in longhand and then type the result, polishing as they go. They claim to choose words more carefully and write more economically if they have to do so manually, rather than on a computer. They maintain that fast, sensitive electronic keyboards encourage verbosity and loose sentence construction, and make writers compose 'off the top of the head' rather than forming and reforming sentences before they write them down, as they would do with a pen and paper.

There are as many writing habits as there are writers (Nabokov, for instance, often wrote standing up; Victor Hugo naked). But there is one habit which is decidedly dangerous - writing the piece without a proper intro and then going back to compose the first paragraph last. The great problem with this is that the process of writing the intro is often what gives you a clear idea of the piece, its construction and the tone you should adopt. If you draft a piece and then go back to write the intro, you may find that the article should have a totally different tone and structure, which means a rewrite.

The only time when this habit may be useful is if the story has a clear, probably chronological, structure and you can start at the beginning of the narrative and then go back and put a summary, declaratory, or some other kind of intro on it. The most obvious instance of this is with major incident stories when you have to start writing before the final outcome, cause or death toll is known. This is called a running story because it is still running when you have to begin writing. With these, it is always best to start at the chronological beginning of the incident and then, just before deadline, add the intro and, possibly, a final few paragraphs.

Process of Interview

Interview has been established as a major technique of getting information in journalism. There is hardly any news magazine which does not carry interviews. Many a time the cover story and some other major stories involve more than one interview.

Text of Interview: The Sunday or the magazine sections of daily newspapers often carry interviews. Sometimes several people are interviewed on a particular subject and different viewpoints are compiled in one feature.

Magazines often supply copies of their exclusive interviews to daily newspapers and news agencies before they hit the newstands so that news content of the interview may appear in newspapers. Transcripts of interviews are sometimes released by the press relations staff of the dignitary interviewed.

The importance of interview has been growing as a news gathering technique over the years. It is now seen more and more in news columns and at times because of interviews a newspaper scores over its rivals in news coverage.

After police action in the Golden Temple (April 30, 1985) Amarinder Singh, the then-Agriculture Minister of Punjab, became the centre of controversy. Resident Editor of the *Indian Express* Chandigarh got an opportunity to interview him and the result was there on the front page of the paper the next morning:

'I'm not a Puppy Who Wags His Tail': Chandigarh, May 3. His is a name to conjure with Amarinder Singh, eldest son of the late Maharaja of Patiala, scion of Punjab's most famous Sikh family. After passing out of the National Defence Academy (NDA) a brief period as an officer in the Indian Army before family business commitments compelled him to resign.

Then as he puts it, "Mrs. Indira Gandhi brought me into politics." A classmate at Doon School of Mr. Rajiv Gandhi (whom

I have known for 25 years), he occupied centre stage soon after Sanjay Gandhi's death. But after "Operation Bluestar" he resigned from the Congress (I) as well as his Lok Sabha seat in protest and joined the Akali party. When it swept into power seven months ago, he was made the minister of agriculture, ranking third in the Cabinet. He was already being widely spoken of as a future chief minister of the state.

However, on Wednesday evening the wheel turned full circle with the entry of the police and commandos into the Golden Temple, a 'mini Operation Bluestar,' a day after the call for 'Khalistan' by the so-called 'panthic committee. 'On Friday evening two members of the Punjab Cabinet, education minister Sukhjinder Singh and Amarinder Singh himself resigned while former chief minister Parkash Singh Badal and former SGPC president Gurcharan Singh Tohra left the working committee of the Akali Dal.

In an interview with this writer the next morning, Amarinder Singh related the sequence of events during these dramatic four days, the reason for his resignation and his future course of action.

What exactly happened and why did you resign?

On the night of Tuesday, April 29th soon after the call for 'Khalistan' was given from the Golden Temple. I understand that Mr. Arun Singh and Mr. Arjun Singh secretly flew down to Mr. Arun Singh and Mr. Barnala and the three of them flew on to Amritsar and then to Delhi the same night....

After a few days Rahul Singh interviewed the chief minister and got another exclusive story for his paper.

Barnala Confirms Amarinder's Charge: Chandigarh, May 13. The beleaguered Chief Minister of Punjab, Mr. Surjit Singh Barnala, whose administration was rocked today by the formation of a new party among the dissidents of the Akali Dal, has confirmed that the minister of state for defence, Mr. Arun Singh and the vice president of the Congress (I), Mr. Arjun Singh, were in Amritsar on the eve of the police and commando action to clear the Golden Temple complex of extremists.

Former agriculture minister, Amarinder Singh, who was expelled today from the Akali Dal had made the charge soon after he broke with Mr. Barnala over the action.

Mr. Barnala also indicated that the document released by the so called panthic committee in which the call for "Khalistan" was given had a 'Pakistani connection'.

The Punjab chief minister, in an interview with this writer yesterday evening at his residence in Chandigarh, admitted that he had not taken any member of his Cabinet into confidence on the exact timing of the police-cum-army action as he did not "want the matter to be leaked out".

The Cabinet meeting at which the call for 'Khalistan' issued by the panthic committee was discussed ended at around 3.15 pm on April 30. The action commenced about one and half hours later.

But he emphasised that the decision, which he described as a very hard one was taken by him alone. There is no comparison whatsoever with what was done on April 30 and 'Operation Bluestar', emphasised Mr. Barnala, 'my conscience is clear.'

Mr. Barnala got the news of the Khalistan call from the Golden Temple when he was attending a meeting of the national development council in Delhi, at which the prime minister was present. He received a message from Mr. Rajiv Gandhi that evening and met him at 9 pm.

"I must act now," the Punjab Chief Minister told Mr. Rajiv Gandhi.

"How can we help in this matter?" the PM asked Mr. Barnala. The Punjab chief minister replied that commandos might be needed, but he first wanted to go to Amritsar to gauge the situation and consult his main officers.

At this point, Mr. Arun Singh and Mr. Arjun Singh who were present asked if they could also come along. The prime minister provided a plane and they arrived at Amritsar at 12.30 pm that night where they were met by the Punjab DG of police Mr. Julio Ribeiro.

Mr. Barnala said that the 'Khalistan' document issued at the Golden Temple was undated, mentioned the Red Fort at Delhi as the proposed capital for Khalistan – whereas previously they had claimed it would be Lahore-and contained certain Urdu words which were no longer used in Indian Punjab but were common in Pakistan.

When questioned about the Rs 2 crore worth of gold that was on the dome of the rebuilt Akal Takht and which was pulled down by the extremists just over three months ago, Mr. Barnala indicated that at least some of it must have been taken away by the militants when they slipped away from the Golden Temple. He said that they had earlier scraped it off the copper plates and tried to sell it to jewellers in the city. But nobody was willing to buy it. But he was not sure if some of the gold was still in the Golden Temple.

Concerning the controversial role of the Speaker of the Punjab Vidhan Sabha, Mr. Ravinder Singh, the Punjab chief minister accused him of "politicking" by holding a meeting of the dissident Akali faction in his house and by flying some of them to Amritsar where they, had gone to enlist the support of the SGPC president, Mr. Kabul Singh, (Mr. Ravinder Singh is an experienced pilot and has his own plane).

"The Speaker should be non-partisan," commented Mr. Barnala but he refused to say anything about action against Mr. Ravinder Singh.

As for his future, the Punjab chief minister declared that he would remain in office only if he had a majority in his own party, though he appreciated the support he had received from the other Opposition parties.

Interview is such a versatile technique that it can be applied to get a story in almost any field. One can have a personality feature or a success story tagged on a news peg as in the following example:

Rock Garden Planned for Bhopal: The creator of the famed rock garden here, Mr. Nek Chand, is planning to set up a similar fantasy garden in Bhopal. The Madhya Pradesh government has finalised an agreement with Mr. Nek Chand a few days back.

The environmental planning and coordination organisation of MP had invited Mr. Nek Chand to create a garden from the waste in an area of 25 acres situated near the state assembly hall. After a recent visit to Bhopal, Mr. Nek Chand has agreed to undertake the project.

Mr. Nek Chand says that he would soon start work on the Bhopal garden. "Initially I plan to lay out the garden in an area of five acres," he added. He said that it was his desire to replicate the rock garden in all the states so that the message spreads. I want the people to realise that what I have done can also be accomplished by them even if it is on a smaller scale.

The world famous artist now appears to be satisfied at the tremendous recognition he is being given within the country.

So far he had laid out a fantasy garden for the children in Washington and also created a *'bhulbhuliyan'* in Paris, for which he was recently bestowed with a medal by the Mayor.

The National Council of Educational Research and Training (NCERT) New Delhi has also approached him for creating a garden in the complex premises. On an invitation of the director of NCERT Mr. Nek Chand had visited the New Delhi Complex and has given his consent. "I expect the director to come to Chandigarh soon to finalise the deal," he said.

The Delhi project would, however, begin after the garden in Bhopal is launched. The MP government has assured him of all physical and material support.

Besides Bhopal and New Delhi, the deputy commissioner of Dehra Doon has also invited Mr. Nek Chand to explore the possibility of creating a similar garden in the valley.

The Ropar thermal plant management is seeking his advice on installing a suitable sculpture at an empty crossing near the resident colony. "I intend to erect sculptures of three or four beggars at Ropar," he said.

Many individuals have approached him for designing the architecture of their houses. Although he is still not sure whether he would undertake the task but thinks that he would at least give an artistic angle to the architecture.

Meanwhile, the Chandigarh administration has started regular payment of his monthly salary. Mr. Nek Chand has been re-employed as a consultant for the rock garden.

A reporter can discuss a circus and get a story:

Indian Circus Facing Extinction: New Delhi, October 27 (UNI). The Indian circus is facing extinction due to the indifferent attitude of the government according to Mr. M. V. Shankaran a doyen of India circus.

Lack of basic requirements, delay in getting permissions and denial of licences were some of the serious problems facing various circus troupes, the former president of Indian Circus Federation told UNI.

Thanking the government for lifting the ban on circus shows in the capital, he hoped that the new government would give priority to encouraging circus which is "an art of physical and gymnastic talents, fun and frolic and feats of trained wild animals all rolled up as a mass entertainment."

He said while the Indian circus art is stagnating in stereotyped and old models, in the Soviet Union, United States, China, Britain, Korea and Germany it is growing to phenomenal heights.

Mr. Shankaran, who is here with his Gemini Circus, pointed out that the Chinese, Soviet and Korean circuses were given all assistance including financial grants from their respective governments.

A reporter has to do more home work for an interview than for a press conference. For, here he is alone to ask all the questions. He is not invited as in a press conference. He has to fix the interview. Unlike the press conference, the success or failure of the interview depends completely on him.

At its best an interview requires that the reporter make a careful choice of the person or persons to be interviewed so that he gets authoritative opinion on the subject at hand. The reporter should do careful advance reading on the subject so that he would neither waste his own time nor that of the interviewee and so that he may go beyond basic, obvious questions and investigate the subject in depth. It requires careful choice of questions, careful recording of replies and objective and effective report on what has been said.

Ideally, an interview should take place in the office or the house of the person who is interviewed. The interviewee should have several days advance notice and should have some idea of what the reporter is likely to ask. There should be enough time possibly an hour or more for the interview. Such ideal conditions are not always possible and interviews at times must be conducted over lunch tables, in cars, in trains, or aeroplanes or at street corners or in the stair cases of office buildings-sometimes neither the reporter nor the interviewee has any advance word and time may be limited to a few minutes rather than a few hours.

After a reporter has identified the person he should interview he has to get in touch with him. This he can do by contacting him directly. He may telephone or write to him identifying himself and the purpose of interview. It may work but it may not, depending on the person who is to be interviewed.

Many a time it is good to approach the person to be interviewed through a third party-through a public relation department if the person is a top executive, through some other person who is known to the executive and tell him that it will be good for him to give the interview. Foreign dignitaries should be approached through their missions. There are ceremonial occasions when reporters meet VIPs. On such occasions he can talk to the VIP directly and ask for an interview. Normally he is told to meet some official whom he can contact with reference to the chance meeting and would get an interview.

The time one should ask for depends on the subject and the purpose of interview and the person interviewed. For a news story – normally ten to twenty minutes may be enough but for a full length interview or a feature an hour or more is required. The typical interview should not last less than half an hour or more than two hours. If you need more time then it should be divided in more than one sitting over several days.

The place of interview is not difficult to decide. It is simply a matter of courtesy that you should go to the person you want to interview – his office or residence-rather than ask him to come and see you. Unless he wants it the other way round.

Preparation of Interview: Advance preparation or homework of the reporter can be in two parts – reading about the subject concerned and preparing questions to be asked.

Once the reporter has decided the general subject to be covered he must decide what information he wants to get. The more specific his objectives, the better will be the preparation. Obviously, he must know the person to be interviewed. If he has written any books, articles or made any speeches about the subject of interview, the reporter should read them. Such material will reduce the time and effort for preparation and help him in framing better and more precise questions. He should check whether any information has been published on the person. He should also find out the environment in which he works or lives.

This background reading will be of great help. He may get answers to superficial questions which he might be thinking to pose initially and new, more fruitful, areas of enquiry may become apparent.

It is always better to prepare all the possible questions and note them down in a logical order. The interviewee may want a list of questions in advance. Some more important questions could be given to him. The rest of the questions can be asked as supplementaries during the interview.

Reporters who do not prepare questions usually run out of questions. While on one hand it is embarrassing on the other, the time available is not utilised properly.

It is not necessary that the interview should proceed according to the order of questions listed with the reporter. The interviewee may reply to question No. 1 and then may start replying to question No. 12. The reporter can easily go back and forth on his list and keep on asking supplementary questions from the answers. A reporter should not hesitate in asking for clarification if he is in doubt about the reply.

Questions should be framed with care. They should be specific and clear. One question should raise just one point. It should not be long and confusing. If it packs too much information or raises many issues it will create confusion and uncertainty about the validity of the answer.

Some open-ended questions should be included to draw out the interviewee. Such questions begin as: What do you mean by? or, what do you think about.... ? or what factors do you think...? This kind of question may put the interviewee in a thoughtful mood. One should not forget to ask basic questions. Sometimes one may get new or interesting insight into old problems. A good reporter should not be afraid of appearing ignorant in an effort to get a worthwhile story.

One should not hesitate to ask tough questions that cause a man to think, reflect and clear up any discrepancies in earlier statements on the same subject. There is no harm in asking uncomfortable questions if they are important. But one should not ask questions that are designed to embarrass the interviewee.

This preparation helps the reporter in many ways. He knows what to ask. He has time to think how best he can ask the question. Besides, he can convince the interviewee that he is interested in him and in the subject through intelligent questions. Many interviewees only cooperate if they know that the reporter is serious enough and can do justice with the interview. Thus the preparation on one hand prepares the reporter for a better interview it also helps in getting cooperation of the interviewee which is so essential for success.

Depending on the person and time given by him the reporter should introduce the subject and purpose of interview in a few words in the beginning. If the reporter feels it appropriate he may devote a few minutes to pleasantries. This is particularly necessary for those who are not exposed to newsmen. Let such people be comfortable before you begin putting your questions.

For dignitaries who keep meeting newsmen it is good to go straight to the point. It will save time which could be better utilised by asking more questions.

During the course of interview, if the interviewee goes off the track, the reporter should bring him back to the subject by politely interrupting and asking another question. The reporter must make sure that he does not lose control over the interview or else he will fail in his objective.

It is always good to take a tape recorder if the interview is planned. It is also good to take notes while asking questions for it will help if the machine fails. Even otherwise it is easy to deal with your notes than to wait for a transcript or replay if the story has to be done quickly. While taking notes one should always note important sentences or phrases which will be useful in assessing the interview and writing the story. A tape recorder helps if the interview is to be given in a question-answer form and if quotes are to be used from it.

If a tape recorder is not available or the interviewer objects to its use after the interview one should note down whatever can be remembered beside what has been noted down during the interview. A reporter should write his story within hours of the interview, but if he needs more information or time then he should write a detailed note on the interview taking into account all that he remembers with the help of his notes.

In chance interviews or background briefings a reporter may not be able to use a tape recorder. Sometimes he may not like to take notes for the fear of disturbing the person who is talking to him. In such cases the reporter must try to commit everything to memory.. He will be able to retain a lot for a few hours. If he can note it down soon after, he will almost reproduce all important things. This habit can be developed with effort and will be very useful.

Closing of an interview is also as important as the beginning. The end should be smooth and meaningful. The reporter should not take more time than he has been given unless he feels that the interviewee is also keen on continuing the exercise. If he has not completed his objective and enough questions remain unanswered then he can ask for another sitting.

The reporter should also tell the interviewee that he may like to check certain facts and may ring him up if necessary. If the interviewee insists on seeing the finished final version, the reporter should accept his request. If there is any difficulty in this he should frankly explain the situation. However, if he agrees to show the script he must abide by it.

Sometimes reporters get 'off-the-record' interviews. Off he record may mean that the information given should not be use at all. But it may also mean that the information can be used wit out identifying in the source. The reporter should make it clear from the interviewee before leaving him what he means by off the record'.

Skill for Interview

An interview is another medium of communication. It is a formal meeting and discussion with someone on a particular subject. A person applying for a job may have to face an interview, or a person with information to broadcast on radio or television. It involves questioning a person in an interview.

The members of the interview committee may interview several for the job. A politician or a public servant or chief of an may be interviewed by press reporters about their activates, programmes, etc. In an interview there must be more than one to have effective communication. Two parties are involved in an interview broadly classified as interviewer and interviewee. Interviewee is a respondent who gives information and facts to questions put by the interviewer.

Interviewer is a person who asks the respondent the questions put to the interviewee or on a questionnaire or schedule. In other words, a person who seeks information for media use, a newspaper reporter, or a television or radio panel show moderator, etc. An investigator who puts questions and solicits answers, information, facts, etc., a person appointed to carry out interviews.

The Objectives

The object of the interview is to sit face to face and to obtain information from the interviewee. It is the best opportunity to assess correctly a particular matter for which the interview is proposed. A good interview depends on planning. The interviewer must be clear before he talks to the interviewee as to what information he wants and what questions will help to bring out that information. Interview is a personal appraisal method of evaluating the persons interviewed.

The Interview: Myers and Myers have defined interviewing, "it is simply a highly specialised form of communication, but one which affects how people are hired for jobs, how they are appraised and told about it, and how they are able to work with others on the job."

James M. Black: "An interview is a conversation, usually between two people, that is confined to a specific subject. The role of the interviewer is to seek information; that of the interviewee is to provide it."

L. Brown: "Is a conversation between two people. It is conversation, yes, but directed to a purpose other than personal, social satisfaction."

Art of Interviewing

S. G. Ginsburg: "The interviewer's questions must explore viewpoints as well as experiences; they must be as tough as the problems that will face the person who gets the job."

Interviewing is an art which demands training and experience just as any other profession does. Much of the difficulty stems from inadequate appreciation of this art. No intelligent businessman would ever purchase an expensive piece of equipment without making a thorough evaluation of its construction, cost, durability and ability to perform the task for which it is intended. Yet the same executive will frequently hire a man for an important job on the flimsiest evidence. He often makes such a personal decision after talking with the applicant for twenty or thirty minutes, basing his evaluation primarily on such surface impressions as appearance, general manners and apparent relevance of experience and training.

However, it is encouraging to note a growing awareness of the importance of the human factor in industry. More and more business leaders are beginning to recognise the tremendous cost of poor selection. Many important selection decisions are being made by untrained employment interviewers.

The most complicated problem of business today is people. Technical processes may be mastered, plans may be devised and offices may be built to exacting specifications, and intricate machines are devised for performing work with fine accuracy, but if the human element in business is disregarded, trouble lies ahead.

Exemplary Drill

Successful interviewing presupposes a flair for dealing with people, drawing them out, analysing and evaluating their strengths and weaknesses. An unselective habit of linking people on sight may distort our judgement. Sympathy is an excellent quality. But if we engage an applicant through sympathy we may have to regret it because our judgement has been so clouded by our attention to the man's needs that we were not alert in estimating his qualifications. The applicant too has a very real stake in this business of selection. He is like a commodity or apiece of machinery that can be purchased on an entirely impersonal basis. In many cases, his whole future may be involved. When any assessor of men makes the decision whether or not a given person should be engaged for an important job or upgraded to a higher level or position, he is assuming a grave responsibility. He had better be right in his decision, equally for the good of the company and for the good of the man.

Types of Interviews: There are many different ways of classifying interviews. Robert Goyer and others have given as many as ten separate categories of interviews. They are:

1. Information getting.
2. Information giving.
3. Advocating.
4. Problem solving.
5. Counselling.
6. Application for a job.
7. Taking complaints.
8. Giving reprimands.
9. Conducting appraisals.
10. Stress interviewing.

Similarly Harold Zelko, etc. have given two categories of interviews. They are:

1. Problem solving and counselling.
2. Informative.

While Myers and Myers proposed three general types of interviews:

1. Information Interviews.
2. Problem Solving Interviews.
3. Professional Interviews.

However, the interviews which are in most use and which the management most frequently uses in communication are discussed as under:

Information Giving Interview: As the name indicates the object of this interview is to provide or supply information. This interview supplies facts, ideas, opinions, feelings, figures, and other matters to the interviewer or to the interviewee. It takes the form of telling how, orientation, and for giving instructions. Information giving interview is meant either to collect information or give information. The interviewer and the interviewee probably already have some information to exchange.

Information Collecting Interview: On the basis of the function of interview, another type of interview is information seeking interview. The interview focuses on receiving information. It is a process of getting information. The techniques involved in getting information are asking, questioning, clarifying, investigating, finding out reasons. Two people interact each other when one seeks information and the other gives information.

Employment Interview: Employment interview is conducted when the organisation wants to recruit new people. It is interview intake, if a person is entering the organisation. The interview should open by putting the applicant at ease and proceed by direct conversation. Interviewer and interviewee interact on each other. In which the interviewer attempts determining the suitability of the applicant for the post. Focus is on collecting information to assess and evaluate to take a decision for selection of the employee. A type of information interview.

Appraisal Interview: Another familiar type of organisational interview is conducting an appraisal interview. It is a performance appraisal interview to do with job effectiveness. The emphasis is on evaluation of performance of the job, need for training, time for promotion, fixing salary, etc.

Counselling Interview: Counselling interview is an advisory type including interviewing as much as providing services. Management counselling promotes good employer-employee relations and brings about a change in the attitude of the interviewee. A two-way process of communication gives participation satisfaction, and improves job performance. It takes place on the job interface that may occur between superiors and subordinates. It covers many areas such as instructing, encouraging, motivating, advice and guiding in problem solving. There are many psychological problems which cannot be successfully handled by counselling interviews. Psychiatrists, psychologists, physicians and counselling personnel can conduct counselling interviews effectively. They render professional services. To tackle the problem.

Managers use some principles. As suggested by L. Brown they are:

1. Empathy – looking at the problems from the worker's point of view.
2. Positive attitude – showing respect, accepting the worker as a person, showing warmth and a clearing feeling.
3. Sincerity – being genuinely interested, honest, and true about feelings and reactions.
4. Concreteness – being direct, accurate, and specific in facts and suggestions.
5. Listening – hearing the other person, giving the other person a chance to express feelings, often helps to create an awareness and recognition of what should be done about the problem.
6. Problem resolution – clarifying the problem, suggesting and evaluating alternatives, modifying and implementing the solution.

Complaint or Grievance Interview: Grievance interviews occur because something remedial has to be done. Employees may seek an interview to find a solution to their problem. When the employees are not satisfied they lodge a complaint and sometimes confront in an interview situation. The interview focuses on coming to an agreement, settling a dispute and differences and remedying the problem. This interview is convened to give the employee a hearing opportunity to come to a solution. The grievances policies and procedures are laid down in the company's manual or handbook.

Disciplinary Interview: When employees who fail to perform according to tasks they are subject to disciplinary action. Any employees who commit costly mistakes or indulge in undesirable behaviour are expected to be involved in a disciplinary interview.

In this interview the causes are identified for changing the behaviour of the person into a right direction. Through joint exploration of objectives the interview finally leads to settlement of a problem, improving the situation and remedying the problem. A person may be given a chance or warning to improve. In a disciplinary interview which; is generally confidential and private between the two persons or between a committee and the person involved, counselling, instructing, correcting, reprimanding and problem solving steps may take place.

Discussion Interview: A type of interview where discussion between people tales place at a fixed place. It is also called as exploratory interview. It is an interview between a small group or large group engaged in interaction with one another in a fact-to-face interview. In this interview members of the group are in interaction with one another. The group reaches a decision after thorough deliberations. It is a place where an exchange of ideas, data, facts, figures opinions and feelings, etc., are openly expressed and opposed through discussion to arrive at a solution to the problem.

Correction Interview: This follows disciplinary interviews. This interview gives a clear statement of identifying disciplinary' areas undesirable or costly errors or alleged violation. Steps are taken *to* rectify the behaviour and put on the line of desirable behaviour. Corrective steps are generally formulated to meet different situations for their implementation.

Evaluation Interview: Evaluation interviews are conducted to form an idea or judgement on a particular subject matter. The members evaluate any functional areas of the organisation, personal and general issues. For instance, evaluation of worthiness, results, performance, events, persons, policies, goals, etc.

Exit Interview: Another familiar type of interview is the exit interview, convened when a person leaves the organisation. This is an interaction between the interviewer and the person leaving the organisation. A face to face conversation to review job satisfaction, future prospects in the organisation, or better prospects outside the organisation, etc. The interview also identifies the reasons for leaving the organisation and to create goodwill.

Goal Setting Interview: In a goal setting interview concentration is mainly on determination of goals. It is a process which marks a beginning of identifying goals, interaction and conclusion. Particularly in goal setting in an area of management by objectives. Here people exchange information. There is a clearly defined problem or goal. Both parties exchange information and finally set goals.

Persuading Interview: Also called a Sales Interview. It is an interview between seller or buyer. The interaction is either as seller or buyer in a persuading interview. It is a highly skilled interview system. It focuses on convincing or persuading a person to action.

Telephone Interview: The telephone can be used effectively to conduct an interview. It is a type of interview over the telephone. In this mechanical oral communication, views, ideas, opinions and facts are exchanged. It can be used to form a conclusion on the subject under consideration.

Preliminary Interview: This type of interview is used in case of employment interview. It is very simple and brief. It is with a view to eliminate the unqualified and unsuitable candidates that a preliminary interview is conducted. Some quick evaluation techniques are followed in , this type like a test, communication skills, impression, etc.

Formal Interview: An official interview which is conducted according to prescribed rules and procedure laid down. Interview procedures are generally laid down in an organisational manual. In this type of interview the interviewer puts a set of well defined questions and takes notes according to requirements. A common interview in social research.

Informal Interview: It is in contrast to the formal interview, again a social research interview. In this the interviewer has full freedom to make suitable alternations in questions. In a formal interview there is no freedom to alter the questions.

Personal Interview: The process of interview is only between two individuals, one is the interviewer and the other is the interviewee. This interview enables one to establish a close personal contact between the interviewer and interviewee.

Research Interview: A research interview is held to collect certain information relating to a research problem. The interviewer prepares a set of questions in advance and by interviewing people he gathers the desired information, facts, figures, data, etc. It is called research interview as the information is gathered for the purpose of research into a problem.

Dummy Interview: An interview conducted in the usual way with a respondent, the data from which is not intended for use in survey results. Used as a training device for interviewers. A type of interview from which the information and data is not intended for use or utility in survey findings. This method is used in order to impart training to the interviewer or investigator.

Other Types of Interviews:

1. Group interview,
2. Diagnostic interview,
3. Treatment interview,
4. Short contact interview,
5. Prolonged contact interview,
6. Qualitative interview,
7. Quantitative interview,
8. Mixed interview,
   a. Focused interview and
   b. Repeated interview.

Techniques of Interview: A conversation between two people is called interviewer and interviewee. They interact each other. They involve in the exchange of facts, figures, ideas, etc. There must be a technique to apply in the interview to make the interview effective. The techniques used usually by both interviewer and interviewee are:

Questioning: Putting questions ensures collection of information but also results in interaction. A question may be an open end question, direct question, indirect question, mirror type question and a loaded question.

Observing and Listening: Listening and observation are the best methods to obtain information and assess the matter. It is a process necessary for understanding and interaction for results. Observation and listening are the simplest forms in seeing and looking into the problem. Observation may be controlled observation and uncontrolled observation. Under this both interviewer and interviewee are involved in observation and listening. Listening to an answer to a question and by observing, the information is obtained. Listening is different from hearing and in the listening process one has to keep one's mind open and attuned to the speaker. From the observer's and listener's point of view it is one sided communication till they react. In observation the observer pays attention to the thinking process like what, why, how, etc.

Evaluating: Evaluation is a process of forming an idea or judgement on a particular matter. It evaluates qualifications, performance, objectives, policies, persons, events, etc. Evaluating technique ensures conceiving and understanding, perspective and logical reasoning. Both interviewer and interviewee evaluate each other on their respective question and answers. Evaluation helps bring perspective on the subject matters relative to logical reasoning. In this, ideas, facts, figures, opinions are exchanged. The technique of evaluation as applied in interviews increases perceptions and understanding.

***Controlling*:** The essential quality of an interviewer is to keep control of the interview. It is a management function in which generally both parties are involved. Leland Brown, on the technique of controlling and involvement, says, "controlling on the part of the interviewer is a management function, but in exercising control, both parties become involved. Thus controlling assures direction to periodic summaries and restatements often provide control of the situation, for they assure direction by stating the main points covered and leading into the next point to be covered. Thus a situation is crystallised. Involvement means participation that leads to results."

Interview Style: Interview is the common method in communication, which helps the management for gathering as well as giving information. This exchange of information is useful in the decision-making process and problem solving. There is an element of participation that satisfies employees and as a result produces a good employer-employee relation. An effective interview depends largely on the style, among other things. Interview style means "the degree or level of patterning of the interactions between interviewer and interviewee. The style can be informal or formal or any modification or combination of the two. The degree of formality is dependent largely on the relationship of interviewer and interviewee."

Interview style may be direct interview, indirect interview, stress interview, depth interview, etc. As given in the definition by L. Brown, a modification or combination of two or more styles involves elements of all the styles employed.

On the basis of practice, the styles of communication we have:

Direct Interview: It is also called direct planned interview. It is a face to face observational method. In this method with the help of questions and answers one measures the attitude, knowledge, suitability of the interviewee. It helps the interviewer to assess personal qualities.

Indirect Interview: It is also called indirect non-directive interview. It is not a straight-forward question and answer method. The interviewee is given an opportunity and conducive atmosphere to feel free to talk. The interviewee plays a role of speaking on a particular issue and the interviewer mainly plays a listening role.

Patterned Interview: In this interview the questions to the interviewee are standardised in advance of fixed questions.

Stress Interview: In the stress type of interview, the worry or pressure experienced by an interviewee in particular circumstances, or the state of anxiety caused by the stress are created deliberately by the interviewer. Under the stress atmosphere the interviewer obtains information to assess the applicant's action and response under it. Stress is created with anger, silence, criticism, etc.

Depth Interview: In this interview a number of questions on a particular area are put to the interviewee. An answer to any one question does not cover full information. A number of follow-up questions are put by the interviewer.

Board Interview: When a group of people propose to interview respondents it is called a panel or board interview, or interview committee. The board collectively is called interviewer. An interviewee has to face more than one person interviewing. Each interviewer has his own area of putting questions.

Group Interview: In group interview a group of respondents or interviewees are allowed to gather to interact and exchange each other's ideas. The interviewer mainly plays an observational and listening role to appraise the qualities of respondents in a group. Sometimes the interviewers and interviewees may sit together for some time or may live together for a few days to know individual and personal habits, conduct and behaviour of the interviewees.

An interviewer is a person who asks the respondent or puts questions to the interviewee. In other words, a person who seeks information for media use, a newspaper reporter, or a television or radio panel show moderator. He who puts questions and solicits answers, information, facts, figures, ideas, and opinions, etc. The interviewer plays an important role in interviewing and as such is a common part of management's routine activities. He has a definite role in the process. He is the person who has to control communication in interview. Interviewer has some data or facts on which information is to be gathered interacting the interviewee. Interviewee is another party in the interview. Interviewee is a respondent who gives information and facts, etc. to the questions put to the interviewee by the interviewer. The interviewer seeks the maximum information possible and for that he has to prepare well for the event.

The Characteristics: The main concern of the interviewer employing the method of interviewing is to get correct and maximum information and to the point on the topics under issue. The interview can be less expensive, economical, effective only if both parties concentrate on the topic and complete without dragging and without deviations. The aim is to succeed interaction with minimum effort and this is possible if the parties follow the principles of group discussion. Accordingly, in order to ensure correct information exchange the interviewer should give maximum freedom of self-expression and should be allowed to describe his reaction. He should be allowed a free hand while describing his response. Usually the variety of responses depends upon the skill and tactful approach of the interviewer. Therefore, there are no hard and fast rules, or rules cannot be framed in this connection.

However, a great responsibility rests on the interviewer as what to do. He has to make correct decisions which involve not only the interviewee's career but other matters. As regards the characteristics of a good interviewer there are different views. Some people suggest traits, which a good interviewer should have. The broad categories of traits are generally intellectual abilities, communication skills and psychological traits. In any type of interview the interviewer occupies a pivotal role. He gathers information and supplies information. The success of interview depends largely on joint exploration or exchange of information. A personal relationship and personal contact emerges between the interviewer and the interviewee, both interact with each other. As such the personality and the abilities of the interviewer are of crucial significance. A man of integrity, honesty, confidence and with skills of logical thinking can successfully conduct the interview.

However, an interviewer should keep in mind the following points while conducting the interview to be an effective interview:

Thorough Knowledge: An interviewer should be thoroughly familiar with the subject and object of the interview. The exchange of ideas, facts and opinions, etc., should be given with full knowledge on the subject.

Narrative: The interviewer should give maximum opportunity of self-expression to the interviewee. He may be allowed to express freely his experience, hobbies and other informal issues.

Background Information: The interviewer should have knowledge in advance of the kind of facts, ideas, opinions, figures to be obtained from the interviewee in the interview. This helps to avoid confusion and no important matters are overlooked.

Time Factor: Time is an equally important factor and should be considered by the interviewer. It is valuable both to the interviewer and the interviewee. But questions should not be put in a hurried manner. The schedule of questions should be prepared in advance to be complete within an adequate time. Sufficient time should also be given to the interviewee so as to enable him to give replies to questions.

Freedom: He should be given full freedom to describe whatever he thinks relevant and reasonable. The interviewer should not interfere in his description if he deviates slightly from the main point and if he gives some irrelevant facts. The interviewee should not be discouraged by imposing checks on him. So long as he remains with relevant subject, he should not be questioned.

Interview Place: An interview should not be conducted in an open place in a disturbed atmosphere, in respect of certain interviews. The interviewer should conduct the interview in a separate room. The face-to-face conversational flow should not be disturbed by holding the interview in an open place. A private room is to be selected to avoid distractions and interruptions.

To Keep Interviewee at Ease: The interviewer should not keep the interviewee in a difficult position. He should not be discouraged with annoying questions and other questions psychologically not good. So the interviewer should create a friendly and informal atmosphere throughout, at the commencement of the interview, during the interview and at the end.

Patience in Listening: Another quality that an interviewer must possess is patience in listening to the interviewee. The interviewer must hear the interviewee with full interest. He should give maximum time and opportunity to the interviewee to speak and express his ideas freely. Therefore, he should not go on speaking but he should be a very good listener and observer. His interference should be limited in order to let the interviewee express himself as far as time allows. He should not give an opportunity to others to guess from his expression that he is bored or that his mind is somewhere else.

Understanding the Level: The interviewer should understand the level, vocabulary and other personal background like educational attitude, etc. Not only that he must adjust and come down to the level of the interviewee so as to assess his abilities and for measuring the ability of the respondent.

No Harshness: It is an accepted principle that the interviewee should be allowed freedom of self-expression. If the interviewee gives some irrelevant facts he must be politely reminded to keep within bounds. Alert direction should not be abrupt and harsh. Under no circumstances can an interviewer afford to offend the interviewee.

Control: In an interview both parties should be under control. The success of the interview depends on planning, and one should plan the interview beforehand. Though the interview is a joint exploration the interviewer has to keep control of the interview.

To Win the Confidence: Winning the confidence of the interviewees the essence of successful interviewing. Basically he must gain the confidence of the interviewee. If there is no confidence in the interviewer the interviewee may not give information fully, freely and frankly.

No Confrontation: When results are not according to their expectations they may confront in an interview. As far as possible an interviewer should not confront an interviewee. Confrontation is needed when incorrect, poor data and weak information is given. It may be a direct confrontation or indirect confrontation.

Training: Interviewing is an art, a special skill and a form of communication. This requires some training and considerable experience to be perfect.

Content: Interview errors occur because of inappropriate content. The interviewer has to plan the questions or the information to be gathered and the sequence. During the interview he should not wander around with questions. Questions should not be on the subject of his own interest and choice irrespective of the subject of the interview. Uniformity in asking the same type of questions is necessary to make a comparison.

No Jumping to Conclusions: The interviewer should not jump to conclusions without gathering full information. Conclusions should be arrived at only after full interaction and satisfaction of both parties.

No Discrimination: The interviewer should be impartial and should not show any discrimination. Equal opportunity should be given, no bias is to be expressed. He should hear all in the same spirit. No place for race, religion and politics.

Appreciation of Interviewee: Listening and appreciation of an interviewee is another quality that he should keep in mind. Appreciation of the interviewee has a salutary effect on the interviewee who then gives full and correct information.

Closing Interview: The interviewer should have a good sense of time and situation to close an interview. He should learn how and when to close the interview. He should use it with mutual understanding, and good relations. Before the conclusion of the interview, he should give a brief about matters not concluded. Thanking the interviewee is a good closing.

Recording: Soon after conclusion of the interview, the interviewer should record the facts and observations made during the interview, as well as his impression and judgement. Recording the proceeding of the interview is good for both the parties and serves as a record for future reference. Recording facts ensures confidence and goodwill among the interviewees. Richard A. Fear has suggested the following qualities for a good interviewer:

1. A warm, engaging manner;
2. Sensitivity in social situations;
3. Reasonable intelligence;
4. Critical and analytical judgement;
5. Adaptability, and
6. Maturity.

Myers and Myers have suggested how to train for those qualities which include the standard sequence of:

1. Telling
2. Demonstrating
3. Supervised practice
4. Evaluation and critique.

Errors of Interviewer: The employment interview should be properly planned, when it is unplanned and unpatterned it will not achieve the objectives and purpose of the interview. In such a case it can be equated to casual or social conversation or chatting, or pleasure talk. It should be concentrated on the purpose and object of the interview. Both the interviewer and interviewee must get as much relevant information as possible from the process. The interviewer must have good knowledge, capacity of listening and best judgement. Generally the interviewer in case of an employment interview commits a number of mistakes resulting in the interview being ineffective. Robert Minter gives a number of sins of the employment interviewer.

The common sins of the employment interviewer are:

1. "Too much talking and too little listening, resulting in sketchy information.
2. Not indicating purpose of interview.
3. Asking irrelevant questions or questions whose answers are already on the resume.
4. Having vague objectives and discussing whatever comes up at the movement.
5. Providing job and company information too early in the interview.
6. Attempting in-depth personality assessment.
7. Providing stress questions and situations in which to observe behaviour.
8. Over-reacting to non-verbal clauses, resulting in stereotyped impressions of the applicant.
9. Not having sufficient information about the particular job for which interviewing.
10. Becoming fatigued by interviewing too many applicants in a short time period.
11. Overemphasising or misusing test results.
12. Attempting a thorough interview in a limited ten or fifteen minutes.
13. Misinterpreting reference letters.
14. Over-selling the job and company, resulting in false hopes and expectations."

Myers and Myers have suggested the following shortcomings of interviews:

Using Untrained Interviewers: The first interview error suggested by them is using untrained interviewers unprepared to take on the situation.

Lack of Interviewer Preparation: An interview plan should be prepared in advance, and questions to be put for the purpose of interview, covering contents.

Inappropriate Content: There is always insufficient or inappropriate content of the subject for interview. Advance interview plan along with questions and sequence should be there. The questions not relating to the object and of his own personal taste and interest should be avoided.

Unwillingness to Confront: In case of weak answers or poor information the interviewer has to confront. Unwillingness to confront an interviewee is a serious error in the process of interview.

Guiding the Answers: Showing discrimination, or bias in the interview by him. They give answers to the interviewee by sign or facial expression.

Doing All the Talk: One of the serious shortcomings of the interview is to talk and talk without giving a chance to the interviewee to give his information. Talking too much by the interviewer should be avoided.

Jumping to Conclusions: Drawing conclusions based on pre-conceived ideas. Anticipating answers, sudden decision to conclude the interview are the defects of the interview.

Poor Listening: Listening is an art and requires a lot of patience, thinking and understanding. This is the most common error often committed by the interviewer.

Inadequate Setting: Lack of general good atmosphere for the interview is termed as inadequate setting. Noise, telephone calls, visitors, lack of privacy, inadequate time and lack of other facilities are the defects of an interview.

Recording and Reporting Error: Failing to follow a form or a logical sequence can produce a weak report. An interviewer has much to do and much to pay attention to during the session and is handicapped by having to take extensive notes.

The Exploration

A good interview depends on planning. The interviewer must be clear, before he goes to the place, about the events and order. Interview should be properly patterned and structured as a two-way communication process. Planning the interview involves a process of determining the major objectives of the interview, and policies and strategies that will govern the conduct of the interview. An interview plan provides a possible range of activities before the interview, during the interview and after the interview. The interviewer has to evaluate both the internal and external environment to help identify strengths and weaknesses. Various factors involved in the interview have to be considered to contribute solutions to the problems. A part of the planning process for the interview is to have full knowledge, to know exactly what information and facts are to be gathered. It involves finding out something about the persons to be interviewed, such as the interviewees, background, interests, expertise, the style of rapport, the questions to be asked, sequence, etc. Thus interviewing is to be carefully planned and structured. The rules for the interviewer and the interviewee are carefully prescribed. It is dyadic planning. Dyadic means two-way process.

Steps in Planning: Richard Huseman and others have suggested the following seven steps in planning the interview:

1. Establishing purpose or purposes to be achieved;
2. Collecting preliminary information on the subject and/or the interviewee;
3. Determining the amount of structure to impose;
4. Identifying, and perhaps recording, the strategic questions or responses that seem to possess potential for fulfilling the interview purpose;
5. Determining time, place and length of time for the interview;
6. Communicating the purpose, time, place and length of time to the interviewee; and

7. Personal preparation, e.g., knowing where one stands on crucial issues and attitudes and predicting points of conflict and resistance.

Leland Brown has suggested the following five steps:

1. To keep objectives in mind.
2. To plan to adapt to the personality and needs of the interviewee,
3. To bring together needed information and to decide how it will be used.
4. To develop lead questions and key questions into a sequential list.
5. To explore possible alternatives and solutions to a course of action or problem.

In many cases interviewing is a dyadic process. It means two persons' activity. Both the interviewer and the interviewee get together and pool their information and interact. The pattern of reflective thinking proposed by John Dewey includes the following sequences :

Definition of the Problem: A definite problem for discussion and exchange of information should be clearly defined. Both the interviewer and the interviewee should agree to the definition of the problem. A successful interview cannot be expected unless there is mutual understanding about what constitutes the problem. Finding a solution to the problem is not possible without clearly defining the problem.

Analysis of the Problem: Interview is a joint exploration of both the interviewer and the interviewee. As such an analysis of the problem also should jointly be attempted.

"If one person (either interviewer or interviewee) gives a fast, off-the-cuff analysis without consultation, then the other should object or at least have the analysis explained."

Alternative Solutions: There may be a number of alternative courses of actions to a given and defined problem. Selecting the best alternative is the objective in interaction with others. Alternatives can be suggested by the interviewer or interviewee in an exchange process. Both have equal opportunities and chances to suggest solutions and discuss them to arrive at a solution.

Evaluation: The solution so arrived at out of alternative solutions as the best possible one should be subject to evaluation. It means to review. Solutions should be evaluated by both persons. There is no domination and say by any person on the ground that one is the boss or superior.

Preferred Solution: The preferred solution should be chosen, relating to the problem.

Educational Features

The term "literary journalism", in the West (in the case, mainly in the United States) can be traced back to the 1930s. In 1937, Edwin H. Ford compiled a bibliography of literary journalism. In the foreword, Ford wrote that the term "Literary Journalism" conceived for the purpose of the bibliography, might be defined as writing which falls within the twilight zone that divides literature from journalism. The literary journalist is the link between newspaper and literature: The reporter gather news which indicates political and social trends. The editorial writer comments upon such news, but within restricted compass. And, when these political and social trends or situations have sufficiently permeated the thoughts and feelings of people generally, they provide the materials from which the mind of the artist creates literature. Through the medium of sketch or essay, of the literary or humorous column, of verse or of critical comments, the literary journalist refashions and evaluates the world about him. The literary journalist is the writer who is sufficiently journalistic to sense the swiftly changing aspects of the dynamic era of our times, and sufficiently literary to gather and shape his material with the eye and hand of the artist.

Today, "literary journalism" refers to a journalistic style a non-fiction literary genre, which combines the skills of interpretative reporting with the technique of fiction writing Literary journalism may be in the form of newspaper feature magazine article and book; and its principal functions are still to inform, to entertain and to educate. However, the writer has more freedom in style and in the presentation of his materials, and as a result, it makes the writing more enjoyable and reading more interesting.

"Literary Journalism" is also another term, a more appropriate term, for the controversial "New Journalism" of the 1960s. No matter what it is called, fundamentally, the literary journalist is still the artist who puts events and phenomena into perspective, and interprets and evaluates the world around him. As Normal Signs in the anthology, *The Literary Journalists,* points out, literary journalism was not defined by critics. The writers themselves have recognised that their craft requires immersion, structure, voice and accuracy. And along with these term "a sense of responsibility to their subjects and a search for the underlying meaning in the act of writing characterised contemporary Literary Journalism".

Ford's early concept on literary journalism seems to apply to a lot of the prevailing journalistic practice in Third World nations. For example, there is a similar genre called "journalistic literature" *(Bao Gao Wen Xue)* in China. The Chinese genre of literary journalism would also include stories based on facts and personal accounts of historical events and exemplary works of revolutionary journalism. However, the concepts, and techniques of Western literary journalists may provide reminders or new directions for the Third World journalist trying to find a more creative and expressive platform for his or her ideas.

Necessary Components

The literary journalist's "craft" as Normal Signs said, requires immersion, structure, voice and accuracy.

Immersion: In researching the story, in order to put everything in the proper perspective and be as accurate as possible, the literary journalist would gradually become immersed into whatever he is working on. To do so he or she has to spend weeks, months and even years in research, depending on whether the writer is preparing an article or a book. For example, John Mills spent five months walking a dangerous beat in New York with a detective to write about his life, in "The Detective;" Truman Capote spent five years researching a murder case in Kansas to recreate the events prior to and after the crime, *In Cold Blood,* Tom Wolfe spent seven years interviewing and corresponding with pilots, astronauts, and their wives and relatives besides delving into the archives of NASA to write about the courage of test pilots and astronauts in *The Right Stuff.* Some even get more personally involved and become participants in the event. George Plimpton joined the Detroit Lions football team to write about the experience of a pro football player *(Paper Lion);* Hunter S. Thompson rode with the Hell's Angels motorcycle gang and nearly got killed in the effort *(Hell's Angels, a Strange and Terrible Saga),* and Normal Mailer was a participant in the Pentagon March, a demonstration in Washington, D.C., in 1967, *(The Armies of the Night).*

In this case, time is a main constraint for Third World journalists. Third World journalists may not be able to spend as much time on a single story or topic as their counterparts in the West; however, the enthusiasm and sheer dedication of literary journalists would serve as a reminder of their own quest, and provide inspirations for story ideas, and possible angles or treatment.

Structure: While the structure of journalism is usually chronological, literary journalism usually takes a more complicated form which is closer to a short story or fiction novel. Literary journalism, as Tom Wolfe summarised, (or "the New Journalism" in Wolfe's terminology) employs the technique of the fiction: scene by scene construction dialogue; point of view - sometimes through interior monologues of characters; and status of life descriptions — such as clothing and mannerisms of characters, details of objects in the environment. In this case, the journalist's eye for detail, keen sense of observation, interview techniques, and language skills would be the prerequisites.

To Wolfe, these are the very devices that give the realistic novel its unique power. Since most of the 20th Century novelists (in the West) have abandoned their "calling" as "chronicles of history" and developed their efforts to myths, fables and forms, the writers of New Journalism have taken their role to become "secretaries of society." Wolfe's own work and others' collected in the anthology, *The New Journalism,* serve to illustrate the variety of techniques and the wide range of subjects of the genre, as well as the changes in styles of living in the United States in the 60s.

The writing styles and some of the techniques advocated by "the new journalists" which seemed innovative at the time have since become standard features of magazine writing. For example the anecdotal opening, is one of the many devices to capture the interest of the reader by, essentially, telling a story; capturing the personality of the interviewee by describing his mannerisms; and in character writing, by imitating the style and manner of speech or writing of the subject character in the story.

The architecture of a story of the literary journalism gene would be thematic, or in the form of flashbacks, storytelling, or even the flow of stream-of-consciousness (as in most of Hunter S. Thompson's works"). Also, by using narrative devices such as association, juxtaposition, and parallel narration, the writer can provide a social and even historical interpretation to ideas and events.

The journalist in developing nations is in effect a "chronicler of history." With the progress of development, or sometimes the inconsistency of government policies, or even the instability of political systems, issues may disappear and problems become more complex. The writings of the journalists soon become records of the changing times before any history book can be written.

Voice: The most controversial aspect in literary journalism would be "voice," as most of the works in the genre are subjective and interpretative by nature. Since conventional journalism in the First World espouses "objectivity," literary journalism lends itself for criticism.

In the Second and Third Worlds, the voice of the jingoist or narrator is the most important aspects of mass communication. As most media are either state-owned, party affiliated or geared towards national and economic development, subjectivity often is a fact of life and not an issue for debate. Standards for fairness and balance in the treatment of subject matters would also vary from county to country. Yet, in the Third World, the voice of the journalist is vital: the voice of the journalist (and or the media), in the form of analytical and interpretative information as well as informed opinions would be invaluable to a public confronting the currents of modernisation and upheavals of development.

This information and opinion would help the people to make sense of their complicated and ever-changing environment.

Accuracy: The main difference between literary journalism and fiction is that literary journalism is presenting FACT using the writing techniques of fiction. That does not mean that the facts are fabricated. The criterion is accuracy. The journalist can be imaginative in the way he or she may present and interpret the facts. That does not apply to inventing facts or taking literary license by twisting the facts to suit the journalist's purpose. In this respect, the note book, or the tape recorder, would be vital to the journalist. In reconstructing the scenes of events or dialogues of characters, the literary journalist would have to be very careful and double check his notes and tapes.

As John Hersey, who had years of experience working with *Time* magazine, wrote that there is no such thing as objective reportage: "Human life is far too trembling-swift to be reported in whole. The moment the recorder chooses nine facts out often, he colours the information with his views."" What the literary journalists is trying to be is to acknowledge this fact, and be subjective in trying to make sense out of this complicated world. Instead of just reporting the facts, he tries to analyse what is going on, to interpret what it means and get at a larger "reality".

Conferences for Press

Press conferences are obviously a special case when it comes to questioning. You are not alone, you are not face to face and you often have little time. If that is the case, and you have to file a story immediately after the conference ends, make sure you or other people ask the questions you need answered. That can sometimes mean being aggressive, shouting your question so that you are sure it is heard, or standing up to ask it.

A lot of people who call press conferences seem to imagine that the event is one where they can hold court before a group of docile note-takers. No reporter should ever let that idea take root. These events may be organised solely for the purpose of generating publicity, but that does not mean you have to play their game. You decide what the story is, not them. Never mind what they think is the significant message, is there another, better story?

If the person giving the press conference is not too grand, and you have some time, you can save your own questions for after the event. In that case, do not let the person who can answer them leave the room until you have cornered them. That can sometimes mean standing between them and the door. Don't be shy of doing that. Any person who regularly gives press conferences will be used to this. You are not there to make friends but to get a story.

Another tip is to watch and try to note if there is another reporter there who seems to know a lot more about the subject. After the conference, engage them in conversation. Most reporters cannot resist showing off what they know, who they know and thereby passing on some valuable leads. Don't take other people's reporting on trust, but you will often pick up some good ideas to follow up from such conversations. This is a reminder that often the real benefit you derive from press conferences is meeting people and making contacts rather than the ostensible story.

Interviews of VVIP's

The bigger the personality, often the less time you will have. Don't waste it by asking questions that can easily be verified by a little pre or post-interview research. Very big stars often have press agents in attendance, who try to set limits to the subjects you can ask about. It is your job to evade such controls where possible, and, if you can't, to tell readers about them. You are a reporter, not a courtier. Don't allow yourself to be flattered that this big star is talking to you; alternatively, don't allow your dislike of them or resentment of their wealth, beauty, brains or success to tempt you to write what you think will be a definitive demolition job. When printed, it will invariably say more about you than it does about them.

Instead, keep it simple. Describe them as precisely as possible and concentrate on questions that will enable you to compare their personality with their public image. As leading British interviewer Lynn Barber says, 'All you have to do is be punctual, be polite and ask questions.' She recommends, and most would agree, that the questions should be as short as possible. The following are often useful probes for unexpected answers, or areas of life that the subject may be willing to open up about. They are based on a list filed by Jeremy Martin to the Compu Serve Journalism Forum.

- What is your first memory?
- What was your mother's/father's best advice?
- Who has had the most impact on your life?
- What was your first job?
- What was your worst job?
- What was your first car?
- Who was your first love?
- What do you do when you are nervous?
- What are you compulsive about?
- Have you got a bad temper?
- What do you eat/not eat?
- Who is your best friend?
- What is your worst habit?
- What makes you angry?
- What do you study?
- How often do you read?
- How many hours a night do you sleep?
- What do you do if you wake in the night and can't get back to sleep?
- What is your ideal day off?
- When do you plan to quit?
- Who would be your favourite party guests?
- Do you like Christmas?
- What is your favourite song/book/film/singer/artist?
- Who do you admire most?
- What is your favourite drink?
- What will you not eat?
- Where is your favourite vacation place?
- Where would you live if you had total freedom of choice?

Methodical Steps

Interview is an oral communication device used to collect information and exchange between interviewer and interviewee. The process or course of interview is a direct one of face-to-face conversation on a clearly defined mutual problem. One interviews someone because one has a message to called and exchange. Executives interview subordinates or equals because they have subjects for interaction with the concerned people. The process may involve exchange of facts, events, opinions, conditions, etc. The interview process may also involve gathering subjective data, feelings, reactions, preference, etc. Sometimes their purpose is for problem solving, panel decision, goal setting, evaluation, investigation, to take corrective action, etc. In brief it may be said that it may help in defining the problem and in planning, investigating, finding solutions. Public relations officers, advocates, consultants, teachers, salesmen, counsellors, etc., are always involved in interviewing several people. Personal and social interactions do not contain problems, solutions, and purposes, hence they do not possess the essentials of an interview.

However, the process of interviewing contains the following stages:

Opening: The first phase is introduction. In this the parties are involved in an exchange of greetings.

Object of Interview: Once the formality of introduction is over the interviewer should explain to the interviewee the object of the interview, the nature of the interview and in clear and intelligible terms what is expected to be achieved.

Beginning of Interview: In the commencement of an interview the atmosphere should be easy and non-stress. Both interviewer and interviewee in a light-hearted manner follow the sequence of questions and topics. The question-answer business will continue.

Free Conversation Atmosphere: Free atmosphere is desirable in the process of interview. A moment of relaxation and easy feeling may be allowed to the interviewee. He should be encouraged to express his ideas freely without any fear.

Recalling Time: The interviewer after observing his facial expressions and feelings may give time to help in recall. The interviewer may give a hint or clue to break the silence which encourages the interviewee to speak.

Objective Questions: It has been found in actual experience that the interviewer puts irrelevant questions and questions of his own choice and interest not relating to the objective. Sometimes the interviewee does not expect such questions. So the interviewer should put such questions which will help to achieve the object of the interview.

Encouragement: The interviewer should not create a situation to feel discouraged on account of certain incoherences in talk. The interviewee should be encouraged in order to maintain a sustained interest in the interview.

Directions: It has already been mentioned that an interview is a joint exploration of both the interviewer and the interviewee. Sometimes they may indulge in an orgy of non-stop talking. It is really a delicate task to attain normality. However, the interviewer should politely and patiently with confidence steer the direction of talk in the desired course.

Note Taking: Recording of interview proceedings is very important as it may create confidence that opinions have been considered in arriving at a decision. And at the same time it is not desirable to rely upon the memory. Writing up of notes is very essential which must be done simultaneously with the process of interview.

Conclusion: As far as possible the object of the interview should be completed in one sitting. However, on certain matters several sittings may be necessary to complete an interview. Concluding the interview takes place with the mutual consent of both the parties. The conclusion should be appropriate to the kind of interview. Both must check before concluding.

Report: Report writing is like minutes writing of a meeting proceedings. Soon after the conclusion of the interview or each sitting a report about it should be put in writing. Taking a long time to write a report is not good as it may lead to errors, omission and forgetfulness in writing a report.

L. Brown has suggested dividing the interview process into three parts. They are opening, body and closing.

Myers and Myers have given suggestions on how to conduct an interview. The check list for an interview consists of:

1. Deciding and clarifying the purpose of the interview.
2. Plan for the interview.
3. Prepare the environment.
4. Prepare the opening.
5. Carrying out the interview sequence.
6. The close should be appropriate to the kind of interview.
7. Write up your notes or report.

Skill for Questioning

Asking someone questions for a newspaper story is a special skill. It may at times resemble a conversation, but it is not one; it may at times be entertaining to overhear or participate in, but that is not its point. Questioning people for newspapers has one purpose to collect information.

Interviews, whether in person or over the telephone, are not scripted and you should be prepared for unexpected answers, to follow their implications and ask follow-up questions. They will often be long, pedantic affairs, as you persist with a question you want answered or something you want to understand. They are not opportunities for you to tell that official what you think of him, show off your knowledge or engage your subject in heated debate.

A lot of interviewing is perfectly straightforward. But there are two particular situations that give trouble: questioning those who are uneasy and reluctant to talk, and questioning those who are positively evasive or even hostile. These situations are looked at later, but first, here are some guidelines that apply to asking questions of any source.

Actual Questions

Know What You Want from an Interview before You Start: You should always have a good idea of the basic information you want from a source before you start asking questions. Think of the final shape that the story might take and therefore the information you will need. During the interview you should continue to think of your report and how the new information you are getting is changing it. Above all, be aware of where the information gaps are in your story, and try at all times to fill these holes. This may sound very complicated but in fact becomes second nature after a while. And do not be afraid to write one-word reminders to yourself on the flap of your notebook. This helps to avoid having to contact the person again for things you forgot to ask in the interview. That is sometimes not possible and you may have to try to write the story without this information.

Do as Much Research as You can before the Interview: You should never be afraid to show ignorance, but that is not the same as being proud of not knowing. Before interviewing someone, find out as much as you can about them, the subject and any other relevant thing. Apart from anything else, this helps to prevent you being hoodwinked or blinded by science.

The Simple Questions are the Best: There is not a single example in journalism where so-called trick or clever questions produced results. Asking questions like that is normally the sign of inexperience or someone more concerned with making an impression than getting the best story. Normally the simple questions are: Who? What? Where? When? How? Why? If you have satisfactory answers to those questions you will be well on the way to having completed your basic research.

In Stories about Events, Build up a Chronology of What Happened: With sources who know in detail what happened, take them back to the beginning of the event(s), or before, and ask them about each stage, step by step. Don't be afraid to keep asking: 'And then what happened?' Get the sequence of events totally clear in your mind. This is vital for incident type stories, like crashes. At the end of your research, you should be able to run in your head a minute-by-minute video of what happened. If you can't, your story has holes.

Take them through Parts of the Story in Slow Motion: On a lot of incident stories you will be questioning people who have actually been part of the event, or witnessed it. Few will be used to giving a coherent account of such things and they may be excited, shocked or distressed. So when you get to the core action, slow them down and get every detail that you can. Ask them what happened at every moment, what they saw, the colours, smells and noises. Ask them where they were standing, what people were wearing, what they shouted, what the weather was like, etc.

Check Names and Positions: Obvious, boring to do, but essential. Ask sources to spell out names, titles, ages and addresses if you need them. Sometimes, if it is an awkward or foreign name, get them to write it in your notebook. You may think that makes you look silly - but not half as silly as you will when you get back to your office and find you do not know how to spell their name.

Get as Many Telephone Numbers as You can: This is as basic as getting your subject's name right. Get the phone number for their office, home, mobile, bleep — whatever they will give you. If their office number is printed on the phone, discreetly help yourself. If not, then ask.

Get too Much Information Rather than too Little: Most of the time you get only one chance to interview an important source. Take full advantage and ask every question you can. The answer to that extra question is often what makes the story. And remember that it is often details that lift a story out of the ordinary. Ask about them.

Do not be Afraid to Look Stupid: We have all been in that situation where someone is talking to us and we sit there nodding and agreeing, even though we do not have the faintest idea what they are talking about. We are afraid that if we ask them to explain we will look stupid. And then we come to write the story and realise that we don't understand what we have spent the last few hours pretending we knew.

Never, ever, be afraid to look silly by asking basic questions. First of all, people, even in press conferences, will rarely be so rude as to snigger at your ignorance. And, if they do, so what? Who is the most stupid: someone who pretends to know, or the person who does not know and admits it? Nearly every source is prepared to explain specialist concepts to reporters and most will be flattered that someone is interested in their subject.

If in Doubt, Describe your Understanding of a Situation: If you do not understand an answer, or if the situation you are reporting on is confusing, then describe your understanding to those you are questioning. Never be afraid to say: 'Can I just go over this. It all began when...', or 'Can I just see if I understand you correctly...', or even 'If I wrote that... would I be right? This is a standard technique. It does not imply that you are slow-witted. And even if it did, so what? Better that than an ambiguous, or wrong, report. The same applies to motives. Do not assume motives. If someone does something and their motive appears to be relevant, ask them, don't assume it. Reporting is not a parlour game.

Ask Questions to Get Information, not Opinions or Reactions: You are talking to sources to get facts and each question should be designed to do that. It is very easy to start asking questions about their reactions to something. But reactions are rarely surprising and so you will not have collected anything that is useful to your story. The knowledge, for instance, that a right-wing politician disapproves of liberal reforms is hardly news. The only exception to this, of course, is when the story is about opinions.

Try to Avoid Asking Cliched Questions: To ask someone who has just been involved in a tragedy 'How do you feel?' is to invite a cliched answer at best, or a flat refusal to answer any more questions at worst. If they have just lost their only son in an air crash how do you expect them to feel? Thrilled? Yet every day you can see in news stories the most predictable emotions ('I was excited to win this money', 'We are very upset to be sacked without compensation') paraded as if they were devastating insights.

Probe for Anecdotes: Good anecdotes can add a tremendous amount of life to stories. Collect them at every opportunity from the people you are questioning. But remember that getting people to discharge amusing, ironic, telling anecdotes is a matter of chatting in a relaxed way, not sitting bolt upright opposite them and saying, 'Now tell me the funniest thing you ever saw/experienced.' They won't. Their mind will go blank. Instead try to get some feel for the areas of their life/work/activity which are likely to provide humour. For instance, if you are interviewing airline cabin crew for a story about a new service and you want a couple of yarns about passengers' crazy behaviour, then don't say, 'Tell me the silly things travellers do.' Instead, naturally edge the conversation around to drunkenness, fear of flying, luggage, complaints about food, kids, strange requests and so forth.

Don't Let them Bullshit You: You should obviously ask for all jargon to be explained. But a lot of phrases that sound like technical talk are, in fact, euphemisms. Each industry, company or bureaucracy evolves phrases to camouflage reality. An airline will talk about 'passenger underflow', when what it really means is that not many people want to fly with them. An investment fund might issue a statement about a 'net liquidity export situation', when what they mean is that their investors have finally rumbled them and are taking all their money out.

Institutions which deal with dangerous materials, like the nuclear industry and the military, are especially adept at developing this kind of bullshit. In America, following a famous accident at Three Mile Island in 1979, the nuclear power industry came up with a potentially bewildering series of euphemisms to describe bad things. Statements talked of an 'abnormal evolution' at a plant which had led to an 'energetic disassembly' and then a 'rapid oxidation', perhaps followed by 'plutonium taking up residence'. What this meant was that there had been an accident at a plant which led to an explosion and then a fire, followed by plutonium contamination — all of which straightforward words and phrases were banned. Unban them. Ask what they mean.

Listen to the Answers: It is easy to be so concerned with rattling off the next question, or taking down the answer, that you fail to appreciate the significance of what is being said. Ten minutes after questioning someone is often too late to realise the importance - or absurdity - of what they have said. This is especially true when people make extraordinary claims in interviews.

The French novelist Georges Simenon once told a reporter from the *Swiss newspaper Die Tat*: 'I have made love to 10,000 women.' The paper duly reported the claim without comment.

However, even the least numerate of brains should be able to calculate that, to reach this total, Simenon would have had to have made a new conquest every other day for about 65 years - no mean feat for a man of 73 who also found time to write nearly 100 books. The real total, according to his tolerant wife in a subsequent interview, was nearer 1,200.

Review the Answers at the End: If at all possible, go back over your notes with people and double-check figures and anything of which you are still unsure. Apart from these overt purposes, this process has two covert ones. First, to see if you can discover any holes or 'information gaps' that have escaped you, and second, to see if you can squeeze a bit more information from the person. Ask them at this stage if there is anyone who can support their contentions.

Never Make Promises to Sources about how Stories will be Treated: Only the editor is in a position to know how a story will be treated and appear in the paper. A lot of the people that you question will ask this question, but you do not need to answer it. Tell them you are 'just a reporter' and give them your editor's name and number.

A lot of people are rather intimidated by journalists. This is not because they find them frightening as people (although some are), but because they are not used to dealing with the press. Even if they are, they may be reluctant to talk because they fear losing their jobs or some other repercussion. As one who has several times been involved in a news story, I know that it can be unsettling to be interviewed. You worry about what you might say, or be quoted as saying.

Often the reporter's first job with people who are uneasy is to persuade them to talk at all. When doing this, you can be friendly, light-hearted, talk about the public's right to know, etc.; in fact, whatever you may think will work. Often, however, you do not have the chance to negotiate first. You are 'cold calling', that is, visiting them without any preliminary telephone call. In these circumstances, just getting past their front door is a problem. The important thing here, as the following quotation illustrates, is to get inside their living room or office. Once you are there, it will be a lot more tricky for the subject to refuse to answer any of your questions. Once inside, the trick is to find ways of staying as long as possible.

This story comes from the book *All The President's Men,* written by Carl Bernstein and Bob Woodward of the *Washington Post* to describe an investigation they mounted which led, eventually, to the resignation of President Richard Nixon. Here, Carl Bernstein is convinced that the woman he is trying to interview is a potentially important source of the activities of her employers. This, and her anticipated reluctance to talk, is why he visited her in her home and did not telephone her first:

A woman opened the door and let Bernstein in. 'You don't want me, you want my sister,' she said. Her sister came into the room. He had expected a woman in her fifties, probably grey; it was his image of a Bookkeeper, which is what she was. But she was much younger.

'Oh, my God,' the Bookkeeper said, 'you're from the *Washington Post.* You'll have to go, I'm sorry.'

Bernstein started figuring ways to hold his ground. The sister was smoking and he noticed a pack of cigarettes on in the dinette table: he asked for one. 'I'll get it,' he said as the sister moved to get the pack. 'don't bother.' That got him 10 feet into the house. He bluffed, telling the Bookkeeper that he understood her being afraid: there were a lot of people like her at the committee who wanted to tell the truth, but some people didn't want to listen. He knew that certain people had gone back to the FBI and the prosecutors to give more information... He hesitated.

'Where do you reporters get all your information from anyhow?', she asked. 'That's what nobody at the committee can figure out.' Bernstein asked if he could sit down and finish his cigarette.

'Yes, but then you'll have to go, I really have nothing to say.' She was drinking coffee, and her sister asked if Bernstein would like some. The Bookkeeper winced, but it was too late. Bernstein started sipping slowly.

The woman talked, gave Bernstein some very useful leads, later spoke again to both reporters and proved to be a valuable contact. This may have had something to do with the fact that Bernstein did not immediately pull out his notebook and begin taking down every word the Bookkeeper said, while pulling faces of delight and amazement. He waited, maybe ten minutes, before slipping the notebook out of his pocket and starting casually to make notes.

If, however, people have agreed to talk, the next thing to think about is how to make them feel at ease. This will help you to get the most information from them. Here are some tips.

Think Carefully about where and how to Speak to Them: Will it be on the phone or face to face? What will be best for them? If it is face to face, where will it be? In a bar? In their office? At your office? Over a meal? In their home? In other words, in which environment are they least likely to feel threatened and, will therefore, be most cooperative?

Adapt to Them: Your aim when interviewing someone is to make them feel relaxed and helpful. This means not intimidating or annoying them. You may have to adapt your behaviour and appearance a little. You do not have to undergo a personality change for each interview, but you should consider your subject. For example, if you are going to interview homeless people on the streets, you would not wear your best suit or dress. That would make your subjects feel uncomfortable. Similarly, if you were going to interview the Prime Minister, you would not wear jeans and a T-shirt. They would probably be offended and think you were more concerned with making a statement about yourself than in getting a good interview - and they would probably be right. With people with whom you would have no natural rapport, you may even have to act a little to feign interest in them or adapt to them. If they are a formal sort of person, be more formal than your usual self; if they are very easygoing, then you can be too.

Make a Judgement about Them: What will get them on your side? Flattery? Friendliness? Jokes? Serious talk? Whatever it is, if they are an important source, do it. What interests them? Whatever it is, take an interest in that too. This is always easier if you are meeting them, especially in their home or office. People surround themselves with what is important to them - pictures of their family, paintings of their favourite places, ornaments and mementos. Use these things, ask them about them. Make the person want to help you. Try to find something you have in common with them, even if it just owning a dog or being a parent.

If you have Time, Try the 'Life Story' Ploy: If your subject is shy, or antagonistic towards you, but seems to have time, try asking questions about their life story. These are basic resume questions - where they were raised, educated, trained, where they first worked, success, achievements, overseas experiences, etc. It may give you some promising avenues for questioning. If not, it will almost certainly put that person more at ease and more on your side. Almost everyone warms to someone who seems interested in them.

If the Interview is in Person, don't Get out your Notebook Immediately: There is nothing that will unsettle the uneasy interview subject more than a reporter marching into the room, notebook open, pen poised over it, ready to take down every word they say. Instead, gradually slide it out of your pocket or handbag when they are relaxed. You can even say something like, 'Do you know, I have a terrible memory, do you mind if I make a few notes' 'Occasionally your judgement is that any appearance of the notebook will immediately stop them talking. In this situation, commit the important things they say to memory and make an excuse to leave the room (such as to go to the toilet or wash your hands). As soon as you are out of their sight, you can write down the highlights of what they have said.

Be Honest about your Intentions - but don't Tell People Everything: You should never fail to declare yourself as a reporter. Neither should you misrepresent your interest in talking to someone. However, you do not always have to explain precisely why you are calling them. If you have a controversial issue or question in mind, you would often be wise not to spell this out when you start talking. Just say: 'I am just making some general enquiries about this subject.'

Do not Come Straight out with your Main Question: Ask some general questions first. These could be questions to which you already know the answer. If nothing else, the subject's answers will tell you what they know and how honest they are. Only when you think they are ready should you ask what you are burning to know. When you do, it may be better to feign indifference to the answer. Dropping your notebook in amazement and exclaiming 'My God! Do you realise what you are saying!' is not the way to react. The thought that they have just given you the story of the decade is liable to produce an almost immediate retraction.

Use the Pregnant Pause: If the person you are questioning does not fully answer the question, try a pregnant pause, accompanied by an expectant look. Sometimes they will respond by adding the extra information you need. There is, of course, a limit to the length of time you can try to out-wait them. Delays of more than a few seconds are liable to be construed as idiocy or the onset of some serious disorder of the nervous system.

If All else Fails, Throw Yourself on Their Mercy: Tell them that you will be in trouble with your editor if you do not get this information. Ask for their help. It often works.

Keep the Conversation Rolling: When faced with 'I can't comment', don't attempt to deal head on with their anxieties. In almost every case you will lose that argument because their reasons are to do with their position or organisation and they obviously know more about that than you do. Instead, keep the conversation going and try several other tacks. First, reassure them that talking to you is no shocking departure, many other people have spoken to you. Then, without pausing, say, 'What puzzles me is... Can I ask you if...'.

Aggressive Factors

Some ways of dealing with uneasy subjects also apply to dealing with the evasive or hostile subject. But, more often, a different approach has to be taken with the potential source who is avoiding you.

Be Persistent: Getting hold of such subjects is sometimes extremely difficult. Never give up. Keep calling them, visit their offices. Make them realise that the only way to get you off their backs is to agree to talk.

If Telephoning, do not be Fobbed off with, 'He will call you back': Many people have no intention of doing so, despite what they or their secretaries or colleagues say. Do not accept this. Say you will hang on, say you will ring them back or, in a few cases, agree to be rung backbut fix a time for them to ring you back. If they do not do so, ring them back. Better still, ring them back an hour before the set time. Many people will say they will ring you back at 4 pm because they know they leave their office at 3.30 pm.

If Someone is Stonewalling Over a Factual Answer, Put Options to Them: If, for instance, you need to know how much the government paid for a certain contract and the person who knows is refusing to give you the answer, try putting sums of money to them: 'Is it $6 million?', 'Is it as much as $12 million?' Such questioning often produces results, or good hints. Yet be careful with this technique, make sure people understand what it is they are being asked. It, and similar verbal games, can lead to confusion.

The most notorious occasion of this was during the *Washington Post's* Watergate investigation referred to earlier. The reporters had a very good story, but only one source for it. Their editor insisted on two before he would publish. So, late at night, one of the reporters rang the only other person who might be able to support the story. He would not do so directly; so the reporter said:

> 'I am going to count to ten, if the story is wrong, hang up. If it is correct stay on the line.' He then began counting, 'One, two, three, four, five...' His voice was now getting excited. '... Six, seven, eight, nine... ten.'

He put the phone down and excitedly told his waiting colleague and the editor that they had confirmation and the story ran. The only problem was, it was not true. The late-night contact had misunderstood the instructions from the reporter and thought if he stayed on the line, he was letting him know the story was not right.

Occasionally, Try Pretending that You Know More than You Do: If you strongly believe something to be true, but cannot get confirmation of it, ring a source and say you are just calling for a comment. For instance, try asking the official *why* something happened, rather than *whether* it happened. He or she will often then start explaining rather than denying. This, however, is something only experienced reporters should do.

Watch out for Non-denial Denials: A non-denial denial occurs when an accusation is put to someone and, instead of denying it, they make a statement which insults the person who is making it, or the reporter, or both. Asked, for instance, if the government contract has been unsupervised and millions of dollars overspent, the subject would reply: 'Your sources do not know what they are talking about.' That is not a denial of the claim. It is often the classic ploy of the person with something to hide - but don't rely on that.

Watch out for Uninvited Denials: Unlike the situation described above, people with something to hide can sometimes go further than your question requires them to go. When asked for a comment, for instance, they deny things you never put to them. Be alert to this, it sometimes comes out of the blue and is the first indication that they have something to hide.

Do not use 'set-up' Questions: These are the questions that try to trap someone, not with information, but with a verbal trick. The fact that the trick is not very original does not stop it being used. It is a variant on the old 'have you stopped beating your wife?' question, to which the unwary might answer 'yes', implying they used to beat their wife but have now seen the light, or 'no', meaning that they still beat her.

One of the occasions when this was used most flagrantly was when rumours were flying around Britain's national papers that Prince Edward, the Queen's fourth child, was gay. The *Daily Mirror* pursued him to New York and, at a public event, shouted out the question: 'Are you gay.' The Prince was naive enough to say 'No', and the next day's *Mirror* appeared with the huge front-page headline: 'I'm Not Gay Says Edward'. The impression readers were left with was that Edward was indeed gay, but was now strenuously denying it. Nasty reporting.

Ask them to Imagine how 'No Comment' will Look in the Paper: If an official is refusing to comment, ask him or her to visualise how this will look in the paper. But don't make it sound like a threat. Make it sound like you are trying to save them from a public relations disaster: 'You know the readers will see 'X declined to comment' and they will think you have something to hide. Now I know that isn't the case, so can I just get your answer to...'.

Finally, remember that a person may refuse to talk to you one day but be more amenable a few days later. If they are an important source, try again.

Subsequent Steps

When the journalist witnesses some great events or makes some observations that cannot be fully expressed in a newspaper or magazine feature, writing a book – non-fiction or fiction – may be an answer.

When novelist Truman Capote first published *In Cold Blood,* he had invented – "the non-fiction novel." No matter what it is called, the work structures like a novel, reads like a realistic novel, but the events in the story actually happened. It is the writer's reconstruction of something that happened, and his recreation of incidents before and after the event. In Capote's case, it evolved around a murder and its victims and suspects. A book of this nature, in effect, is a case study, and a vehicle for social comments.

Hunter S. Thompson took the idea even further. Thompson fused facts and fantasies and created 'Gonzo Journalist," a highly interpretative and personally involved style of writing in the New Journalism stream. His parodies on the 1972 US Presidential campaigns are witty and entertaining, but damaging for the political candidates when they appeared in *Rolling Stone* at the time.

Some writers in the Third World could only envy the luxury of such freedom of expression enjoyed by their First World colleagues. Sometimes when the social and political climate of a country is such that the reporter runs the risk even in straight reporting – merely relating the facts and quoting the exact words of officials – let alone interpretative reporting. To fuse facts and fantasies like Thompson would be highly dangerous for the writer.

However Journalists and other media workers in such advertises are usually very resourceful. They know how to circumvent the scrutiny of censors and work around the constraints. They write fiction, stories in the form of fantasies, fairy tales and fables. They use cartoons, popular songs, chants and verses, and wall posters. The puppet theatre becomes the stage of the voice of the repressed, and street drama, the vehicle for social and political criticism.

And then, there is nothing wrong with wanting to write a novel or produce a play to express some personal observation of life in general, or even just to suit the creative fancy of the author (provided that the author is an ethical and socially responsible person).

In any case, journalism is not necessarily "more true" than fiction. It may be, as Hunter Thompson in his more serious moments wrote, that both "journalism" and "fiction" are artificial categories, and that both forms, at their best, are only two different means to the same end.

Humour: As media workers, we often remind ourselves that we have this serious responsibility of informing and educating the public we serve; and we tend to forget that, at times, something in the comic mode might be more effective in getting the message across.

Humour is more than a literary or narrative device for the creative person operating in a repressive environment: It is the pretext and platform of expression, and the weapon of the oppressed. For those who have lived under colonial rule or experienced oppression, reading between the lines and sensing the meanings of parodies and allegories is a means of survival.

As Emir Rodriguez Monegal said,"...laughter is the weapon of the oppressed used to parody and destroy the solemnity of their oppressor." He points out that the tradition of laughter has a long history in Latin American literature, whether be it Peruvian, Brazilian, Argentinian or Mexican.

"Satire in colonial literature," wrote Monegal, "is both a literary technique and way of preserving personal integrity." To him, the greatest Latin American writer of the 20th Century is Jorges Luis

Borges, ' 'the parodist, deconstructionist, reducer of philosophy to science fiction and metaphysics to fantastic literature." And among those writing in the Latin American tradition of laughter include Nobel Prize winner, Brazilian, Garacia Marquez *(One Hundred Years of Solitude)*, and the Cuban author, Guillermo Cabrera Infante (*Three Trapped Tigers*).

Latin American literature is only an example of the functions of humour. The form or medium of expression may vary from culture to culture, yet laughter is an essential part of our lives. At times, humour – in the form of irony, satire or parody – may be the smiler with the knife under his cloak, for the underdog and repressed. It can also reduce tension and provide relief for the man or woman after a day's hard work in the fields, at home, at the factory or office; or the catalyst of self-reflection for a society enjoying economic and political stability.

Telenovels: As laughter can be a useful tool, entertainment can be the vehicle for important messages. That does not mean to negate the functions of news stories, or radio and television newscasts and documentaries. The traditional categories of media entertainment, such as humour columns, cartoons as well as radio and television dramas can complement development such as government health programmes, or bringing about tribal understanding or religious tolerance among the people.

Latin American countries, especially Mexico, are quite successful in developing the potentials of television entertainment, through *Telenovels*, in connection with national development. The *telenovela*, a type of soap opera developed during the 1950s and 60s, is the dominant genre in Latin America, In a study on the success of *Telenovels*, Rogers and Antola pointed out that themes emphasising upward social mobility, and educational and other goals in addition to entertainment are among the characteristics of *Telenovels* compared to their US equivalents. And, these series capture the mass audience, unlike soap operas in the U. S. where viewership is predominantly female and mostly for day-time viewing.

In the 1970s, in Mexico, Televisa produced several popular *Telenovels* with themes towards social improvements in line with government projects and campaigns. They include: *Come with Me (Ven Conmigo)*, fostering adult literacy training; *Accompany Me (Accompaname)* promoting family planning; and *Let's Go Together (Vamos Juntos)*, combating child abuse.

According to the production company's research, during the year in which *Accompany Me* was broadcast (1977), the number of family planning adopters in the country increased by about 560,000; and the research also suggested that the one-year broadcast of *Come with Me* helped to bring about an increase of enrolment of about 1,000,000 in adult literacy training classes.

These Mexican educational soap operas were inspired by the success of an extremely popular Peruvian *Telenovela of the* 1960s, *Simple Maria (Simplemente Maria)*. A modern Latin American version of Cinderella, *Simple Maria,* is about a girl from the slums who started as a maid of a rich family, and eventually becomes a fashion designer due to hard work and her ability as a seamstress. The show made profits for the production company, and enhanced the sale of sewing machines in Latin America; and it also presented an educational theme that contributed to national development.

The results of the Mexican programmes, in turn, have inspired other Third World countries to produce educational soap operas. India, for example, has produced a series, *The People (Hum Log)*, on family planning. It was broadcast on prime time in mid-1984 and enjoyed a rating of 90, which sparked other production of soap operas. Other Third World countries are also planning to use this form of entertainment to promote national development goals such as family planning and the equality of women.

What attracted the audience to these educational soap operas, according to Rogers and Antola, is their fast-moving and emotionally charged stories: "the audience see them primarily as entertainment. These programmes do not try to "teach" family planning or literacy. They are subtle and indirect in their approach. For example, in *Accompany Me,* the characterisation of positive and negative role models was based on family planning behaviours promoted by the Mexican Government; and *Come* with Me tried to show low-income individuals participating in adult literacy classes.

From the Mexican experience, we can learn that something educational does not necessarily have to be solemn and dead serious. As William C. Miller advises aspiring script writers: an issue is often a challenging starting point for a script; however, the writer should moderate his zeal and avoid being too obvious or preachy. Subtlety is the key. In producing educational radio or television dramas, the message has to be natural to the context. Also, any transformation or conversion of the characters – for example, when the reluctant traditional farmer finally decide to participate in a farming programme advocated by the government, or the mother forgiving the daughter for marrying someone from a different social class – should be developed with a plausible story-line and in line with the personality of the character(s).

The Recitation

Men have been telling stories since pre-historic times. The tribesman tells of the boy who walked bravely into the jungle, ready for his first hunt... The old man under the banyan tree speaks of the young man who journeyed to a distant mountain to seek training from a legendary master swordsman. The *Wayang* master enacts the tales of the *Ramayana* in which the hero with the help from the gods defeats the evil force of the demons... No matter in what form or medium, past and present, there is always a purpose, a message somewhere. Myth, legends, folk-tales, fairy tales, fables and parable, whatever the term or category it may be, they are subtle carriers of moral codes, values and models of conduct of the culture.

In many ways, as journalists, writers, or writers/producers of radio and television programmes, we are essentially "storytellers." First, our editors, publishers, producers, or production managers, have to "buy" our story. Then we have so attract and retain the attention of our audience. Otherwise, whatever jewels of wisdom we have would be lost.

As communicators working in a developing nation or newly independent country, we are constantly working to establish a solid cultural identity in our work to counter the possible "cultural invasion" of the developed countries. May be one of the solutions would be to get the inspiration and foundation from the different narrative and poetic forms of our indigenous culture. We need to know our audience, as well as what is the best way to reach them, and how to get our messages across. It is important to examine the prevailing social climate in order to understand the mind-set of the people. However, it is also important to be retrospective and to learn from history and traditions. Proverb and parables are useful tools for putting certain ideas into the perspectives to which the audience can relate. In the realm of beliefs and moral values often the answers are embedded in myths, legends, folklore and popular stores at the time. They can provide ideas for the theme and contents of stories, or used as analogies to news events or description of news makers. At the same time, they are valuable sources of ideas for presentation and form.

Child development and cognitive psychologists in the West have found that children develop the sense of the plot of the story during grade school (primary school according to some school systems). They expect a certain sequence from the story they heard. They would tend to understand and recall a story better if the stories are told in the "ideal order". May be structural and content studies of the stories in folklores, myths, popular arts, and/or other narrative forms would be an appropriate topic for communication researchers in Third World countries. For example, Dan Ben-Amos, in a comprehensive study of African folklores, defines the functions of different forms of African tales as well as proverbs and riddles, and discusses studies of other researchers concerning the structure of African narrative forms. Perhaps different "ideal forms" can be developed to suit the audience of different cultures.

Principled Features

There is no entertainment per se. There is always a purpose behind the storytelling. It depends on whether the story is used for a good cause or for selfish reasons. It is understandable that in a community where literacy prevails, the word becomes more sacred; and in a nation which worships technology, voices from the radio or images or television would be expected to embody the truth. A journalist or media person should caution against being wrapped up in the myth of his or her own power. Ethics is personal and cultural. There is no fixed standard as there is no definite way to present a message. To have an open mind and continue to be receptive to the needs of the community and ideas for solution; to serve humanity and maintain persons integrity are some of the appropriate guidelines. Just remember that in a world of flux and instability, people tends look to the media for information, guidance, inspiration and moral support. Words of encouragement, and stores the spreads the ideas of tolerance, understanding, love and peace and generate hope, are some of the motifs.

The Opening

The intro is the most important paragraph in the story. It can make people want to read to the end, or it can turn them off and send them hurrying to another article. And they will not be slow to do this. Newspapers are often consumed quickly, by people with little time to read them, in places and conditions not designed for relaxation and contemplation - trains, cars at traffic lights, offices, the street, etc. There is a good chance that if the first paragraph does not grab their attention, they will never get to the second one.

That progress is not always determined by the quality of the intro. Other factors play a role: a good headline will sometimes inspire people to dig beyond the intro, and a strong interest in the subject matter may force them to plough on in case the story perks up. Readers are also influenced by the size of the paper (one of 96 pages obviously offering more alternative articles to sample than one of 12). As a journalist you cannot influence or have foreknowledge of these factors. (And don't say you know the size of the paper. Of course you do, but the reader may be buying several others.) The only way you can make a reader get beyond the intro is to make it a good one.

Journalism by Cooperation

The advertisers led the way: they discovered the technique of producing irrational belief. What the person who cares about democracy has got to do, One thinks, is deliberately to construct an education designed to counteract the natural credulity and the natural incredulity of the uneducated man: because the uneducated man has these two opposite defects, that he believes a statement when no reasons are given for it, and equally he disbelieves it when reasons are given. So that you have two opposite tasks to cause people not to believe when there is no reason, and also to cause them to believe when there is reason. The credulity and the incredulity are exactly wrong in the natural man. One thinks if there is a department for original sin, it is perhaps in this direction, in the ways in which we come to believe and to disbelieve things.

One should start very young. If one had to run an infant school, I should have two sorts of sweets, if one was the teacher — one very, very nice and the other very, very nasty. The very nasty ones should be advertised with all the skill of the most able advertisers in the world. On the other hand, the nice ones would have a coldly scientific statement, setting forth their ingredients and consequent excellence. One should let the children choose which they would have one should, of course, vary the assortment from day to day, but after a week or two they would probably choose the ones with the coldly scientific statement. Bertrand Russell, in an address, reprinted in *Power.*

Irrational beliefs forms a large bulk of the furniture of the mind, and is indistinguishable by the subject from rational verifiable knowledge.

Categorised Publications

Apart from preparing publicity material-news items, articles, features, advertisements, etc. for newspapers, the publicist in the government departments, public sector undertakings, business houses and other organisations is also required to bring out publicity journals. Most of these are House Journals or Trade Journals or a combination of both.

A House Journal is a medium of communication intended to project the image of the organisation, both within and outside the organisation. The purpose is to improve the morale of the employees, create favourable climate for the working of the organisation, and promote and provide opportunities for creative expression. While internal House Journals are meant for circulation within the organisation, external Journals are circulated outside the company or organisation such as dealers, consumers, shareholders, etc.

Journal for the House: The Trade Journals disseminate information about a particular trade, equipment or technical progress. Unlike House Journals, they are not meant for image building of the organisation. There are publications which are a combination of Trade and House Journals. They give technical information about the particular trade, and also news about the employees and the organisation.

The House Journals are, generally, in magazine format size 81/2" × 11". They deal with the welfare of the employees as well as other activities of the organisation. The House Journals, in many cases, accept advertisements. However, they should not be commercial in appearance since their primary purpose is to promote goodwill. Generally, the House Journals are not priced.

Early Phase: Under the Press and Registration of Books Act, 1867, for bringing out any newspaper (any printed periodical work containing public news or comments on public news) which covers House Journals, the printer and publisher have to make a declaration before the District Magistrate or Sub-Divisional Officer within whose jurisdiction such newspapers are printed or published. The declaration is made in a prescribed form giving all relevant information, such as title of the paper, language, periodicity, retail selling price, publisher's name, place of publication, printer's and editor's name, etc. It is necessary to file a fresh declaration whenever the place of publication or printing is changed or when the publication is temporarily suspended. Six copies of the declaration are filed. The declaration is, however, not necessary in the case of government journals.

Clearance of Titles and Delivery of Copies: Before making the first declaration, it is necessary to ascertain from the Press Registrar, New Delhi, through the concerned District Magistrate or SDO, as the case may be, whether the title of the journal is available. This formality is necessary in the case of government journals also.

After the declaration is filed, the Magistrate forwards one copy of the declaration to the Press Registrar, who then issues a certificate of registration to the publisher.

Every publisher is required to send a copy of the publication, if it is in English, Hindi or Urdu, to the Registrar of Newspapers for India, New Delhi. In case of other languages, copies are required to be sent to the Press Information Bureau of Government of India as given in Rule 5(2) of the Registration of Newspapers (Central) Rules, 1956. A certain number of copies are also to be sent to the addresses mentioned in the Rules, made by the State governments under Act 25 of 1867.

House Journals are, generally, printed either on art paper or printing paper. Most frequently used standard sizes of the House Journals are crown (15" × 20") and demy (18" × 23").

Newsprint/Printing Machinery: The publicist has to apply, for the allocation of the paper, to the Registrar of Newspapers for India, New Delhi, in a prescribed form every year. The newsprint policy is revised every year and the quantum of allocation depends on the number of copies printed, frequency of the journal, number of pages and other details.

The Registrar of Newspapers should also be approached if the organisation, publishing such journals, would like to import printing, composing and allied machinery for bringing out the journals.

Sales Tax and Postal Concessions: The company publications, distributed free to employees, are exempt from sales tax (entry No. 4 of Schedule A of the Sales Tax Act, 1959).

House Journals can be posted at concessional rates provided they comply with the conditions laid down in Rule No. 122 of the Post Office Guide, Part I. The conditions are that it should be registered with the Registrar of Newspapers for India, and bear in print the RNI Registration No. on the Journal. For bringing out House Journals and other publications, the publicist should know different printing processes: types of paper, use of type faces and the art of proof reading.

The printing processes are mainly of three types-Letter Press, Lithography and Offset Lithography, and Gravure. The selection of a particular printing process depends on the type and size of the publication, the quality aimed at, the number of colours involved, the print order and the time and money available for the project.

Letter press is the most popular printing process. Printing is done through the relief method, where the raised printing surface of type or block is inked with rollers. The impression is then obtained on printable surface (paper, board, plastic sheet, etc.) by contact. This is a speedy and economical process, particularly for small runs. Newspapers, most of books, magazines and commercial printing jobs are done by letter press.

In lithography and offset lithography or photographic printing, the text or the image is transferred to a flat slab of stone or metal plate with greasy crayons or ink. The surface is then damped. Because of the mutual repulsion of water and oil, the greasy parts repel moisture but catch the ink when rolled on. The image is then transferred to paper. Gradually, the metal plate is replacing the stone slab and the printing matter is generally transferred to it photographically. Offset lithography is a further improvement on this process. This process is generally used for posters, calendars and long-run colour jobs.

In gravure or intaglio printing or photogravure, the impression is made from ink deposited in engraved areas or 'depressions' in a plate. The matter or the image is transferred to a copper sheet or roller by photography and etched with acid, the desired depth of colour being determined by the depth of etching. The surface is covered with ink and the surplus ink is wiped off, leaving it in the 'depressions' which are impressed on paper. This process is increasingly used for illustrated magazines in many colours, requiring large runs.

Printing Paper: For the printing of House Journals, there are generally two types of paper-coated or art paper and uncoated paper. The quality of art paper depends on the type of finish (coating) given to the paper. The uncoated paper is mainly of two varieties-rough (antique) and smooth (calendared).

Printing paper is available in sheets of various standard sizes foolscap (17" × 27"), crown (15" × 20"), demy (18" × 23"), and royal (20" × 25"). To obtain pages, the sheets are to be folded once to obtain 'folio', subdivided twice to obtain the 'quarto' and thrice to get the ,octavo'. Different quality of papers are not available in all the sizes. For instance, art paper, map litho, offset and newsprint or poster paper are available only in crown and demy which are, in fact, most used standard sizes in India.

Since the cost of paper normally accounts for as much as 50 *per cent* of the total expenses of the publication, it is economical to fit the publication into one of the standard sizes. This avoids wastage when the paper is trimmed for printing. This is particularly important in the case of the publication with a large circulation.

While deciding the size of the page of a journal, it should be kept in mind that at least ¼" is allowed on each outer edge for bleed or trimming, after printing and binding the sheets.

Type Faces: An intelligent and clever use of different type faces not only helps readability, but also gives better 'look' to the publication. Generally, one type face is used for the text and not more than two or three for headlines. The mixing of too many 'families' of types results in chaotic situation.

Most type faces can be used in at least four different ways. Bold characters are used for headlines, subheads, and for giving emphasis to an important paragraph in the text, while italic variety of type face is suitable for captions and subheads. The headlines can be varied by printing some of them in upper/ lower case, and others entirely in capitals. Capital letters in the same type face as the text may also be used for subheads in articles and for other purposes.

The size of the type, whether hand-set or machine-set, is designated in units of points (a standard typographical measurement is 1/72 inch or point). The point size applies to the height of the type, as measured from the front to the back of the metal shaft bearing the letter. The width of the type line, column or page is expressed in terms of 'ems' (a standard measurement for printers-approximately one sixth of an inch).

Proof Reading: It will greatly facilitate the publicist's work, if he has some knowledge of the art of proof reading. The use of standard marks of proof correction is of great help to printers.

The author's corrections should be kept to the minimum as the corrections cost money and cause delay. A few words added or deleted may mean the recomposing of a large number of words by the compositor, or even resetting the entire paragraph. It may also affect a number of pages. All this can be avoided to a large extent, if the publicist carefully checks the type-script before type-setting. As far as possible all additions, deletions and corrections should be carried out in the type-script. This saves considerable time and money.

The Standard: According to the British Association of Industrial Editors — and that is a pretty authoritative body — a house journal is a publication issued periodically and not for profit, by an industrial undertaking, a business house or a public service.

The first-ever house journal to make its appearance was the *Lowell Offering* which came out in 1840 and very appropriately from the Lowell Cotton Mills of America, a country that may be said to have fathered the concept of public relations.

What Public Relations is? Public Relations — or PR as it has commonly come to be known in its abbreviated form — took a great deal of time to gain respectability. In its bare essence public relations is an attempt to inform, persuade or adjust to engineer public consent for an activity, cause, movement or institution. The definition is provided by Edward Burneys and it is as good a definition as any. The aim is clear: this is to make whatever activity it is that one wants to promote, quickly and painlessly acceptable to the general public. For any kind of public relations there has, first of all, to be a public to cultivate relations with.

Public relations as a concept may be new, but it has always been practised down the centuries. When Cleopatra welcomed Mark Antony in regal splendour on the banks of the Nile, she was practising a subtle kind of public relations. When Tata established the Tata Charitable Trust and publicised it, he was doing PR. When Mahatma Gandhi called on King George V at the latter's residence at Buckingham Palace clad only in the peasant's dhoti and shawl, he was practising public relations for Indians poor *in excelsis. Chamchas* of politicians, the hangers on that crowd the outer offices of ministers also do public relations, albeit a little unsavoury, of sorts. In the modern world public relations has become an essential function in almost all spheres of life, whether of education, business, trade, commerce, international relations, industry, administration and even day-today dealings. Every organisation has a PR man.

If PR is — as Edwin Emery has pointed out — a planned effort to influence and maintain favourable opinion of the public through acceptable performance, honestly presented and with reliance on two-way communication, how is it best conducted? This, it might be said, depends on what audience wants to persuade, influence or convince.

The Readership: Primarily, there are three kinds of audiences: the internal, the external and the internal-external. And the most suitable way of reaching out to them is through house journals. In the circumstances, house journals themselves can be divided into three types: the internal house journal, the external house journal and the internal-external house journal.

Internal House Journal: The internal house journal is intended primarily for the internal consumption of an industry, business house or organisation. Its aim is obviously to enlist the cooperation of employees through a variety of ways: by providing them a forum to vent their grievances, by giving them an opportunity to exhibit their talents, by supplying them adequate information about the aims and objects of the institution concerned, even by educating them about various matters regarding the organisation they are serving.

Briefly, the internal house journal (IHJ) projects the image of a company as a good employer who cares for the interests and well-being of the employees. The IHJ publishes events of personal interest to the employee such as transfers, births, deaths, marriages and other social events. Promotions, retirements are grist to the IHJ mill. Is the company about to put a new product in the market? The employees will be about the first to be told, possibly through the IHJ. Are there certain problems that need to be resolved and demand employe attention? More likely they will first be discussed in the IHJ. Not only inter-work, inter-staff and inter-department news meaningful to the IHJ, so is intra-work, intra-staff and intra-department news of absolute validity.

Without Reserve: Consider this editorial in *Without Reserve,* the appropriately named house journal of the Reserve Bank of India (October-December 1978):

In April-June 1978 issue, while discussing avenues for participation in management by individual employees we had made a passing reference to the Staff Suggestion Scheme. We then realised that this subject is important enough to deserve separate, exclusive treatment.

The Staff Suggestion Scheme introduced in the Bank in August 1969 (initially covering only staff members but later encompassing even officers) will soon be completing a decade of its operation. The experience gained over the year makes an interesting study. It need hardly be emphasised that the scheme is based on the firm belief and conviction that creative ideas for improvement are not the prerogative of top echelons alone. Rather, there is abundance of talent available at all levels and this untapped reservoir of ideas should be allowed to contribute to improving the working and image of the Bank and take pride in seeing this happen. In a way, it also provides a channel of communication between the management and the employees and serves as a modest tool in giving impetus to the style of 'participative management'.

Coming to the actual operation of the Scheme, it provides for a specially designed form to enable the suggester to first put forth the problem as he sees it, then the solution which he seeks to offer and lastly the advantages and benefits that should accrue by implementing the suggestion. The Management Services Division, which administers the Scheme, examines each suggestion critically, holds discussions with suggesters and wherever necessary modifies or develops the ideas in consultation with the concerned operational department.

The recommendations are then submitted to a high level committee consisting of the CM, CA, and the Director, MS Division. This Committee decided about the acceptance or otherwise of the suggestion and awarding of the prizes, which vary from a minimum of Rs. 50 to a maximum of Rs. 2000 in cash. Needless to say, the evolution of the suggestion takes into account the visible savings as well as the invisible/intangible benefits resulting from it in the areas of customer service and employee morale, etc. In case the suggestion does not qualify for a cash prize, a certificate of merit is presented to the suggester.

A survey recently conducted, reveals that of the total number of 3008 suggestions received upto the end of August 1978, about 285 have been accepted. This works out to nearly 10 per cent acceptance ratio, compared to about 5 per cent in some of the private industries. Although difficult to calculate actual savings, rough estimate of potential savings is over Rs. 2 lakhs. In terms of cash prizes, the Bank has so far disbursed about Rs. 12,500: the maximum individual prize being Rs. 750. Another interesting feature of the survey is that suggestions relating to operational/general side departments were roughly twice in number than those pertaining to all the other departments put together. Again, of the 3008 suggestions involved, as many as 1900 came from Class III staff, 171 from Class IV staff and the rest 937 from officers, including 605 Staff Officers Grade A.

The above features are sufficiently indicative of the fact that the Staff Suggestions Scheme has generally made a good beginning in the Bank. Its continued success will, however, largely depend upon the ungrudging support from the staff at all levels. Needless to say, every member of the staff owes it to the institution to make it stronger, efficient and of greater use to the community and the nation at large. Suggestions to improve the thrust and content of the suggestion scheme are most welcome.

This is an excellent example of the institution seeking the cooperation of its employees. The editorial does several things: it informs the employees of a Staff Suggestion Scheme that had been inaugurated a decade earlier. It provides factual material regarding the progress of that scheme.

It entices the employees to be more cooperative by referring to the cash incentives provided by the Reserve Bank and it further challenges even those at the lowest levels of employment to come forth with ideas, giving the example of others who have so done in earlier times. In sum what the editorial does is to inform, encourage, induce and exhort employees to give of their very best. This is exactly what an IHJ is expected to do.

The Reserve Bank of India's house journal is a good example of what an IHJ should be. In the first place it is beautifully produced, no doubt because it has the necessary financial backing. In the second place it is bilingual and carries articles in Hindi as well in order to reach a larger slice of the Bank's employees. Finally, it is amply illustrated and is a visual delight. Let us examine its contents:

It carries an editorial, a page of letters from staffers, a "portrait gallery" that introduces up-and-coming staffers, an informative piece called "Know Your Central Office", a feature called "From the Balcony of Memories", another on a wife's eye-view of her officer husband, a note on a two-week seminar held for officers dealing in foreign exchange, four entire pages of pictures of staffers engaged in a variety of activities, two pages devoted to photographs taken by staffers, two more pages of marriage photographs under the rubric "Love Means Not Taking Each Other for Granted", a page of obituaries and some three pages full of pictures of staffers' children, young and old. In sum, the journal Touches all bases.

The usefulness, indeed the relevance of an IHJ is best gauged by the kind of reaction it elicits from its in-readers. Consider some of the letters published in *Without Reserve:*

The delayed appearance of WR has become proverbial. A lot of jokes are exchanged on it. It is said that a marriage photo is published along with that of the first-born and a baby's photo is published along with that of its passing some exam, etc. All such jokes go to reveal the truth that the readers are anxious to have the journal on the due date.

What is the use of bedecking a bride in a grand manner and thereafter delaying her joining the hands of her husband? Does not all her beauty go in vain? Similarly, don't you think that all the efforts in making the journal enjoyable go to waste, if it is unduly delayed to reach the hands of the readers?

H. Krishnamurthi, Correspondent, Madras.

Cut down news regarding transfers/promotions. Some such important news reaches us already through the RBI Newsletter, Bank's Circulars and Officers' List. The space so released can be utilised for 'ventilating' what the Bank is doing for the betterment of the employees and their families and other developmental aspects.

It appears that whenever there is a shortage of material, you leave blank spaces here and there. I feel that these spaces can be beautifully filled up with corner designs – plenty of them are available in the currency notes issued by the Reserve Bank.

– Amaresh Kumar, Gauhati

Synergy: Not all IHJ's, of course, are such marvels of design as the Reserve Bank's house organ. Some of the over 790 house journals produced in India by public sector and private sector organisations are poorly produced, either for want of financial support or proper staff. Take the journal of Indian oil Management Academy called *Synergy* which is "for Private Circulation Only". Its editorial for January 1980 issue said:

> The first bulletin of IMA, fresh with birth marks, — a few stencilling smudges and possibly typing errors — seems to have been received well. Quite a few letters have come in, encouraging us and suggesting some improvements. We reproduce some comments without revealing the source to protect copyright interests!

To each one who cared to write back and tell us, our sincerest thanks. Brickbats are as welcome as bouquets. So please keep giving us your impressions. We need to feel our way.

Instead of calling it a Bulletin, we would now be calling it a Journal. The cover pages are printed but the contents are cyclostyled. One step at a time and we are sure each footprint will be stronger and better defined.

We would like you to pass on material you consider your colleagues could read, enjoy and learn from — if one likes to learn, of course. For this issue, we had to lean heavily on the quarterly Journal brought out by the Management Training Centre of SAIL. We are very grateful to them for sharing their good work with us. A meeting of two phases, in fact, solid steel and normally liquid crude. The bond — hopefully must grow mutually — steel to drill out the oil from the bowels of the earth and oil to protect steel from rusting.

The editorial highlights the problem that most editors have to face in bringing out an IHJ. Lack of financial support and lack of staff support in the shape of news, articles, comment, etc. Both can be — and frequently are — crippling. Editors have to coax, cajole and control writers to fill IHJ columns which means that they have to be in constant and continuing touch with employees at all levels. It is by no means an easy task. And there is often not enough money for printing the IHJ. Companies put an IHJ at the lowest priority level.

Zinc News: *Without Reserve* is an internal house journal. So is *Synergy*. So are *Accumulator* (house journal of the Standard Batteries), *Gesco News* (Great Eastern Shipping Company Ltd.), *H.P. News* (Hindustan Petroleum), *Bharat Refineries House Journal* (Bharat Refineries Ltd.) and *Zinc News* (Hindustan Zinc). To give an idea of how the editor of *Zinc News* gets his material for his 12-page house journal from various units of Hindustan Zinc Ltd., here is a letter addressed to all staffers that was prominently published on the last page in a one column cut box:

Dear Reader,

February issue of Company's House Journal is in your hands now. Are you in it? If not, we would very much like you to be in this publication through your activities and achievements on the job as also your social and cultural life in HZL.

To maintain a direct communication, correspondents in each unit have been named and you can always forward material for house journal through them or address the same to the Editor, Zinc News, HO....

Possible subjects are summarised below. However, if you have something else in your mind, please do not hesitate to share the same also with us:

1. Important events in units and corporate set-up during the month.
2. Promotions, transfers, appointments, retirements, deaths, etc.
3. Labour welfare and sports activities.
4. Important achievements in studies or extra-curricular activities of employees' children with photographs.
5. Awards to or achievements by employees.
6. Visits by VIPs, dignitaries, etc.
7. Important notifications regarding employees.
8. Engagements/marriages.
9. Cultural activities and celebrations on National Days and Independence Day each year.
10. Small poems, quiz, etc. from children.

Which roughly sums up what an IHJ would need and which simultaneously tells how this is sought to be obtained.

Internal-External House Journal: If the intention of an IHJ is to seek the total involvement of the employees in the work of the institution or organisation they serve, the purpose of an internal-external house journal (I-EHJ) is to meet the needs of an extended family that comprises not merely of company employees but of an external audience as well. *Sandesh* is an example of the I-EHJ brought out by the Shipping Corporation of India, a public sector undertaking. It is a tabloid size journal and its audience consists of company employees, government officials, Union Ministers, other shipping companies and news papermen. Besides disseminating all the news pertaining to the Corporation, *Sandesh* also seeks to build up a favourable corporation image among its readers. The November-December 1978 issue of *Sandesh* carried an image-building story on its front page: *SCI Tankers Carry India's Total Crude Requirements.* The story pointed out how no single tanker of the Shipping Corporation was laid off when there was a tanker crisis, although many tankers were laid off in other shipping companies.

External Journal: Hoechst Pharmaceuticals Ltd. has both an IHJ and an I-EHJ. The IHJ of Hoechst Dyes and Chemicals and Hoechst Pharmaceuticals Ltd. is known as *The Hextonian: A Window to the World of Hoechst,* and carries the usual quota of articles by and on its employees, and states clearly that it is "Published for the Employees" of the two associated firms. *Hoechst Trade Bulletin,* however is clearly intended for chemists and druggists and is an example of an external journal — EJ. The January 1980 issue of the *Bulletin* carries a front-paged message from the Managing Director of the Company to its clientele which reads as follows:

Dear Readers,

Greetings and best wishes for a Happy and Prosperous 1980 from the Editorial Board of this Bulletin, from Hoechst Pharmaceuticals and myself!

Looking back over the years preceding 1979, I do find cause for satisfaction. Our chemist friends and distributors have stood by us through thick and thin. 1979 particularly has been not a very easy year for us but we have come out through it unscathed largely due to your support. We look forward to similar unstinted support from our customers in 1980 and also in the years to come.

We have strived to make this magazine as one of the chemist and by the chemist. With this end in view, we have been giving coverage to chemists in different areas in every issue of the Bulletin. We have also been introducing to you our various Distributors by publishing write-ups on their organisations and on the people managing them. The idea is to bring our Distributors and Chemists closer to one another and to ourselves. From time to time, we have been keeping you informed of the changes in packing, prices, products and our organisation through this medium of communication.

At present we have over 30,000 chemists on our mailing list. These chemists are served by our Distributors and Stockists which number over 250 throughout the country. In this family of 250, we have over 60 veterinary preferred stockists and over 70 outlets to handle our agro-chemicals. These outlets are catered to by our eight Branches and four Depots.

As the years go by, more chemists will come into existence and many more will be added to our mailing list. The same applies to the medical profession which is equally important to our business. We have been gradually expanding our distribution network in order to be able to cater to the growing number of chemists and doctors.

While a Company's distribution network is a link between production and the chemist, it is the latter which ultimately joins consumers to this link and thereby to the manufacturer. The role that the chemist has to play in the entire chain of distribution can, therefore, never be overemphasised. While prescription business originates from the medical profession, a manufacturer depends more on chemist for his over-the-counter (OTC) products.

It is physically impossible to meet each and every chemist in this vast country but we have tried to reach as many of them as possible through our Trade Bulletin. We have tried to come closer to you, to know you and to make ourselves known to you. We hope that 1980 will bring us all still closer and will be a fruitful year for you, for our Distributors and ourselves.

Trade Bulletin: The above letter is a perfect example of what an external journal – EJ – is meant for. To quote from it: "To come closer to you, to know you and to make ourselves known to you." The front page of the *Trade Bulletin,* carried, in addition to the Managing Director's message, a report on the silver jubilees of three of the company's "able and experienced Distributors in the Bombay Branch territory". The report stated that "in accordance with our practice, the three Distributors were given a reception and presented with Silver Plaques as a token of our twenty-five years' association and cooperation with them". Inside pages contained information on other distributors under the general rubric: Meet Our Distributors. Each report was accompanied by a photograph. Sample reports:

Frank Ross and Company was established jointly by Mr. Frank and Mr. Ross as far back as 1890 simultaneously in Calcutta and Darjeeling. With the expansion of their business, they opened Branches in Bombay, Delhi and Madras. After Independence, Frank Ross was Indianised and converted into a public limited company, assuming the present name of Frank Ross & Company Ltd.

Over and above owning a number of retail counters, they are also Distributors for a number of pharmaceutical firms. They also deal in toilet goods.

The Darjeeling Branch is looked after by Mr. M. G. Vora, Manager and Mr. S. K. Dutt, Assistant Manager. Both of them are qualified pharmacists and have long experience in pharmaceutical business.

Frank Ross & Company is a member of the North Bengal Chemists and Druggists Association as well as its governing body.

Messers Ramesh Medical Stores was started way back in 1969 and in the initial phase they were operating as wholesalers. With their sincere hard work and dynamism within a short time they became one of the best wholesalers in the Madhya Pradesh pharmaceutical trade. It was at this point that many pharmaceutical companies saw a potential Distributor in them. Gradually offers started coming to them. It was in 1973 that they were appointed Hoechst Distributors. At present they have distributorships for 12 companies. Their annual turnover was approximately Rs. 3.7 million in 1978-79.

The establishment was started by Messers Chetan Das Rajpal and Ramesh Kumar Rajpal. Mr. Chetan Rajpal is now abroad and runs a cloth business there. The present active workers associated with the firm are Messers Ramesh Kumar Rajpal, Chandrabhai Rajpal, Sudhuram Rajpal and Narain Rajpal.

Ramesh Medical Stores are one of the most reputed Distributors in Ujjain and they are one of the best Distributors we have in Bombay Branch. The establishment is managed by Ramesh and Chandrabhai Rajpal with the able guidance of Sudhuram Rajpal. They are very young and enterprising people. Though Mr. Ramesh is 28 years old and Chandrabhai 23, they are conducting their business with maturity, dynamism and efficiency.

The firm's area of operation incorporates a major part of western MP in which the major towns are Bhopal, Ujjain, Indore, Ratlam, etc. For the effective coverage of this large area they have salesmen but even Mr. Ramesh goes on regular tour to improve this business and to continuously develop cordial relations with the customers thus improving the image of the firm in the eyes of the chemists.

In addition to the pharmaceutical business, the family has got other business interests, cloth wholesaling and photography. They have also one of the best studios of Ujjain.

Mr. Ramesh Rajpal is an active member of the Ujjain Jaycees.

In addition to giving information on its chemists and distributors, the *Trade Bulletin* also carried information on the company's products. Here is an example:

The critical role of brand names in assuring the quality and safety of a drug was strikingly illustrated recently in respect of Furosemide, a diuretic which helps eliminate fluids from the body. Furosemide is taken by patients with heart and kidney diseases, cirrhosis of the liver or high blood pressure.

There are four manufacturers of the drug in the US. However, only Furosemide marketed by Hoechst under the brand name Lasix is approved by the Food and Drug Administration. The FDA recently advised patients taking the prescription diuretic furosemide to be sure that the name Hoechst is on the tablets. Patients taking furosemide tablets that do not have the Hoechst name on them should ask the pharmacist for a replacement. Patients who are unsure whether they have the Hoechst product should contact their pharmacists, according to the FDA.

Consider what an EHJ does:

1. It informs clients about their links with the company.
2. It enlightens them about their numerical strength and likely influence.
3. It introduces them to each other.
4. It gives them incentives to do better than ever.
5. It tickles their vanity.
6. It provides product information and guidance.
7. It also educates them in matters pertaining to their own field.

The Trade Bulletin, for example, carried a brief article on the new edition of *Indian Pharmacopoeia* that chemists, druggists, stockists and distributors would not otherwise have known about.

The second edition of Pharmacopoeia of India (The Indian Pharmacopoeia) has just been published. Compiled by the Indian Pharmacopoeia Committee, the IP is the official book of standards for drug manufacture in the country.

The second edition incorporates a number of new monographs, although a substantial number of monographs included in the first edition has been retained. Among the new monographs special mention may be made of the following:

Antibiotics: Bacitracin, Neomycin. *Antihistaminics:* Cyclizine Hydrochloride, Meclizine Hydrochloride, Phenindamine Tart-rate. *Neo-plastic Suppressant:* Busulphan. *Tranquilliser:* Mepro-bamate. *Hormones:* Prednisone Acetate, Prednisolone Acetate, Thyroxin Sodium. *Muscle Relaxants:* Gallamine Trieiodide, Tolazoline Hydrochloride. *Hypnotics:* Amylo-barbitone, Amylo-barbitone Sodium. *Central Nervous System Stimulant:* Bemegride. *Antidiabetic:* Tolbutamide.

For the first time standards for three drugs used in indigenous systems of medicine have been included in the Indian Pharmacopoeia. They are: 1) Jatamansi (*Nardostachys jatamansi),* 2) Rasna *(Alpina officinarum)* and 3) Vidang *(Emblia ribes).*

Priced at Rs. 94.50, the publication is available from the Manager of Publications, New Delhi.

The Shalimar Standard (Shalimar Paints Ltd.) is an example of a house journal that meets the needs of both internal and external clients. Published from Calcutta, Vol. XXXI No. 1 carries the usual message from the company's Managing Director, a report on the ninth All India Paint Conference and Exhibition, plenty of pictures of the conference (on the sure grounds that photographs speak much better than the written word), photographs of wedded couples, staffers who have retired or died and a page devoted to dealers.

ICI Magazine: Some house journals are specifically intended for house employees only but because they are so beautifully produced and carry articles of interest to a wider audience, the organisations that put them out are willing to make them available to outsiders "on request". Such a journal is the *ICI Magazine* published by Imperial Chemical Industries Ltd., London. The imprint line of the magazine says that it is published "for the interest of employees of the ICI Group worldwide" but that "copies are available to readers outside the Group on request". While most journals make no mention of payments for articles published, the *ICI Magazine* specifically states that "payment will be made for articles commissioned and accepted" and invites employees "to submit suggestions for articles arising from or related to their membership of the group or reflecting special and uncommon activities or interests or ideas".

The ICI is a multinational corporation and has branches all over the world and its magazine cannot, in the circumstances, carry the usual quota of pictures of married couples or reports on company's activities. By its very nature, it has to be selective and sophisticated. The February 1977 issue of the *ICI Magazine* carries the following articles:

Shining Bright: In an emergency, seconds count. Strong and effective visual warning of actual or potential danger is vital. And, as this article shows, that is where the new ICI florescent safety paint makes its contribution.

A Reader Remembers: Trevor Richards became an indentured apprentice in 1923 at Castner-Kellner Alkali Co. Ltd., was appointed Works Safety Officer there in 1934, and subsequently, in Safety

Departmęnt, Millbank, played a major part in drafting and editing ICI Engineering Codes and Regulations. He retired in 1966.

Orchids in Indonesia: Miss Hing Widagdo is an accountant with ICI (Export) Ltd., Jakarta, Indonesia — one of the many members of the staff there who are ardent orchid enthusiasms.

Polymers — are they Worth the Energy? A.H. Woodhead retired from R & D Department, Millbank, at the end of 1976 after 25 years' service with the Company, mainly in Fibres Division where he had been Research General Manager. Before joining ICI he had research and production experience in both government and private sectors. His article is based on a paper he gave to the British Association last year.

To Russia with Films: Gordon Begg, Managing Director, Millbank Films Ltd., has made films for ICI and others since 1947. He is married with two sons, lives in Chelsea and rides to work on a moped. Here he writes of a cultural exchange visit to Russia as one of a small group of leading British industrial film-makers.

Business Sponsorship of the Arts: Albert Frost was Finance Director of ICI when he retired from the Company in March 1976 after 27 years' service, and is now a director of Marks & Spencer, "Warburgs and British Airways. An accomplished musician, he puts in this article the case for industrial sponsorship of the arts and describes an organisation set up to foster it.

A.L. Mudaliar, Chairman, ICI (India): This month's profile as much of ICI India itself as of its chairman — is written by Dilip Mukerjee.

After taking a B.A. (Hons.) degree at Lucknow University and spending some time in industrial public relations, Mr. Mukerjee became a journalist with *Economic Times* in Calcutta. Among other senior journalistic posts, he has been India correspondent of *The Economist* and chief of bureau of *The Times of India.* He is now senior writer for the *Business Times,* Kuala Lumpur, Malayasia.

World of ICI: The regular miscellany of items about ICI people, ICI products and ICI places.

Though it is clear from the art cover that *ICI Magazine* is not something that you get at the magazine stalls, its format, layout, design and contents could well mark it out as a general purpose magazine and even when its approach is ICI-oriented, the articles are so crafted that they would appeal even to an "outsider" who has nothing whatsoever to do with the multinational. And that is the secret of good public relations.

That, indeed, is the technique followed by some other organisations like Diners Club whose magazine *Signature* is available for Diners Club members and member establishments (annual subscription Rs. 24) and for non-members.

Signature is a quality magazine as opposed to *a glossy* like *The Taj* (the magazine of the Taj Mahal group of hotels) or the *Soma* (an Oberoi Hotels publication). Unlike other house journals, these magazines accept outside advertisements no doubt to balance the high cost of production. They are priced and subscriptions can be taken for them though neither *The Taj* nor *Soma* mentions price or subscription rates while *Signature* does. These magazines carry articles of general interest. Consider the contents of *Signature.*

Diners Club News

Lying About Your Age is Lying to Yourself by Wendy Haskell Meyer

Kumaon: Lake Land for all Seasons by A.D. Mod die *House Journals as Journalism*

Berlin: Fun City on the Wall by Arturo Gonzales Jr.

Fly or Die: A Review of the Concorde by Richard Witkin

Warding Off the Office Politician by Caroline Donnelly

Men, Women and Rape by Jeroo Gorimar

It will be noticed that though this is a Diners Club magazine, the articles do not necessarily deal with the Club all the time. Understandably one article deals with Club news and elsewhere, as in *Travel Forum* attention is drawn to the Club card.

Is it possible to fly Bombay/Colombo on a direct flight? Can this ticket be charged on the Diners Club card?

Ans: Swissair operates direct flights from Bombay to Colombo.... Swissair offices in Bombay, Delhi, Madras and Calcutta accept the Diners Club card for the fare.

The Taj Magazine and *Soma* are real glossies and obviously operate on the theory that quality counts and that the quality of service at the Taj group of hotels and in the Oberoi chain is on par with the quality of the magazines they produce. Let us examine the contents of these two magazines.

Soma (Vol. 8 No. 3) carries the following articles:

The Taj Magazine (Vol. 7 No. 3) had these articles:

The Taj Magazine like *Soma* or *Signature* is not on sale at magazine stalls. It has a particular clientele in view and it is the needs of that clientele that this magazine seeks to meet with style and sophistication.

Other Magazines: There are still other magazines that do not fall into the general category of house journals whether IHJs, I-EHJs or EHJs. These are college magazines and trade journals and these have their own formats and readership.

Monetary Publications

Trade journals come in various sizes and are clearly market-oriented and have as their aim the provision; of product-information, whether the product be a film, a book or a painting. Most pharmaceutical firms have their own trade journals. So have book publishers. Vikas Publishing House Pvt. Ltd. has its own journal *Vikas News* which is available on subscription. So have Jonathan Cape, a British publisher, or Chatto & Windus. These trade journals keep the publishing outlets informed of upcoming books, giving details of the books, their authors and their price. It is also customary, though the custom is not always observed, for publishers to mention the size of the book- and the age group it is intended for. At times a brief comment — always commendatory — from a distinguished writer or reviewer is also appended.

The information on the book may be in the form of a review or an extract from it. Sometimes, the author himself is invited to introduce his work. Take this example from *Vikas News* published by Vikas Publishing House, New Delhi:

Naked Triangle: A man's love has many triangles — the triangle of a wife and a mistress; the triangle where the mistress betrays for another lover; when the betrayed wife seeks solace elsewhere. In this autobiographical novel set in the landscape of corruption and sex-hungry society, the triangle changes with the ever-changing emotions.

Gargi describes the innermost layer of mental tortures, the glory and degradation of love, its insane pleasure, beauty, cruelty and the evil chained in our flesh, the source of creative energy.

The action is set in Bombay, Delhi and Chandigarh. The backdrop of the university campus infested by pompous educationists lays bare the corrupt human nature with gleams of idealism and noble moments. He describes the inside life of contemporary painters, actors, writers, politicians — shocking and exciting — caught in a vortex of passion. A writing that is fired by truth which is roguish, chilling, saintly.

Says Gargi:

> My narrative does not follow a strict chronological order. Flashbacks and flash-forwards intermingle. The

> events and images are telescoped. My eyes looking at a horse do not register it from head downwards, but may be from its flying mane or kicking hooves.
>
> The theme betrayed. How men and women deceive each other when they make love; how they betray. In their search for truth; how being disloyal to one makes them madly loyal to the other... the power and torture of sex, its ecstasy, its destructive nature... how geniuses are blinded by it, and how they lust to be destroyed by their women.

My characters are naked, the living people... my friends whom I adore... My friendship is their punishment. The women I have loved are stripped to be worthy of the altar. There is no other comfort than the warmth of one's own skin. I have used real names, characters and situations... women I have known... men with whom I have dined... my friends. A few faces I have covered with a thin gauze... to deceive so that I could speak the truth and share with you the magic of sex, the truth of desire, of creation, of my nightmares and their dark taste.

> "Full of raw passion and a sense of loneliness... critical, honest, brutal, interlaced with Indian compassion. I enjoyed reading it." — *Elia Kazan.*
>
> "Balwant Gargi has had the courage to submit himself to self-examination. He goes into forbidden areas and has literally taken the lid off... the most daring book."
>
> — *Mulk Raj Anand.*
>
> "Gargi spares neither himself nor the women he loved. He exposes himself with the same ruthless candour as he denudes them of their pretensions and pettiness. His character portrayal is very much like that of an artist of the impressionist school. What at first sight appear as artless dabs of the paint brush reveal themselves in perspective as carefully worked out combination of colours to illustrate the theme of love and lust gone sour by familiarity and misuse."
>
> — *Khushwant Singh.*

And this from Jonathan Cape (Autumn and Winter Books August 1979-February 1980):

> Karma Cola is a highly entertaining, if sobering, look at what happened when the West invaded India in reckless pursuit of mind expansion and obscure salvation. Just when Indians were becoming excited about rock and roll, washing down their contraceptives with Coca Cola, the Americans turned their backs on Elvis and Bill Haley and pointed East, declaring that's where it was at.

Allen Ginsberg and the Beatles opened the floodgates, the hippies turned it into a state of emergency, the Guru Maharshi filled the Houston Astrodome, while an Indian national airline advertised 'Nirvana for $ 100 a day'. Even today, after being told often enough that the experience of the East is simply not accessible to the Western mind except after an almost total re-education, tourists pour into India, scrabbling for mantras like clothes in a market stall, transplanting popular Californian therapies into leather-padded cells in Indian ashrams under the eye of gurus with a rare gallow humour. The British, still self-conscious about the lines of Imperialism, seek the hair shirts of the slums; the Canadians and Australians, trapped by-fear of provincialism, follow the caravan with an eye on the price-tag, while the Germans, who are certain they know more about Hinduism than everyone else put together, go to the snow-peaked mountains and try to be supermen.

Gita Mehta's biting wit does not obscure the sensitivity and thoroughness with which she has approached her subject: the close observation and interviews with victims, both. Eastern and Western, of this commercialism of culture. She colourfully recreates scenes from within the ashrams which have come to resemble everything from beauty parlours to full-scale orgies; she visits the holy crematorium at Banaras where passport rackets and the drug trade flourish. She examines the use of irrelevant language both East and West have adopted to camouflage the fundamental contradictions of what they shouldn't be trying to say — the complicated philosophical concepts that have become part of every day slang. Ironically, for a generation disenchanted by war, none has greater currency than 'karma', which now means anything from a nice personality to *deja vu:* it was Krishna's word for war.

The author. Gita Mehta has researched, produced, scripted, and directed television films for Thames, Granada, ATV and NBC. She spends her time in India and England.

D8 gives out measurement of the book which is 8 3/4" x 5 5/8". "October" suggests when the book is marked for release. XCUSA suggests the sales territory which is entire world excluding Canada, USA, dependencies and Philippine Islands. If (W) is used, it would mean the whole world is sales territory.

Here are examples of advance notices in Chatto & Windus, The Hogarth Press (Autum 1979).

David Halberstam

The Owers That Be

Chatto & Windus September

0 7011 2467 9 XCUSA $ 9.95

Met Royal 8vol. 784 pp

The Powers That Be is a dramatic analysis, from behind the scenes, of the influence of the American media on the making of American history. This is the fascinating story of the President-makers, the policy-shapers and the newsmakers behind the news. David Halberstam shows where the power in American politics really lies, who the power brokers are, how they rule and what it is that inspires their decisions.

The story starts in the Thirties when the press was tame and the newly-established radio (Roosevelt's metier) was beginning to 'personalise' the presidency. Incident by incident, the entertainment needs of the media took over. Presidential campaigns became 'a new art form' linking advertising, political and television skills. When Lyndon Johnson was in the White House in the Sixties he complained, "All of politics has changed because of you... you guys in the media". In the end, when Nixon was forced to resign, it was the press that brought down the very politician that its needs and methods had created.

Halberstam unfolds this astonishing reversal, illuminating every aspect of the American media as he does so. In the limelight are the politicians: Roosevelt, McCarthy, Eisenhower, Kennedy, Lyndon Johnson and Nixon. The events of which they were a part — the Depression, the Second World War, the Vietnam War and Watergate — are dramatic enough. They are more than matched by the great American commentators of the time, from sober Ed Murrow to the abrasive Woodward and Bernstein. In the background stand the real manipulators, individual corporation men of wealth and huge influence, acting out their hopes, dreams and obsessions: William Paley of *CBS,* Henry Luce *of Time Inc.,* Phil and Kay Graham of *The Washington Post* and the Chandley family of *The Los Angeles Times.*

Halberstam's eye for the telling detail and his gift for the telling anecdote is quite unmatched. In this magnificent book, as in his famous *The Best and the Brightest,* he is writing at the height of his immense powers, the powers of one of the outstanding journalists of our time.

"An important and admirable book... *The Powers That Be* will remain stirring history" — Richard Rovere, *The New York Times.*

Cinderella

0 7011. 2417 2

Aladdin And His Magic Lamp

0 7011 2416 4 Chatto & Windus July

XUSA Each £ 1.50

171 x 135 mm Full colour illustrations

Ages 4-7.

Two of the best-loved fairy tales, *Cinderella* and *Aladdin and His Magic Lamp,* are at last available as Peepshow Books. Each is brought magically to life in five brilliantly coloured three-dimensional scenes, and tied up into a star-shaped mobile a design that is unique to Peepshow Books and has contributed to their huge popularity.

Writing brief reviews for publishers' lists is an art. The reviews should be — like women's skirts — short enough to be interesting and long enough to cover the body. Take this example from George Allen & Unwin's January-June 1980 list:

The Hands: A fascinating amalgam of anatomical, biological and historical observation and comment.

This book is an intimate account of that most intriguing of appendages – the human hand, a subject on which Professor John Napier is a leading authority and which has been of abiding interest to him for over thirty years. For, after serving as an orthopaedic surgeon during the War, he concentrated on research on the function and anatomy of the hand (coining the terms power- and precision-grips, now known as Napier grips, and publishing scientific papers on many aspects of the hand), before embarking on a second equally distinguishing career as a zoologist and anthropologist, with a special interest in the hands of apes and monkeys.

The infinite dexterity of the human hand clearly distinguishes man from animal. Yet the hand's basic structure has remained unchanged for over two hundred million years. In these pages Napier presents the essence of what is known about the hand's evolution, structure and function. He also touches on such absorbing subjects as fingerprints, fossil remains, handedness, gestures and tool using and tool making, ancient and modern, which will be of particular interest to the general reader. The book is written in a style accessible to the layman, as well as the host of people with a professional need to know about the hand, among them orthopaedic specialists, physiotherapists; osteopaths, physical education instructors, biology teachers, detectives, dancers, magicians, painters, sculptors and musicians. It will also be invaluable reading for a wide range of other people in the medical and scientific world, including anthropologists, archaeologists, forensic scientists and pathologists, anatomists, surgeons and physicians.

> 'Dr. Napier is one of the small but notable band of British scientists equally well-known and distinguished for their scientific work... and for their ability to popularise their work without distorting it.'
>
> – Desmond Morris.

> 'Napier examines evidence with sceptical tolerance...his comments make delightful reading'
>
> — Books and Bookmen.

Every publisher has his own code. In the above case, the A in the last line suggests that the price of the title is published separately in the USA. Where the letter B follows the price, the book cannot be supplied to Canada and if the letter is D then the book cannot be supplied to Australia and New Zealand.

Magazine for College

In addition to the journals discussed above, we have specialised journals that do not easily fall into the categories of IHJ, EHJ and I-EHJ but are in a class by themselves like *Communicator* (Journal of the Indian Institute of Mass Communication) or *The Word* (published annually by the Rajendra Prasad Institute of Communication Studies) or *Siddha* (published yearly by the Siddharth College of Arts and Science). These are essentially college magazines and are usually of a high academic standard. Contributors to these magazines would include both teachers and students. Editors would invariably be the principals or the colleges concerned or professors, though students may be included on the editorial boards.

The purpose of college magazines, of course, is to maintain communication between the staff and the students and, hopefully, the parents as well. The contents of a typical college magazine would include an annual report on the working of the college, an account of the achievements of students past and present — but mostly present — and articles of general interest. Some college magazines would have separate Hindi, Marathi, Gujarati and other Indian language sections depending on college locale. Here are the contents of a typical college magazine published by Bombay's Siddharth College of Arts and Science for the year 1978-79:

Thus Spoke Dr. Babasaheb Ambedkar

Editorial Notes 1

From the Principal's Desk — Principal P.N. Choudhari 8

Obituary Tributes 10

The St. Xavier's College Magazine, 1980 is a more sophisticated affair and its contents are more revealing. In addition to carrying all the regular features SXC Magazine 1980 also carried a Mini-Mag edited by one of the college students. A run-down of the magazine shows the following contents:

What interests students? The student editorial in the SXC Magazine is revealing. It is signed by two students, members of the Magazine Board one of them in the senior year B.A. and the other from first year B.A.

In India today, the youth appear to be quite divorced from the major events of the times. One of the most critical challenges facing us in the next decade is to involve the general body of students in the mainstream of national life inculcating in them political and social awareness, which would be expressed through active participation in these spheres.

The current state of affairs, however, does not indicate that this challenge will be successfully met. The modern day Indian student has become a victim to the present age of materialism, and seems concerned only with issues relating to his personal profit or economic gain. The patriotic Indian student of pre-independence days, passionately devoted to his motherland has, in thirty-three short years been replaced by one who is blissfully indifferent to the happenings around him.

Independence gave this country a democracy, and a set of Fundamental Rights, bequeathed and safeguarded by a glorious Constitution. In recent years, however, these privileges have been criminally abused, wasted, and have even been repealed. Moreover, since the 1950s, national unity has been threatened, and lessened, by linguistic, regional and caste differences; which are being played up by communal factions with a view to causing disharmony. The uneducated populace of this nation is being ruthlessly exploited and deliberately misguided into indulging in violence, strikes and indiscipline to further this end. The enforcement of law and order has become a major problem. And all these fissiparous forces and activities are being met by silence on the part of the student community, a silence of indifference. (Those few student movements that have taken place have been characterised by indiscipline chaos, and unnecessary noting, and have achieved nothing rely worthwhile.)

Herein lies the tragedy of our nation. Right now, the destiny of India hangs on the sort of leadership that will emerge in the 80s. And this leadership will come from the current student body. Our country is in a state of flux and crisis, which can be resolved only by firmness, true awareness, and dedication. India is in need of men and women of sterling worth. Will the students of today meet the desperate needs of the country tomorrow? A look at the normal student, especially in colleges like ours, forces one to answer with a regretful 'No'.

The history of the world, and our own nation, shows that in a country's hour of need, her students always rise to defend and support her. It cannot be said that India's hour of need is yet to come – it is too alarming to even consider the prospect of things getting worse. How then can one account for the apathetic attitude prevalent in the student class today?

It is not (or should not be) a lack of education. Most students are familiar enough with Politics, Economics and Sociology *to* have a knowledge of the problems this land has to overcome. However, a knowledge of problems does not necessarily imply a desire to solve them. It is the cause for this lack of desire that needs to be examined.

The cause does not lie in family or personal factors. The student of today is, by and large, as responsible as the student of yesteryear, and a whole generation of parents cannot have gone wrong in their method of upbringing. The difficulty lies in the fact that the very system that needs to be demolished has induced those very attitudes which will facilitate its continuance.

Chaos and indiscipline prevail in every area of student life – from the bus stop to the University, which, as an academic institution, has repeatedly failed the students. Examinations are not held on time, results are long delayed and often wrongly declared, papers are commonly misplaced, and to cut a long story short, a university result is no indication of a student's knowledge and ability – it need not even be his/her own result! In such a situation, a youngster of 17 or 18, who should be enthusiastic and optimistic regarding the life before him, is a disillusioned cynic who sees no sense in trying to fight a hopelessly corrupt and degenerate system.

Though this is understandable, the student of today must be made conscious of the power he wields. He certainly has the power to influence decisions and will soon be in a position where he will be making them, either by virtue of office, or through the responsible exercising of his vote. It is only if the entire student community takes a positive and unified stand that the salvation of this country will be assured.

We have just had a mid-term poll and it is too soon to make a comment on the choice our nation has made. It is our hope, on the threshold of the 80s, that the student community will prove an active force and pull its weight in the next decade, and do its best to realise the rich potential that is India. For it will be in our country's prosperity that we will find our personal happiness.

Some college magazines accept advertisements, some either don't or can't get them. They are either subsidised by the college or a magazine charge is levied on students.

For an Embassy

In an entirely different class from the rest of the magazines are those which foreign embassies put out as part of their information services. These magazines are usually published on a reciprocal basis. *SPAN*, for instance, is published on behalf of the American Embassy, New Delhi. For obvious reasons its editor and publisher are American Embassy officials. But the rest of the staff is Indian, starting with the Managing Editor. Use of *SPAN* articles in other publications is encouraged, except when copyrighted, in which latter case, of course, permission for reprinting may be sought from the editor and is usually given. *SPAN* is available to subscribers.

SPAN does not carry advertisements; it doesn't need to. Its main purpose, understandably, is to present America's social, cultural and economic life and where possible present the American point of view, without antagonising the host country. In its particular field *SPAN* has no rivals. It is objective, high-class and carries articles not only by Americans on America but by Indians on America and has a lively Letters to the Editor page as well. It has hosted Indian short story writers, Indian writers on science and technology and one of its purposes is to foster Indo-American understanding. In that it has eminently succeeded.

Some sample articles carried by *SPAN* over the years: *Do Americans Speak English?* – Book Review by Nergis Dalal *Young American Poets* by Shiv K. Kumar

America Is India's Major Trading Partner — FICCI President

M.V. Arunachalam interviewed by Malini Sheshadri

Jimmy Carter Attends a Town Meeting

What Are We To Do About Deserts? (decertification experience in the United States) by Harold E. Dregne *Robert Francis Goheen – The New American Ambassador to India*

How Did Developed Countries Develop? — Simon Kuznets interviewed by John J. Harter.

The Attainment

There is a great deal said in favour of the empire, as no one can fail to be aware. The arguments for empire find sufficient expression in the Press and on the wireless and seem to be held with only slight variations by Conservatives and Labour alike. But it does not seem likely that when a person is influenced by appeals to preserve the empire, he has the reasons well balanced in his mind. It is more certain that the word is exerting an emotional pull; the hearer may have been brought up on history textbooks and juvenile fiction in which the idea of empire is presented in terms of heroism, pioneering, independence and self- sacrifice. This is a somewhat one-sided picture and needs to be corrected by Edward Thompson's *The Other Side of the Medal* and Norman Ley's works on Kenya. For some people too the word is associated with the long history, the magnificence and the civilising work of the Roman Empire. Possibly also the instinct of self-preservation is brought into play, and the safety of the empire connected with the individual's prosperity.

This book will have failed unless by now someone has accused it of propaganda. There are two main meanings of the word. In a derogatory sense it is applied to attempts to bully or emotionally persuade people into some fresh belief or action. It also describes the presentation of views and facts. Often those who are quick to resent the latter, because they meet with something new and feel perhaps a little insulted, breathe in the former like air — it is as pervasive and unnoticed. Of propaganda in the first sense there should not be any in these pages; there may be some of the second kind.

The common meaning of the word propaganda itself has changed recently. A few years ago propaganda was something discreditable; only Reds resorted to it, and it was all underhand and heavily financed by Moscow. For instance Major Ralph Rayner, M.P., wrote a few years ago that "The greater part of the English people are sick and tired of the impertinence of Communist propaganda, based as it is upon that Marxian creed, which was always false, and which is now demode, old-fashioned, and out of our way to discredit Communist ballyhoo on all possible occasions, and to help that grand chap, the British workman, who has to bear the main brunt of their unpleasant campaign."

But in recent months the government in response to pressure has founded the nucleus of a propaganda department and developed broadcasts to other countries; and it is constantly being urged to develop propaganda for the British Empire, or against the Nazis. The word has lost its bad smell.

'Defence' and 'Democracy': The first word is used by everyone, from Communists to archbishops, to justify alliance with other countries, internal reorganisation, an increase in armaments, and all kinds of widely differing policies. It is an unrivalled means of begging the question. It might come also under the heading of arguing by analogy, because the underlying idea is that of a single person defending himself against burglars and bullies. We admire and sympathise with such an individual, the peacefully minded victim of aggression.

The word is then transferred to the defence on one nation, which cannot be equated with an individual, against another, by mechanical and chemical means, which again are very different from the fists and muscles of a human being. So that in some uses of the word we are being asked to give a nation involved in modern warfare the same respect that we show towards an individual who puts up a good fight.

Some of the implications and assumptions involved in common uses of the word will now be considered. However long and tediously it is discussed, we shall have no more than skimped the problem; a small library is needed for a thorough survey. The purpose is to show how different meanings lurk behind the simple word.

First, what general policy underlies the defence of this country? One widely accepted is that of the "Big Fist," though it is often given gentler names; Britain must be so strong that all will be afraid to attack her. Some questions may be put:

1. Is that possible?
2. Germany and Italy appear to share the same view. Great Britain increases her forces, Germany follows, Italy must keep up with Britain. Is there an end to the process? and what end? It assumes that other nations are likely to be crowed. Are they actually intimidated? Is there any justification for this low estimate of the foreigner's courage?
3. This policy is often associated with the view that Great Britain and the empire should isolate themselves from the rest of the world. Is this possible now that the world is a single economic unit, except for the USA and the USSR? The fable of the Members of the Body may be a fair analogy to apply to the world Today; it is said that the Argentine and Denmarkare still economically parts of the British Empire, to a greater degree than some nominal constituents of the latter.
4. This policy is backed by papers which have urged courses of action which ended disastrously, and whose methods, especially in controversy, are dishonest. Is it reasonable to expect that for once they are right? They sometimes come round to the view shown by events to be correct, but it is then twenty years too late.

Then there is the policy required by membership of the League of Nations. Obviously it has far more to commend it than the last; it is more rational and generous, and works by cooperation, not by fear and intimidation. A society of nations is necessary for the same reason or at the isolationist position is sentimental and impracticable. The achievements of the League are solid and considerable, and include the prevention of war. But there is no hope of "collective security" either becoming collective or affording security, though it was a theory very attractive before the situations arose which required that it should be put into practice. It has a large and increasing number of genuine supporters, especially since Hitler occupied Prague, and a number of half-hearted believers, who see in the League a means of furthering Imperial interests.

Third, the pacifist view of defence is that military methods do not secure defence, and that this is only attainable by attention to the economic and psychological roots of war, and immediately through the removal of the war guilt clause and other features of the Versailles treaty. By this policy Great Britain would lose prestige and economic advantages.

As for the methods of defence, Earl Baldwin's statement is quoted, because he was then making public the conclusions of experts, and nothing has happened since then to invalidate them.

I think it is well also for the man in the street to realise that there is no power on earth that can prevent him from being bombed. Whatever people may tell him the bomber will always get through. The only defence is in offence, which means that you have to kill more women and children more quickly than the enemy, if you want to save yourselves.

Both the isolationist and the believer in military sanctions have to support an armament programme to implement this kind of 'defence.' But these meanings of the word are not meant to be thought of when for example we are invited to join the Territorials and defend our homes. Practically, the word has reversed its meaning; the politicians have found the word invaluable because its original sense (the preservation of something) commends itself to everyone.

Another proposal, Non-menacing Defence, is Mr. Jonathan Griffin's. He argues that to increase our menacing navy and air force is the best method of provoking an attack, and actually aggravates the vulnerability of an exceptionally vulnerable country. In his view money should be spent on granaries instead of navies, and a genuine attempt made to provide anti-air raid precautions. It is perhaps the only reasonable, coherent and not panicky defence policy advocated at present, although it may be argued on the other hand that to make any preparations for war is to increase its likelihood. Finally, what are we going to defend? Our personal selves and these islands? For the reasons suggested by Mr. Baldwin that cannot be done with certainty, though Mr. Griffin argues very persuasively.

The empire and its trade routes? "The distinction between defensive and aggressive preparations has no validity where the empire system is concerned. If we maintain safe passage through the Mediterranean, we only do so by acquiring the power to deny it to all other countries. If we secure the safety of Britain's food supplies, we only do so by acquiring the power to blockade and starve our potential enemies, and to destroy their commerce" (Leonard Barnes). Democracy against Fascism? This is a very popular slogan among all parties at the moment of writing, and deserves some consideration; remembering all the time that it is the meaning behind the word, its implications in a particular context, that we are trying to detect.

We shall have to leave democracy undefined, and assume that in its genuine form it is worth defending. I am assuming also that Russia is not at present a full democracy, and that our own country has at least the forms of democratic government. Democracy might be even more worth defending if it offered a good example of civilised life, treated its colonial peoples well, showed economic sense and goodwill, and implemented some of the wordy good intentions of its statesmen.

History suggests that democracy can be defended. Greek democracy was defended by force of arms against the Persian tyranny with complete success at Marathon and Salamis. It did not last permanently in Greece, but the idea was not destroyed and is alive in several countries Today. However there is no parallel between defending democracy in 480 BC and 1940 AD. It may be possible to defend the British Empire by present methods of warfare, but it is impossible to preserve democracy in this way.

By joining in a race with the dictators we inevitably make for the same goal as they do.

Something like an attempt has been made to preserve it. The early aims of this country in 1914 were to wipe out Prussianism and make the world safe for democracy, and explicitly not to add any territory to the British Empire. The war was won. But now Prussianism is more vigorous and rampant than ever, the democracies fewer and rather ineffectual; and approximately one and a half million square miles of territory were added to the British Empire. All wars start with the most excellent of aims. In some past wars, fought with comparatively small professional armies, it is possible that the aims were kept in sight throughout the campaign. But in modern warfare there are many reasons why the worthy paper aims are soon lost sight of, if indeed they were ever genuine. It is 'totalitarian,' involving every member of the nation, it spreads more widely, it lasts longer with a greater intensity. The entire change in the methods of fighting puts a different complexion on every theory and all the practice of war; yet eighteenth-century ideas are being applied to twentieth-century weapons. The ratio of defence to attack is no longer constant.

The 1914 attempt to save democracy (which was quite as genuine as any repetition is likely to be) failed for many reasons. Idealists were deceived by the fallacy of the "personal state" — "There shouldn't be war — but what's to be done but fight Prussia? I've seen the half-million refugees in the night outside Antwerp; and I want, more than before, to go on, till Prussia's destroyed." (Rupert Brooke, letter to Lowes Dickinson.) The error of making an image of a country is well exemplified in Europe at present.

It can be observed in Socialist and Conservative declarations; dislike of the governments of Germany or Russia leads people to a condemnation of all Germans and Russians. This habit obscures, amongst other things, the fact that in the attempt to 'defend' good democrats at home you must kill perfectly good democrats abroad. A selective bomb for killing only dictators and their supporters has not been invented. This implication of 'defence' against Fascism is commonly ignored, except by a few honest supporters of rearmament. But any real defence against dictatorship should begin at home.

This discussion of the meanings underlying the word 'defence' has gone on rather long, but one more of its neglected implications must be mentioned. The country which seeks to combat dictatorship by its own methods ends by being Fascist itself. Characteristics of a dictatorship, right or left, are: organisation of the whole country on a military basis, through the schools and in voluntary ('fitness') associations, repression of opposition and criticism, perversion of truth, regimentation of opinion, decay and impotence of Parliaments, centralised control usually in military hands. Observers detached from politics see some of these features well developed here.

At the moment politicians of all parties are making great play with the phrase "defence of democracy"; and those who do not wish to be victims of propaganda should consider one way in which the word 'democracy' is already being used as a propaganda to further policies which seem anything but democratic. We are asked to accept as 'democratic' most of the changes mentioned in the previous paragraph. Most Englishmen have a deep emotional faith in democracy, and approve of anything which is described as democratic. This gives a perfect opportunity to the propagandist. At a recent youth conference of X party a speaker urged his listeners not to allow Y party all the advantage of the word, but to make good use of it themselves.

Thus the word which should denote a vital principle becomes a mere label used to encourage the people of one side to get together and beat the others. The powers that be also realise that the word has a strong emotional pull, which can be exerted to manipulate public opinion and behaviour, in much the same as the Nazi propagandists secured mass support by repeating clever catchwords. This is most strikingly shown in Sidney Rogerson's *Propaganda in the Next War,* a book incidentally in which there is more than a trace of the propagandists' cynical and scornful attitude towards the people they delude.

The author (an advertising expert) is giving directions on how this country should use propaganda in war: "We shall do well to press the loud pedal on the democratic stop in our home propaganda. This is calculated to be the most telling in a future war as it was in last." And on another page: "When we agree that propaganda control is necessary, we shall impose it instantly, and label our control machinery 'democratic' or 'voluntary' in large letters. Meanwhile, we are preparing ourselves for the change by loud assertions that we should never tolerate such a control." This should convince us that the words 'democracy' and 'democratic' cannot be examined too closely; writers use them with very different aims and meanings.

For further discussion of the word 'defence' Bertrand Russell's *Which Way to Peace* and Norman Angell's *Menace to Our National Defence* can be recommended; they come to different conclusions. Some of the varied uses of the word 'defence' can be seen in the quotations that follow:

> Field Marshal Sir A. A. Montgomery-Massingberd... said he never wanted to see another war in Europe, but there were even worse things than war. One thing that was worse than war was a degenerate people who had lost the spirit and power to defend their women, children and homes. He could not understand the man or woman who persuaded the younger generation not to fight for the defence of the country. Defence of the country and loyalty to the King were things that ought to be outside politics.

A warning that purely passive defence must not be regarded as of the same importance as the active defence services was given by Sir Walter Kirke. "In the present world conditions it is only fear of reprisals by our armed forces which will prevent the disturbances of peace who believe that they have everything to gain by another world war. Our armed forces must be strong enough to create the idea that they have also something to lose."

Observer, 22 Jan., 1939.

Most theologians in the past had... held it a duty to society to assist in just wars or wars of defence. "This conclusion, even if we agree with it, does not help us very much, for it is fairly certain that any war that broke out would now be represented on both sides as being a just war and a war of defence."

Dean of St. Paul's, *Daily Telegraph*, 23 Jan., 1939.

'Patriotism': The fact that this word is so frequently abused should not be the excuse for dismissing patriotism as "the last refuge of a scoundrel." Human beings are naturally patriotic and often rightly so; they tend to form attachments for place or institutions. A true patriot, presumably, is one who loves his country and considers how that love may be most effective. A merely emotional patriotism may cause harm; we would regard as stupid the parent who never sent her child to the dentist because she could not bear to have it hurt.

An intelligent patriotism may cause a person to take a line of thought or action which will bring unpopularity or danger upon him; many figures whom the history books describe as patriots were very differently thought of in their own time. A purely emotional patriotism may release a flood of feelings which will leave the country worse after it has passed; this may be the reason why some people whose patriotism does not appear in peacetime are ready to claim the title in war.

Since the word can be used to discharge strong charges of feeling, it has been much exploited by propagandists. Advertisers have always employed it; "British Made" is a label that has been applied to goods merely assembled in this country, or produced by British workers, British materials, British brains, British capital. It does not always mean all of these things. Because of this and other abuses the word 'patriotic' has become almost a term of derision like 'jingoist.'

To reveal some of the layers of meaning which underlie the word, some question may be considered. What does a popular newspaper mean by patriotism? Is its conception adequate? Why is the word used more in war than in peace? Can it be shown in peace? And by what actions? Does love of country require that we should love and obey the government for the time being of the country? To what loyalties if any should patriotism be subordinate? Is it true that national patriotism is unreal without a local patriotism? What are the claims of the following to be patriotic? – Conservative, Liberal, Arms Manufacturer, Socialist, Pacifist, Communist, Fascist?

The reader is asked next to read the following extract and consider the questionnaire in order to follow the implications of the statement:

1. "There is universal abhorrence...." Is bombing from the air a method of barbarism, literally or otherwise? If possible, answer Yes or No.
2. "It would involve women and children...." Can you share the writer's indignation?
3. "It would be the bankruptcy of statesmanship...." Can you think of a better instance of the bankruptcy statesmanship?
4. How would a short summary, not more than 100 words, of the passage, bring out the implications, the meaning between the lines?

Finally there is universal abhorrence of the idea that civilized nations should sink to methods of barbarism to the extent of making war upon one another by bombardment from the air. It is sometimes lightly argued that bombardment from the air is no worse than artillery bombardment. Materially and morally it is infinitely worse. Its destruction must be more indiscriminate, and once action had been engaged it would involve women and children and the accumulated wealth of civilization in slaughter and ruin. It would be the bankruptcy of statesmanship to admit that it is a legitimate form of warfare for a nation to destroy its rival's capital from the air, and that the correct procedure of the attacked nation is to destroy the attacker's capital and all the life in it with high-explosive, noxious and bacteriological bombs.

The Times, leading article, May 9, 1934.

Any utterance takes certain things for granted; it is impossible to carry on any kind of conversation without making assumptions, and usually we do not suffer much if they are ill-founded. If we examined all the assumptions made in everyday life the mind would soon give way through over-work.

But there are plenty of examples from the past of widely-accepted assumptions leading to unwise action or lack of action. During part of the last century it was taken for granted, and even exalted into the will of God, that the "self-chosen activities and aims of each would add up to the benefit of all." It was used to justify child labour and other cruelties and injustices. Everyone can now see that the doctrine was wrong, if only through the visible evidence of misshapen towns, slums and the desolate industrial areas.

There must be equally misleading ideas floating about Today. There are quite recent instances of newspapers and politicians advocating policies which failed not because of any fallacy in their argument but because they rested on groundless assumptions. A healthy opposition and a more critical public would be of great assistance to politicians here; the lack of informed and constructive criticism makes for inefficiency.

Examples of questionable assumptions are found in the current admiration of millionaires, promoted by nearly every considerable paper whatever its politics. We are expected to applaud their energy and resource in making money and their generosity in giving it away. The medieval church preached that the makers of big profits were likely to be damned. The following considerations should also be taken into account. It is never asked whether the millionaire's activities contribute to the general good (perhaps they were the making of armaments or trivial luxuries), whether the lives of his employees could be said to have been usefully and happily spent, whether or not he increased human misery.

It is assumed that his high profits are a just measure of his services: it is not mentioned that public resources and public activities have cooperated with his own endeavours. It is not mentioned that the growth of industry, the shift of populations, local improvements at public expense, all contributed to his wealth, to say nothing of tariffs and other expensive public policies. "Whatever comes to a man from the favourable play of the market belongs to him by right, though the sources of this favourable play may lie wholly outside his control or his prevision." (J. A. Hobson.) The millionaire's achievements are ascribed to his own unaided efforts: the support and the protection afforded by the social order which makes his achievement possible are forgotten. Forgotten, too, are the skill of inventors and technicians, the labour of thousands of workmen — for millionaires as a whole do little but exploit the inventions of others.

An American writer makes further points. "It is a complete mistake to assume that without philanthropies of the Rockefeller type, the world would have been without the educational, medical and religious institutions and activities which their gifts brought into being.... The Rockefellers of Today 'give' colleges, hospitals, foundations, just as the medieval barons used to 'give' monasteries, nunneries, chapels, and the Rolman senators used to 'give' baths and amphitheatres. But in reality they 'give' nothing. They merely return a part of what they were acquisitive and powerful enough to seize" (Ralph A. Borsodi).

The Imagination

Newspapers, of course, have their reasons for making these assumptions about millionaires. They advertise. The Press thrives in an acquisitive society, acquisition must be glorified. But even if acquisition were creditable, and even if the laboratories we hear so much of were due to one man's work, we should keep a sense of proportion. The seller of cheap cars is not to be compared with the founder of a religion, a considerable poet, the inventor of an antiseptic, or with anyone whose ideas, beneficence and vitality will last long after the cars are scrap.

The Church's doctrine that usury (most of the means leading to wealth came under that head) was a deadly sin is now dead. It is am instance of belief which pervaded society and became an assumption on which conduct was based. It influenced the course of past history. Future history also would take a different turn if some current assumptions were generally seen to be invalid, and if statesmen tried grounding their policies on a fresh set. Many people, for instance, who want peace, assume that this end can be secured by violent means.

If they are wrong in taking this for granted, the results of policies now in operation are not likely to be satisfactory. Others contend that the means shapes the end and that military force, apart from being an undesirable method, as even statesmen perceive, is also an ineffectual way of attaining objects. Expressions of this belief may be found in many pronouncements on current affairs: "If we continue to pile up armaments to the utmost of our economic strength and beyond it, we shall perpetuate the evils from which we suffer Today and bring the world nearer to an even greater disaster than that from which it is only just beginning to recover." (Mr. Eden,.1937). "Whichever side in Spain wins will not be the better for having had to fight for its victory." (Mr. T. S. Eliot) If there is anything in this belief it might, with luck in the turn of events and some distinguished supporters, have far-reaching consequences.

Other assumptions on which many topical arguments are based need inspection. Those, for example, concerning the ownership of territory, the capture of trade, the transfer of wealth or trade by military power. Sir Norman Angell's books are recommended as models of fair, painstaking and illuminating controversy, not as authorities.

There is abundant matter for discussion to be had from uncovering what lies beneath such phrases and sentences as "We are a great and united nation, a first-rate power, etc." "Disaster is inevitable, unless the present decline in population can be arrested." "This wave of crime can only be ended by a decided increase in the severity of sentences."

The reader is also invited to consider the following current assumptions: That England is a democratic country. That Russia is a Communist State. The English love of fair play. That advertised goods are good goods. That the unemployed are idle, that it is wrong to marry on the 'dole,' etc. That England is a refuge for exiles. That criminals are a separate order of human beings. That slum-dwellers like dirt. That Progress is constant. That free speech is allowed in England. That captains of industry 'create' employment. That work is in itself good.

A common method of argument is by analogy. The apparent or agreed resemblances between two cases are used to argue that further similarities exist. The fable of the Members of the Body has been cited to show that there can be no equality in a state, that different functions must be performed by different strata of society, that order must be preserved, and so on. To argue by analogy is easy and pleasant, but by the scrupulous it needs to be used carefully. In dishonest or careless hands it can be perilously misleading; it is often a way out for the lazy thinker. Either an analogy which holds good up to a certain point is pressed too far, or an argument is founded on an analogy which is quite inapplicable.

Thus the example just quoted might be adduced in support of the view that people must do the work for which they are best fitted. That may be acceptable, but it can be carried further by the assertion that everyone should be content with that station of life in which he was born, and acquiesce in the state of things as they are. In another field Buff will contend that it is absurd and unnecessary for nations to have armaments on the ground that individuals have long ceased to carry weapons about the streets: whereas Duff will say that navies and armies are necessary to police the world. Both are trying to apply to the state what is true of individuals.

That weapons are no longer carried is due partly to the fact that the police prevent the kind of crime against which weapons are of assistance, and partly to changed views about the personal use of weapons — no civilised person wishes to restore duelling. Buff is wrong in that he forgets to mention the introduction of police to protect individuals; to look after the nations there is nothing analogous to a police force. But he may be right in suggesting that we should be much better if the nations as collections of individuals could through their governments show as much goodwill, trust and readiness to cooperate as individuals in most nations show towards each other in daily life.

Duff uses the same analogy as Buff to advocate an opposite course of action, and he is not more justified. He makes some invalid assumptions: that some nations are criminal, others good, which is not true because so far as we know the proportion of 'good' to 'bad' persons is roughly the same in most countries. A police force can only operate if it has a government and a judicial system behind it, but Duff, somewhat arrogantly, is putting in the hands of one nation the right to act as police and judge as well. There are countries where this happens more regularly than it does in England, but Duff would disapprove of that as being undemocratic.

This gives an opening for chasing the analogy further. If Duff's country is to act as police force it must have an army and an air force. But the police in the country Duff admires most have more moral than physical force behind them, and when they use violence, against strikers, for example, and at political meetings, they lose respect and authority. How far the police force does in the last resort depend on force, physical or military, can be left for discussion.

Many analogies are embedded in the language as metaphors, and they do not always lead to clear thinking. When a writer, for instance, declares that in the next war "the teams will line up as before," he may cause us to regard war rather less seriously than we should, by presenting it as a game.

The following analogies are offered for examination:

1. War is nature's pruning-hook.
2. Christians must be ready to take up the sword in defence of their principles:
3. The exercise of mastery inevitably entails on the master himself some sort of slavery more or less pronounced. The uncultured masses and even the greater part of the cultured will regard this statement as absurd, and though many who have read history with an eye to essentials rather than to trivialities know that this is a paradox in the right sense — that is, true in fact though not seeming true — even they are note fully conscious of the mass of evidence establishing it, and will be all the better of having illustrations recalled.

   Let me begin with the earliest and simplest which serves to symbolise the whole.

   Here is a prisoner, with his hands tied and a cord round his neck (as suggested by figures in Assyrian bas-reliefs), being led home by his savage conqueror, who intends to make him a slave. The one you say is captive and then other free. Are you quite sure the other is free? He holds one end of the cord and, unless he means his captive to escape, he must continue to be fastened by keeping hold of the cord in such a way that it cannot easily be detached. He must be himself tied to the captive while the captive is tied to him. In other ways his activities are impeded and certain burdens are imposed on him. A wild animal crosses the track and he cannot pursue. If he wishes to drink of the adjacent stream he must tie up his captive, lest advantage be taken of his defenceless position.

Moreover, he has to provide food for both. In various ways he is no longer, then, completely at liberty; and these worries adumbrate in a simple manner the universal truth that the instrumentalities by which the subordination of others is effected themselves subordinate the victor, the master, or the ruler.

Herbert Spencer, quoted in *Prussiansim and its Destruction.*

4. "We must be able to destroy the hornets in their nests." (From a discussion on Air Force policy.)

Symptoms: In buying a used car certain signals put the purchaser on his guard; the appropriate noises convey "piston-slap" or worn transmission. Similarly if one examines some of the reading matter which thrusts itself upon us, certain symptoms of unreliability occur. It often happens that the user of metaphors, outworn and impotent because they no longer draw vitality from everyday life (We have put our hand to the plough, He drove a straight furrow) has ideas which are equally inapplicable.

Comrades, list to the clarion call. The plank of progress is now ripe for plucking. Soon we shall see the Socialist avalanche descending from the mountain tops and, with its mailed fist, crushing beneath its iron heel the capitalist snake in the grass, which is barring the progress of the flood-gates of democracy from walking hand in hand with the British lion over the rich fields of prosperity from which we draw the sweet milk of iron, coal and cotton.

The speaker may hold excellent economic views, but his speech, the only evidence we have in most cases for evaluating politicians, suggests that we should not without further evidence trust a mind so muddled. The metaphors clarify nothing; they are used to impress, or to cover the speaker's emptiness. On the other hand it is merely pedantic to seize on mixed metaphors; they are abundant in Shakespeare, where they show an uncommonly swiftly-moving mind, able to illustrate a theme by seeing resemblances which no one else could have thought of. When we come across metaphors we need to ask why they are being used, especially if we are expecting a statement and receive images. Many in everyday use are 'dead'; the figure has lost force and the literal expression would be better. When we read of a statesman "laying down the reins of office" we do not visualise a man with a horse, and so far as plain sense is concerned 'retired' would have been much better; though the writer's purpose may have been other than conveying mere sense. It is impossible to get through a day without using numbers of these 'dead' metaphors. But if we find a speaker or writer, who has some pronouncement to make, relying on metaphors which do not clarify his meaning, but are on the contrary worn-out and commonplace, the language may reflect the mind that uses it. Overworked figures of speech also come under the heading of 'cliche.'

These are handy, ready-made and hackneyed phrases. They are very common in conversation, where like mass-produced tools they are easily used and do ordinary work well enough. Always in stock, they save much labour of thinking out precisely the right expression. ('Precisely' in itself a cliche — it is at least often used in a wrong sense. Judge: "You saw the accused come out of the shop?" Witness: "Precisely.") When we read a politician announcing the policy of his party or government we expect something intelligible and clear-cut.

But because the mass of people do not require from their rulers the precision they expect in the making of their cars, leader writers, clergy, politicians and others are able to hand out stale and damaged goods. Inevitable in conversation and impromptu speeches, in books and considered statements they are reasons for suspecting the motives or intelligence of their author. A speech which is peppered with torches of freedom, grave difficulties, deliberate efforts, fundamental satisfaction, profound gravity and ultimate results rings hollow.

With these is connected another characteristic of political speeches — circumlocution. This is used to give an appearance of profundity or caution, to cover poverty of material or to conceal something with a verbal smoke screen, or to take the sting out of an unpalatable truth. For the last purpose an abstract instead of the concrete is often preferred. Fascist and Communist regimes "liquidate their political opponents;" that is, they shoot them. The expression "military sanctions" used to make war appear less unattractive. A Labour Premier once urged the miners "to make a contribution towards meeting the difficult situation with which the industry is confronted" — in translation, to accept a wage cut. The secret of politicians' English, as of advertisers, is to give actions or motives such pleasant, misleading and impressive names that we do not consider whether they are really the right names. With the aid of politicians' English it is possible to make high-sounding speeches, full of nobility and good intentions, but in entirely abstract terms; the audience is left, according to its disposition, with a comfortable feeling of uplift or in a state of bewilderment and exasperation if they expected any instruction on how to get peace. "I do not think that there is a worse sign of the times than that the sacred subject of Peace should be dragged down into the political arena." (Earl Baldwin, March, 1935.) The practical implications of that are worth considering.

In its relations with politicians the public shows a low degree of vigilance and short memory. The art of saying nothing while appearing to say something and the habit of saying something and contradicting it very soon are highly developed.

What are we to say of a country which accepts without protest these utterances from four prime ministers of three parties:

Mr. X referred to what the Government had done for housing, and remarked that he thought they could say the housing problem was solved except for two strongholds — the destruction of the slums and the extinction of overcrowding.

The Great War lasted so long because the respective war aims of the two sides were incompatible, and neither side was prepared to give way until compelled to do so.

(Next two declarations by the same statesman in the same year:)

The Labour Party stood in their heart of hearts for our Constitution and our free Parliament.... The Labour Party as a whole have helped to keep the flag of Parliamentary Government flying in the world through the difficult periods through which we have passed. (May.)

The Labour Party remains a party which would attack our social system at its roots, destroy the fabric of the Constitution, and seek to bring the country to a ruthless Socialism through crisis and chaos. (December.)

Schemes must be devised, policies must be devised if it is humanly possible to take that section *(i.e.,* those unemployed who are unlikely shortly to be reabsorbed into industry) and to regard them not as wastrels, not as hopeless people, but as people for whom occupation must be provided somehow or other, and that occupation, although it may not be in the regular factory or in organised large-scale industrial groups, nevertheless will be quite as effective for themselves mentally, morally, spiritually and physically than, perhaps, if they were included in this enormous mechanism of humanity which is not always producing the best result, and which, to a very large extent, fails in producing the good results that so many of us expect to see from a higher civilization based upon national wealth. That is a problem which has got to be faced.

To the Greeks a tragedy was a dramatic poem about the deeds and the noble end of a dignified and impressive figure, and an epic was a long narrative in verse of the adventures of a hero. These words are now used by the Press to describe a violent or sordid death or an advertising flight. Tragedy was first used in this debased sense to get a kick out of a jaded reader; and as a result of overstrain it has no power left in it now. This debility of language is evident in any newspaper, but much less so in conversation because people are more self-conscious in speaking than in reading.

It is like taking stimulants; after a time you need a bigger dram to get the same result. "It is with gratitude that we...", then "with real gratitude," and finally "with very real gratitude." "I want you all to make a very definite effort to attend this absolutely unique meeting." The attempt to be forcible ends in being feeble. Public speeches and sermons abound in examples; and exaggeration has for years been pronounced in the film and book reviewing pages of the Press. Small local papers at least merely reprint the blurb sent out for the purpose by the film distributor. The advertising publisher must be given good value for his money, with the result that words like 'great,' magnificent,' 'stupendous' and 'masterpiece' have no edge left. One reads of reviewers who have sat up all night reading a detective novel, read a book twice through from start to finish, gone without food, nearly lost their lives through crossing a road while reading the book of the minute. Words like roads are common property, and if they are wrongly used and not kept up by public care they break down and become useless for everyone as well as for those who have done the damage. This example comes from Mr. Owen Barfield's *History in English Words:*

> We can see clearly how the two kinds of Platonism...combined to beget the infinite suggestiveness which is now contained in such words as *love* and *beauty.* Let us remember, then, that every time we abuse these terms, or use them too lightly, we are draining them of their power; every time a society journalist or a film producer exploits this vast suggestiveness to tickle a vanity or dignify a lust, he is squandering a great pile of spiritual capital which has been laid up by centuries of weary effort.

Finally a symptom that should stir more suspicion than any other. An appeal to one's better nature is very often a sign that the reader is "being got at." This includes attempts to flatter one's good sense, moderation, originality, taste, normality, etc.

"Every sensible person will admit. "The more broad-minded among us." This extract is quoted from Mr. Harold Stovin's *Totem:*

> But fortunately for the nation there is a quiet, commonsense, middle lot of men in between the extremists who, though they don't talk loud, think quietly for themselves: sensible workmen, humane employers and public-spirited benefactors; in other words, a citizenship that is out for fair play and mutual forbearance for the good of *The Whole.*

While I do not wish to say anything disrespectful of the Press, I know that they had some idea that we were contemplating a large advertising scheme if we got a reduction in the beer duty, as the Press, particularly the commercial side, came and asked me all sorts of questions about this. I said that first we had to get a reduction in the duty, and I think there is no doubt whatever that this had some effect, because the commercial side are always pestering the editorial side. In the same way, if we begin advertising in the Press, we shall see that the continuation of our advertising is contingent upon the fact that we get editorial support as well in the same papers. In that way it is wonderful how you can educate public opinion, generally without making it too obvious that there is a publicity campaign behind it all.

Director of the Brewers' Society quoted in *The Observer.*

The place of advertising in the economy of the country, some of its appeals and effects, are touched on in *Culture and Environment.* Since then the invention of new types and the development of others have produced some exciting specimens, which deserve analysis.

Up and down the world, wherever you go, you will find that proverbial wisdom prescribes the wine of the country as the best drink of all, and what could be more logical than to assume that men will thrive best upon the fruits of that self-same land that bore them?

Here in Britain our native wine is beer, brewed from the finest barley-malt, with hops, sugar and yeast. This, as befits our climate, is a mild, luxurious, and heartening beverage; as apt to restore the body that a bleak northeaster scourges as to quench the parching thirst of summer — as grateful in the sunshine of June as in December's firelight.

When next you drink a glass of beer, give a thought to the elements that went to the brewing of its amber contents. Barley-malt for digestion, hops for appetite, sugar for energy, yeast for vitality. What could there be more wholesome? What more indeed could the body or the heart of man desire? Rejoice then in the good liquor that our honest forefathers did use to drink of — the wine of our country — beer!

The original of this was spaciously set out in good types with a border of barley ears and agriculture implements, which helped to evoke the emotional aura associated with the Good Old Days. "Up and down the world, wherever you go...." One seasoned globe-trotter, with his feet on the mantelpiece, is yarning at ease with another — the reader, who is flattered by this tribute to the extent of his travels. Then the writer emits the respect in which proverbial wisdom is held, and the mention of wine (clinched at the end) puts the whole affair on a much higher plane than that of mere pedestrian beer-drinking. People are growing shy of advertisements, so 'logical' is added to show that there are no monkey-tricks; then the patriotism key is lightly touched.

"Here in Britain" – again one needs the thick-and-rich gravy voice of the newsreel commentator to bring out the unification. The slow movement, the deliberate manner, give the effect of leisure and space; the imitation richness of the prose helps to convey the ideas of wealth and security with which advertised goods must be associated. In connection with the concluding paragraph, it would be of interest to know how much hops actually does go into beer, and what proportion of the barley is British. It would have to be considerable to justify the bluff heartiness of the affected last sentence.

If it is thought that this analysis is overdone, and that too much has been read into the piece, a deflated version would meet the objection: "Foreigners have their national drinks, so we should drink beer. It is good at all seasons because its ingredients, malt, hops, yeast and sugar, promote appetite and energy." Again, in discussion of such writing it is sometimes said that analysis is waste of time, and that it is not likely to influence any reader of this book. On the other hand the extracts considered here have all appeared in newspapers appealing to an intelligent public. It is known that the collective advertising of the brewers has been effective, and advertisers in general are not going to spend on frills what would otherwise go into profit. (Against this it should be added that one of the reasons why brewers, certain banks and insurance companies advertise it to get rid of surplus profits on which they would otherwise have to pay income tax.) The influence may not be direct; it is usually subtler. The one just quoted works on suggestibility; the reader may think he has forgotten it, but at a tired or thirsty moment the suggestion comes into play, and the drinker feels he is behaving like his honest forebears.

The Aggressiveness

Aggressiveness is also said to be part of the normal human make-up; most people, for example, will have found themselves at times beginning to contradict a statement for the mere sake of opposition – almost before the speaker's words were out of his mouth. Aggressiveness and hatred both crop up at moments when one is off one's guard. A sophisticated person, proof against the more obvious attempts of the propagandist to stir the aggressive impulses, will yield to them, when driving a car for instance – being overtaken by another car is enough to bring them into play. It is easy to think of other examples. Especially we must beware of those, including ourselves, who cover their underlying but unconscious motives with a quantity of reasons. I may *think* it is a disinterested quest for truth that makes me to go to a political meeting and heckle....

Rationalising is an insidious habit. Some pacifists, for example, who profess peaceful aims and methods on paper seem to be an incarnation of aggressiveness in their cries for belligerent preparations; or even if they oppose an armament programme, consisting mainly of weapons for attack, they conduct their campaigns against other parties inside the country with a ferocity easy to diagnose. We accept as sincere the profession of Christianity from a man who behaves in a recognisably Christian, mild and forbearing, manner: we suspect the person who says the world is not yet ready for the application of Christian principles. Similarly, it may be reasonable, other things being equal, to expect that the most workable peace policy will come from those who start by being peaceful here and now. Probably by now some readers suspect the author of this book of rationalising his destructive impulses in compiling it. The suspicion may be well founded.

It has been suggested that to support a belief or action for emotional reasons is not enough, and that one should be suspicious when one's emotions are brought strongly into play during discussion. Perhaps it was implied that beliefs supported only by emotion are undesirable, but that is clearly wrong; one can back a perfectly "good cause" under the influence merely of strong feelings, though it is doubtful whether sustained support will result from feeling alone. One wants reason combined with the emotions. The visiting preacher at a school chapel spoke on slum clearance and housing schemes in the East of London; he was charming and clever, told good stories and gave a sincere and moving picture of life in that slum. He ended by hinting that though he was not allowed a collection the boys would perhaps "get together" of their own accord and send him some money. The result was that over £ 20 was collected next day. But it is doubtful if as a result of that sermon any of his listeners gave slums or their causes a second thought. It often happens that the indignation or sympathy of an audience is worked up by a broadcast or at a meeting; their goodwill and righteousness are warm for the moment, but evaporate when it comes to giving support in money or active help.

To enjoy the luxury of sympathy or momentary despair ("Where is the world going to?") is only a way of evading one's responsibilities. While this is being written, the newspapers are united in horror at the bombing of Shanghai by the Japanese. But most of their readers are in such an intellectual muddle that they do not see any inconsistency in attending protest meetings against such warfare and in voting for the building of planes designed for the same 'defensive' work as the Japanese carried out.

In private life, as we all know, when we are miserable and particularly when at the back of our minds we are half aware that our misfortunes are in part due to ourselves, the instinct to turn angrily upon someone or something and to find a scapegoat is almost universal. "To blame it on the cat" domestically is so common as to have become a standard joke. The man who smashes the glass, china and furniture when he feels angry or thwarted or who breaks his golf club when he is playing badly has gone half-way back to the mental condition of the savage who believes in magic and does not distinguish between the responsibility of inanimate things and animate beings.

There are abundant examples of the working of that principle in propaganda and in the Press, in past history and the present; the Nazis found in the Jews and Communists a scapegoat for their troubles, politicians here make their opponents responsible for everything that is wrong at home, and we are all of us inclined nowadays to put the blame for everything that is wrong upon the Nazis. In home and foreign affairs the habit of finding scapegoats enables people to escape responsibility, and to enjoy a feeling of self-righteousness. Above all it makes it more difficult to solve any problem.

Irrational factors generally are only just beneath the skin in apparently civilized people. Some of them may have served a useful purpose once; for the herd to keep together was a biological necessity on which the safety of the individual depended, and the jumpiness and unreasonable fears one has when alone in a house for any length of time may be survivals of a time when to suspect every leaf movement was a condition of existence. But they do no help in deciding matters of home or foreign policy under more complex conditions. A little reflection will show how much of our behaviour is due to instinct or emotion.

At the cinema, one finds tears gathering, lumps rising, etc., at suitable moments of pathos or excitement. The choice of a car or shaving soap or M.P. even may be determined (if we examine our motives) by the fact that we knew and liked a person with the same name as the particular product on sale. Recently I read a speech by a politician named Morrison; I thought it was nonsense, being under the impression that he belonged to party X, which I do not like. Then I found it had been made by another politician of the same name belonging to Y party which appeals to me more. At once I found myself making excuses for the speech, the views seemed fairly sane after all, etc., etc.

Obviously this section does not even give a complete list of irrational factors; but once aware of their existence one can find plenty of examples of their working in one's self and elsewhere. It would be impossible to eradicate them, even if we wished to, but it is an advantage to be conscious of their influence when an important choice has to be made. Self-knowledge is generally considered desirable; and a step towards it can be made by a study of everyday reading matter, through learning in what light the propagandist writer regards one, and by catching one's self on the point of surrender to a specious appeal or accepting a fallacious argument, because it is pleasant or convenient to do so.

Description, Genesis and Evaluation

The habit of easy credulity is closely allied with the habit of responding to emotionally charged words instead of thinking.

During the Spanish War for instance it was difficult for anyone who wanted to make up his mind to decide about the English policy of non-intervention, because the issue was confused by partisan and sweeping terms. Opponents of the government denounced it as 'spineless,' 'lethargic,' 'dilatory,' cowardly' and 'inert: supporters described the same action as 'prudent,' 'determined,' 'level-headed' and the work of 'far-sighted statesmanship.' If the parties in Parliament had changed places before the civil war one can imagine the discussion being carried on in the same terms. Two different sets of words describe the same actions. Those who use them may be able to substantiate them by rational argument; the words can have a solid meaning. But as it is they are used as a substitute for argument; they convey not facts but the speaker's feelings. Both sets of words cannot logically be appropriate.

In this case there is no need to impute dishonesty to either party. But it is clear an unsatisfactory method of carrying on controversy, and one likely to have serious results. To return to the terms 'Bolshevik' and 'Red' as used by the *Daily Mail.* They are not strictly accurate in fact. It is possible for a newspaper to print direct falsehoods, but it would become obvious in time that it was untruthful if it persisted in saying that 2+2=5. If, however, it claims that two Englishmen equal four Bolsheviks, it commands (or used to command) a good deal of assent. Carried too far the method is funny: a Fascist paper, *Action,* said that *The Times* grows each month more 'Red'; and that appears absurd because there is no grain of plausibility about it.

The terms are used most effectively where one per cent of truth enables the emotional charge to work violently. The *Daily Mail* reader knows vaguely that the Bolsheviks were people who in Russia seized power, shot their opponents, dispossessed property owners and so on. He hates violence and oppression when exerted by the wrong people, and the words applied to these people become charged with emotions which it is easy to touch off when the temperature is rising. They can thus be used to blast anything the *Daily Mail* dislikes — Liberals, Socialists, Trotskyites, a school of thought or art, though those to whom the word is applied may disapprove of Russian methods as much as Lord Rothermere himself. The factual content of 'Bolshevik' is negligible; very few people who use the word in the emotional way could tell you the difference between a Bolshevik and a Menshevik. Similarly Mr. Chamberlain is called a 'Fascist' by some of those who think that the government of which he is a member has totalitarian leanings.

Of course there is no objection to emotionally charged words as such. Literature could not exist without them. But they should be used with full knowledge of their working by writers and readers.

Some of the finest specimens of the creation of irrational belief crop up at election times. If your own party changes its plans it is "showing the requisite flexibility:" but if your opponents do so they are indulging in "opportunist shillyshallying." We meet the emergency with "prompt resourcefulness," but the others resort "rash make-shifts." The following list (from a letter by Miss Margaret Cross to the *Manchester Guardian)* consists of phrases of the kind discussed; the blanks are left for filling up the complements.

Your own party makes a challenge The other party indulges in tactics

conducts a campaign	....
issues a message	....
indicts the others	....
makes a pledge	....
is faced with a problem	....
replies to its critics	....
maintains its attitude	....
deals in facts	....
----------------------------------	makes an insidious move
----------------------------------	prejudices the electors
----------------------------------	is emotional
----------------------------------	is panicky
----------------------------------	makes a defence
----------------------------------	picks holes in your plans
----------------------------------	aims are exposed
----------------------------------	is merely electioneering.

Perhaps one reason why people do not more frequently see that they are being misled is that they are habituated to emotional beliefs by advertising, which has always found the trick profitable. It is very common to find a simple, standard product or substance called by an impressive or suggestive name. You could sell water if you bottled it and called it Vitaquence, it is the name that sells a certain brand of raisins, and other examples are not far to seek. A car of course works much better if it goes to a "car valetting station" than if it is just taken to a shed which says "Cars Greased." In the same way undertakers in the USA call themselves 'morticians.'

Advertisers and propagandists work on very similar lines and are in fact often the same people; the campaigns for Guinness, Gold Flake and the National Government Publicity Bureau (to say nothing of Johny Walker, the Treasury, Austin Cars and the War Office) were in the hands of the same advertising agency. A difference is that advertising is more intensive and pervasive because there is more money to spend; by comparison propagandist bodies do not spend large sums on publicity. But when we come to choose our policies and our leaders we do so with habits of thought and feeling carried over from advertising.

Both advertisers and propagandists tend to use flattery, promises, appeals to fear, group feeling and snobbery. An electorate which buys its soaps because they are advertised by the portraits of film stars naturally votes for a candidate whose chief asset is a charming wife and baby. By the use of slogans advertising accustoms us to the tabloid thinking of elections. This was illustrated by the preliminary propaganda which enabled Hitler to seize power; it ran on the same lines as an advertising campaign, repeatedly using the phrases found most effective: "Germany, awake!" "Perish the Jew" "November Criminals" "National Pride" "Voice of the blood" "Red sub-humanity." E. A. Mowrer suggests that if Hitler had not become a politician, he might equally well have been an unequalled advertising manager. Hitler claims to have learnt his propaganda lessons from England, and it must be admitted that the misleading slogans and emotional half-truths handed out by advertising and the Press are not on a much higher level than those just quoted.

Developed Suggestions: This section develops some of the suggestions just made. So far as politics or international affairs are concerned these emotionally charged rebels confuse thinking and perpetual antagonisms. Attitudes, policies and actions are based on catchwords which depend for their power on being unexamined. In the past "It is God's will that..." may have been used as a substitute for thinking; Today spokesmen of all parties tell us that "It would be impossible for the empire to exist if..." and that is expected to clinch the argument. Any questioning of the catchphrase is unexpected, and in argument usually causes a rise in temperature. (Overheating in a disputant is often a sign that his argument is weak, or that though sound his belief is not held for intellectual reasons.)

In the same way writers of the Left use the word 'Capital' in a vaguely derogatory way, not making it clear whether they are referring to men, money or engineering plant. In the dictatorship countries and here to a less extent we find the word 'State' used as a catchword: "The interest of the State demand..." that we should think or do something which does not seem in our best interests. If we find ourselves influenced by the phrase we should bear in mind that the State is an abstraction, and does not exist except as a collection of individuals. "Because living human beings are realities, the alleged good of the State, as such, is not worth the suffering of a single individual." (C. E. M. Joad.)

It is often possible to catch oneself using labels instead of thinking. Thus we tend to judge views and proposals, not on their merits, but on the source from which they come. The words 'Conservative' and 'Socialist' are enlisted to dispose of what might receive a good hearing if the label happened to be different or absent. Probably this book will be dismissed as propaganda for the Left by organs of Right views, and as 'Fascist or 'reactionary' by reviewers at the other extreme, because it criticises both sides.

"The Price of Empire is External Vigilance." "The defence of the empire requires...." I think these are the utterances of the *Daily Mail* watchdog and of a Labour peer respectively. Both were basing certain proposals on the assumptions that the empire exists, is desirable, is unquestionable, is sacrosanct. In reports of speeches the mention of empire often seems to have provoked applause;

elsewhere 'Fascism' suitably stressed produces groans and hisses from the audience. As the former word is so strongly charged with feeling, it is worth considering for what reasons we should admire and defend the empire. It consists of the colonies, of the dominions, of India, and of this country.

The greater part of the colonies are in Africa; some of them are profitable because it is possible to force natives to work at very low wages by imposing taxes to pay which they must find an employer. The dominions are independent countries. "Broadly speaking, there is little to differentiate Britain's relations with the Dominions – from her relations with foreign countries whose day-Today intercourse is close and, in the diplomatic sense, friendly" (Leonard Barnes, *Skeleton of the Empire,* a brief and on the whole anti-Imperial survey). They are attached strongly to this country because they owe it a great deal of money. As for India it has for years been regarded as a property and a market; some moves have now been made in the direction of self-government. So far as 'Defence' is concerned a great deal is spent on that to "make sure that they do not become the debtors of someone else" (Leonard Barnes).

Error Correction

Once upon a time, newspapers did not make mistakes. If that reads like the beginning to a fairy tale, that's because it is one. Newspapers did make mistakes; it's just that they did not admit them - or at least not unless forced to do so by lawyers. For decades, the Press preferred to be confident liars than seekers after the truth.

Text Correction

Punctuation Rules

1. Aim at writing sentences that are clear without the help of stops.
2. When you feel convinced that it is necessary to use stops, use no more than are essential to express your full meaning. Over-stopping is a very common fault and may seriously hinder the reader.
3. Do not use stops in an attempt to rectify a badly constructed sentence. The only remedy for such a sentence is to rewrite it. The legitimate purposes for which stops may be used are: to denote the grouping of closely connected words; to represent the inflection of the voice; to give emphasis or express emotion.

4. As certain alternatives in punctuation are permissible, decide which of these alternatives you intend to adopt, and keep to them. In other words, be consistent.

The Full Stop

Rule I. The full stop is used at the end of a complete and separate sentence that is not in the form of a question or an exclamation. (A sentence is a group of words making complete sense.)

Rule II. Sometimes the full stop is used after groups of words that are not complete sentences, when the words omitted can be readily supplied by the reader.

Example: Better late then never.

(The practice of writing such 'sentences' is not recommended to the beginner.)

Rule III. A full stop is placed after an abbreviation, including initials and titles.

Notes:

1. When the last letter of the abbreviation is the same as the last letter of the complete word, the use of the full stop is optional; as, Mr. W.W. Jacobs, Dr. Johnson, Messrs Spenlow and Jorkins.
2. A full stop was usually placed after the Roman figures I., II., III., V., etc. The recent tendency is to omit it.
3. A full stop is not usually placed after the Arabic numerals, 1, 2, 3, 4, 5, etc. When, however, these figures are used to enumerate various points of a subject, in a tabular form (as in this section), or to introduce side-headings, the full stop is necessary.
4. No full stop is required after 1st, 2nd, 3rd, 4th, 5th, etc., as these are looked upon as symbols, not as abbreviations. 5. If an abbreviation occurs at the end of a sentence, only one full stop is to be applied.

The Comma: The comma is the most frequently used of all stops. It denotes the lightest break and the shortest pause in a sentence.

Rule I. The comma is used to mark off each word or phrase in a series of words or phrases.

Example: He was a tall, thin, gentlemanly fellow.

Note: When the last number of a series is preceded by 'and' 'or' some writers omit the comma before these words; but this practice sometimes leads to lack of clarity, and is not recommended.

Rule II. When two adjectives occur together, and the second is more closely associated than the first with the noun it limits, the comma is omitted.

Example: Tennyson was a notable English poet.

Rule III. When the words or phrases in a series of words or phrases are joined by conjunctions (usually and / or), commas are not used.

Example: John and Mary and Tom are sure to be there.

Rule IV. When such words as however, therefore, indeed, too, now, of course, again, no doubt, moreover, thus, hence, are inserted into a sentence, and could be omitted without altering its sense, they are usually marked off by commas.

Example: I was, as a matter of fact, on my way to see you.

Rule V. When certain of the kinds of words mentioned in Rule IV be omitted from a sentence without altering the sense, the comma is not used.

Example: However great the danger, he was always in the forefront of the battle.

Rule VI. Commas are often used, instead of brackets, to mark off a parenthesis.

Example: The instrument can also be used, and very often is, for several other purposes.

Rule VII. As a rule, a comma should not be used to separate a subject from its verb. When, however, the subject is exceptionally long, a comma is permissible.

Example:

1. Henry the Eighth was then about twenty-five.
2. A man who has had all that experience, is the very man we need.

Rule VIII. A comma is often used after a phrase or clause that is placed out of its normal order, unless it is very short.

Example: From the top of the old tower, we could now see the distant town.

But –

On Mondays the castle is not open to visitors.

Rule IX. The comma is used to denote the omission of some word or group of words that is 'understood'.

Example: We are going to the lakes; he, to Ireland.

Rule X. The comma is sometimes used for rhetorical purposes; that is, to give emphasis or express emotion.

Example: For these services he gave the man, six pence.

Rule XI. The comma is used to mark off words that denote the person addressed.

Example: Tom, where are you?

Rule XII. The comma is used: (a) to separate the month from the year, (b) to mark off the items in an address, (c) to mark off every third figure in a large number, counting from the right.
Examples:

1. The letter was dated 3rd October, 1991. (3 October, 1991 and October 3, 1991 are also correct).
2. Mrs. William Black, 3, Brook Street, London, S.W. 1. (The use of the comma between the number and the name of the street is optional).
3. The total number of people who voted was 8,576,823. (Round numbers, such as, 'two million', are usually written in words.)

Rule XIII. The comma is used to mark off a phrase in apposition to a noun.

Example: The speech was read by Mr. Beale, Clerk to the Council.

Notes:

1. If a noun in apposition represents part of a title, the comma is not required; as, William the Silent.

2. In phrases such as 'my son John', 'the poet Shelley', where the common noun precedes the proper, the comma is omitted.

Rule XIV. The comma is used to separate two coordinate clauses, unless these are very short.

Example: A Saturday afternoon in November was approaching the time of twilight, and the vast tract of unenclosed wild known as Egdon Heath embrowned itself moment by moment.

But –

Come and find me.

Rule XV. Commas are used to mark off the explanatory words he said, she said, he replied, etc., introduced into conversation.

Example: 'You yourself must know,' said Lothair, 'that the whole statement is founded on falsehood'.

Rule XVI. The comma is used to introduce or mark off a short direct quotation; that is, where the exact words of the writer are given.

Example: As Washington Irving observes, 'The only thing that never grows mellow with age is a tart tongue. '

Rule XVII. When, however, there is no break in the sentence, but the introductory words and the words quoted run straight on, no comma is used.

Example: The witness explained that he was 'barely ten yards away at the time'.

Rule XVIII. A comma is used to introduce words which, although not a direct quotation, are in the nature of one. The sentence quoted begins with a capital, but it is not placed between inverted commas.

Example: All I would say is, Remember.

Rule XIX. A comma is used to mark off words or phrases that occur in pairs.

Example: Dickens and Thackeray, Tennyson and Browning, Carlyle and Macaulay, are the Victorian writers usually compared for purposes of criticism.

Rule XX. When the same two words or phrases come together in a sentence, a comma is used to separate them.

Example:

1. Let us call a spade, a spade.
2. Whatever is, is.

Rule XXI. When two words stand in contrast, and are joined by conjunctions such as but, yet, and though, no comma is used. *Example:* It was a small but charming house.

Rule XXII. The comma is always used to mark off an adverb clause when it comes first, and usually when it comes elsewhere in the sentence.

Example: If it is possible, you may be sure that the work will be done.

Rule XXIII. When the adverb clause is short, and comes last; or where there is no break in the run of the whole sentence, the comma is omitted.

Example: I will go when he returns.

Rule XXIV. The comma is put to mark off a series of noun clauses or adjective clauses, excepting the first.

Example: They said that they did not accept the explanation, that they would make further enquiry into the matter, and that he would hear from them again.

Rule XXV. A comma is used to mark off a phrase in the absolute construction.

Example: The rain having stopped, play was resumed.

Rule XXVI. A comma is used to mark off a non-defining adjective clause.

Example: The three men, who were just returning from work, did all they could to help us.

Note: With a defining adjective clause no comma is used; as, 'This is the plumber who is going to repair the pipe.'

The Semicolon: A semicolon is a stronger stop than a comma, but is not so strong as a colon or a full stop. It consequently indicates a remoter degree of relation between the parts of a sentence than is indicated by the comma.

Rule I. A Semicolon is used to separate two or more different statements which are not joined by conjunctions, but which are connected in thought.

Example: To give advice is bad enough; to give good advice is absolutely fatal.

Rule II. The semicolon is used to mark off the two main sections of a sentence, when each of those sections contains parts of its own sub-divided by commas.

Example: The surrounding country is smooth and green, it appears; and pleasant country roads, bound for distant towns and villages, strike through it in all directions.

Rule III. The semicolon is used to lay stress upon a series of clauses which would otherwise be separated by commas.

Example: This is the man who had promised to defend his country; who had held a high office; and who was in a position of sacred trust.

Rule IV. The semicolon is generally used to mark off clauses joined by conjunctions such as for, then, yet, so, otherwise, still, therefore, which introduce an inference or express opposition or contrast.

Example:

1. By now he was utterly worn out; yet he struggled on for another mile.
2. You are sure to succeed if you try hard enough; so why not persevere?
3. Come early; then we shall get good seats.

The Colon: It is, now mostly used for various miscellaneous purposes, such as to mark an anti-thesis, or to introduce a quotation or an enumeration of details.

Rule I. The colon is placed between two statements, not joined by a conjunction, the second of which helps in some way to amplify, illustrate, or explain the first.

Example: But we are not to think of their expectations: the question is what you can afford.

Rule II. The colon is used to mark a sharp contrast.

Example: Art is long: time is fleeting.

Rule III. Enumerations of details are preceded by a colon, particularly when a word or phrase such as, viz., namely, i.e., that is, e.g., for example, for instance, is understood but not actually given.

Example: Among the most famous of Sir Walter Scott's novels are the following: Ivanhoe, Kenilworth, The Bride of Lammermoor, The Talisman, and old Mortality.

Rule IV. The colon is used to introduce a quotation.

Example: As Emerson well remarks: "It is easy in the world to live after the world's opinion; it is easy in solitude to live after one's own; but the great man is he who in the midst of the crowd keeps with perfect sweetness the independence of solitude."

Notes:

1. If the quotation is short, and there is only a slight pause after the words introducing it, a comma will be found sufficient to mark it off.
2. If the words that mark off the quotation do not stand first, but are placed somewhere else in the sentence, the comma is used.

The Question Mark or Note of Interrogation.

Rule I. The question mark is used after a direct question; that is, a question in which the actual words of the speaker are given.

Examples:

1. Does anybody here know poor Rip Van Winkle?
2. He is getting much better, don't you think?

Rule II. When a question asked by a speaker is repeated by another person in the form of a statement, the question mark is replaced by a full stop.

Examples:

1. They asked the stranger where he was going.
2. She enquired how long he was likely to remain.
3. The strikers roughly demanded to know what I meant.

Rule III. A question mark is used after each separate question in a series of questions.

Examples: Where is my accuser? With what crime does he charge me? What proof has he of my guilt?

Rule IV. When the questions in a series represent parts of what is really one whole question, and when combined require only one answer, the question mark is placed only at the end of the sentence, and not after each separate question.

Example: Can a man be honest and behave in this way?

Rule V. When a sentence is a statement in form but a question in meaning, the question mark is used. In spoken English, the fact that the sentence is intended to be a question is denoted by the tone of the voice.

Examples:

1. You are Mr. Smith?
2. He did say that he was coming this afternoon?
3. I suppose they will agree to our conditions?

Rule VI. A question mark is used after a word or expression, often a date, to indicate that there is some doubt as to its accuracy, or to suggest that a statement made by the writer is intended to be taken ironically.

Example: The names of the injured, as given to our representative, are: William Chester, Charles Pellit (?), and John Kingston.

Exclamation Mark

Rule I. The exclamation mark is used after interjections; that is, a single word that expresses the emotions of admiration, wonder, fear, surprise, etc.

Examples:

1. Ah! that explains everything.
2. Oh! I see what you mean.
3. Hurrah! we've won the match.
4. What! you can't see how the two cases differ?
5. At Lima, alas! they were just too late.

Rule II. The exclamation mark is used after phrases and complete sentences that are exclamatory. When an interjection introduces a phrase or sentence of this kind, the exclamation mark is placed, not after the interjection, but at the end of the phrase or sentence.

Examples:

1. Why, bless my soul! you look younger than when I last saw you.
2. How many fleeting impressions that path had shared with me!
3. Alas for his dreams of boundless dominion!
4. To think that he should do a thing like that!

Rule III. An exclamation mark is used after each exclamatory word, phrase, or sentence, in a series of exclamations.

Examples:

1. The whale! There she blows! there! there! she blows! she blows!
2. What sighs have been wafted after that ship! what prayers offered up at the deserted fireside of home! How has expectation darkened into despair!
3. What a piece of work is man! How noble in reason! how infinite in faculties! in form and moving, how express and admirable! in action, how like an angel! in apprehension, how like a god!

Rule IV. The exclamation mark is generally used after words of a address preceded by O.

Examples:

1. O friend! I know not which way I must look.
2. O my dark Rosaleen!
3. O soft embalmer of the still midnight!

Note: These, of course, are all poetical usages; but sometimes the exclamation mark is used in prose, when the name of the person addressed is not preceded by O; as 'Arthur! I want to speak to you for a moment.'

Rule V. The exclamation mark is used after a phrase or sentence to indicate that the writer wishes his readers to know that he regards the statement as (a) absurd (b) ironical (c) deeply impressive.

Examples:

1. And this is the type of man we are all asked to admire!
2. This brave (!) man ran away after the first shots were fired.
3. Sound, trumpets, a mournful march!' Fall, dark curtain, upon his pageant, his pride, his grief, his awful tragedy!

Brackets

Rule I. When a clause is inserted into a sentence of which it really forms no part, and from which it could be omitted without materially affecting the sense, brackets should be used to enclose the close.

Example: I remember that I drove in a hansom (it was before the coming of the taxi) from Ealing to Marble Arch in record time.

Rule II. Brackets are used to enclose an explanatory reference.

Example: The heat increased rapidly towards two o'clock (42°C), by which time every voice of bird or mammal was hushed:

Rule III. Occasionally a parenthetical sentence is not inserted into another sentence, but forms, a parenthesis in a paragraph. In that case, the first word of the parenthesis should begin with a capital, and the stop at the end should be placed inside the bracket.

Example: Nor was Mrs. Amelia at all above the pleasure of shopping, and bargaining, and seeing and buying pretty things. (Would any man, the most philosophic, give two pence for a woman who was?) She gave herself a little treat, obedient to her husband's orders, and purchased a quantity of lady's gear, showing a great deal of taste and elegant discernment, as all the shopfolks said.

Rule IV. Square brackets are used to enclose an explanation or observation inserted into a sentence by someone other than the author or speaker quoted. There is no need to break the quotation marks to indicate the insertion.

Example: 'The Prime Minister [Mr. Gladstone] himself made the announcement,' says the writer.

The Dash

Rule I. The dash is used, as an alternative to the comma, to emphasis a particular word.

Examples:

1. And so you are reduced to doing — this.
2. Such was the work of — a patriot.
3. Mountains were in labour, and there crept forth — a mouse.

Rule II. The dash is used, as an alternative to brackets, to mark a parenthesis.

Example: He may be a little flighty perhaps — many of us are that-but he is not mad.

Rule III. A dash is used to denote an abrupt break or sudden change in the construction of a sentence.

Example: I think it was Mr. Brown who — But wait a moment; wasn't he away at the time?

Rule IV. The dash is used to indicate hesitating, agitated, or faltering speech.

Example: Well, I don't know - I suppose-er - if you say he did it, he-er-must have done so.

Rule V. The dash is used to indicate that a name or word has been intentionally omitted. Sometimes the name or word is suggested by the use of the first letter, or the first and the last letters.

Example: We have received a donation of one hundred dollars from Mr. C - B-, of Bristol, who desires to remain anonymous.

Rule VI. The dash is used to summarise several subjects all belonging to the same verb.

Example: English, French, German, Italian — they suffered alike the extremes of misfortune.

Rule VII. The dash is used before a word that is repeated in the manner of an echo.

Example: It was gold — gold that he had found.

Quotation Marks or Inverted Commas

Rule I. Quotation marks are used to denote direct speech; that is, the actual words used by the speaker or writer.

Example: Walter Bagehot says: 'I can imagine nothing better in theory or more successful in practice than private banks as they were in the beginning.'

Rule II. When in the course of a conversation that is being recorded, explanatory expressions, such as he said, she said, they replied, are introduced, quotation marks are placed before and after each part of the interrupted quotation.

Example: "It is but a ring of lead," he cried, "nor has it any value. Therefore take thy half of the treasure and go from the city."

Rule III. When the words quoted are not the exact words of the speaker or writer, but are repeated indirectly by another person, no quotation marks are required.

Example: Walter Bagehot says that he can imagine nothing better in theory or more successful in practice than private banks as they were in the beginning.

Rule IV. A word that is used in some new or special sense, or that it is referred to merely as a word, should be placed within quotation marks.

Example: On most ships there is a small engine called a 'donkey'.

Rule V. Quotation marks are used in the titles of books, periodicals, plays, films, etc., as an alternative to italics.

Example: "The Vicar of Wakefield" is one of the most charming of all English novels.

Rule VI. When quotation occurs within a quotation, double quotation marks are used for the inner quotation and single quotation marks for the outer.

Example: 'But, my dear Frank, you know what Shakespeare says: "My lord, beware of jealousy".

Note: Frequently double quotation marks are used for the outer quotation and single quotation marks for the inner; but the practice suggested is preferable. However, both are correct and one of them should be chosen as style and should be followed.

Relative Position of Quotation Marks and Stops: Often some difficulty is experienced in deciding what is the correct position of the question mark, the exclamation mark, and the four main stops, in relation to the quotation marks, when a passage is in direct speech.

First, then, as regards the question mark and the exclamation mark:

Rule I.

1. If a sentence which is not in the form of a direct question or a direct exclamation ends with a quotation which is in that form, the question mark or exclamation mark is placed before the final quotation mark, because the question or exclamation mark belongs to the quotation.

Examples:

1. After a few moments, he said, "Shall we go down to see them now?"
2. When Shaw had ceased speaking, Winter exclaimed, "What an extraordinary story!"

Rule II.

2. If a sentence in the form of a direct question or a direct exclamation ends with a quotation which is not in that form, the question mark or exclamation mark is placed after the final quotation mark, because the question mark or the exclamation mark belongs to the complete or containing sentence.

Examples:

1. Why is that Socrates was always saying, "Know yourself"?
2. What a curious thing it was to say, "Know yourself"!

Rule III.

3. If a sentence, in the form of a direct question or a direct exclamation, ends with a quotation which is also in that form, only one question mark or exclamation mark is used, and this is placed outside the final quotation mark.

Examples:

1. Why is it that he is always asking, 'What can we do to earn a little more money'?
2. How futile a thing for him to exclaim, 'What a pity it is that I didn't seize the chance when I had it'!

As regards the placing of the four main stops (full stop, comma, semicolon, and colon) in this connection; most printers, in the interest of neatness, put the stop before the final quotation mark, and, although this is sometimes open to question it is advised to follow suit.

The Apostrophe

Rule I. The apostrophe is used to show that a noun is in the possessive case; that is, the case that denotes ownership or possession.

(a) If the noun is in the singular and does not end in s, then *'s* is added. If the noun is in the singular and does end in s, then *'s* is added, provided that this does not result in three s sounds coming together, or is otherwise unpleasing to the ear. In that event, only the apostrophe is added.

Examples:

1. Mr. Weston's opinion was then asked,
2. She was reading Burns's poems in St. James's Park. (b) If the noun is in the plural and ends in s, only the apostrophe is placed after the s. If the noun is in the plural and does not end in s, then *'s* is added.

Examples:

1. The Smiths' house is very conveniently situated.
2. The soldiers' and sailors' quarters were far from comfortable.
3. The men's health was not good, and the women's was even worse.

Rule II. The apostrophe is used to denote the omission of some letter or letters from a word.

Examples:

1. When you sleep in your cloak there's no lodging to pay.
2. Where ignorance is bliss 'Tis folly to be wise.
3. 'Don't ask him,' cried Madame Duval; 'your best way is to ask Mr. Smith; for he's been here the oftenest. '

Rule III. The apostrophe is also used when a letter or number is counted more than once.

Examples:

1. Nine 8s are 72.
2. There are two c's and two m's in the word accommodation.
3. He was told to mind his P's and Q's.

The Hyphen

Rule I. The hyphen is used to form compound words.

Examples:

1. They took a house-boat for the summer months.
2. His daughter-in-law was learning French.

Rule II. The hyphen is generally used between a prefix and the word to which it belongs, when the prefix ends and the word begins with a vowel (usually the same vowel), the object being to denote that each vowel must be pronounced separately.

Example: Their cooperation was eagerly desired.

Rule III. The hyphen is used to denote the division of a word.

Example: Pre-sume, pur-pose, ex-claim, confidence, formation.

Rule IV. The hyphen is sometimes used to join the words that form an adjective phrase, when the adjective phrase precedes the word it limits.

Example: They came at last to a little-known, but extremely picturesque, hamlet.

Rule V. When, however, the adjective phrase follows the word it limits, the hyphen is not used.

Example: They came at last to a hamlet, little known but extremely picturesque.

Rule VI. The hyphen is used to join the cardinal numbers from twenty-one to ninety-nine, and the ordinal numbers from twenty-first to ninety-ninth, when those numbers are expressed in words.

Example: This remark occurs on chapter forty-three.

Rule VII. Similarly, a hyphen is used to join the parts of a fraction expressed in words.

Example: He obtained one-quarter of the stipulated sum at once.

Marks of Ellipsis or Omission: Three dots (...), or three asterisks (***), are used to denote a broken sentence or a broken paragraph; that is, the intentional omission of some words from the beginning, the middle, or the end of a sentence or paragraph.

Example:

1. ... as I saw the ship staggering and plunging among these roaring caverns, it seemed miraculous that she regained her balance or preserved her buoyancy.

   (Here, the words 'The thunders bellowed over the wide waste of waters, and' have been omitted from the beginning of the sentence, as will be seen from the next example.)
2. The thunders bellowed over the wide waste of waters, and as I saw the ship staggering and plunging... it seemed miraculous that she regained her balance or preserved her buoyancy.

   (Here, the words 'among these roaring caverns' have been omitted from the middle of the sentence.)
3. The thunders bellowed over the wide waste of waters, and as I saw the ship staggering and plunging among these roaring caverns, it seemed miraculous that she regained her balance...

   (Here, the words 'or preserved her buoyancy' have been omitted from the end of the sentence)

Italics

Rule I. Italics are to emphasise words and phrases.

Examples:

1. I am *not* going to receive any help from him.
2. *So that is* what you have been doing.

Rule II. The names of books and periodicals are usually printed in italics, and the names of ships.

Examples: Pride and Prejudice, The Daily Telegraph, India Today, INS Vikrant.

Rule III. Foreign words and phrases are printed in italics.

Examples: Billet doux, adagio, proforma.

Note: When foreign words have become more or less anglicised, they are printed in roman type; as, 'She made her debut when she was scarcely twenty. '

Capital Letters: The following words should begin with a capital letter:

Rule I. The first word of every sentence.

Example: She is not the rose, but she has lived near the rose.

Rule II. The first word after every full stop.

Example: It is painful enough to discover with what unconcern they speak of war and threaten it. They do not know its horrors. We have seen enough of war to make us look upon it as the germ of all evils.

Rule III. The first word after a question mark or an exclamation mark that occurs at the end of a complete sentence. If the question mark or the exclamation mark follows a word or a phrase, then the next word requires no capital.

Examples:

1. How delightful it is to be back again! It seems only a few months since I left.
2. Ah! that action is not so easily explained.

Rule IV. The first word of a direct quotation.

Example: Benjamin Franklin says: 'Wealth is not his that has it, but his that enjoys it. '

Rule V. The first word of every line of verse, although there is a tendency to discontinue using capitals for this purpose.

Example: No coward soul is mine.

No trembler in the world's storm-troubled sphere; I see Heaven's glories shine.

And faith shines equal, arming me from fear.

Rule VI. Proper names and the adjectives formed from them.

Example: Patrick Clare was partly English and partly Irish by birth, and this may explain much that was curious in his temperament.

Rule VII. Nouns and pronouns relating to God.

Example: These are the men that have loved our Lord, When they were in the world, and that have left all for His holy name; and He hath sent us to fetch them, and we have brought them thus far on their destined journey, that they may go in and look their Redeemer in the face with joy.

Rule VIII. Personification.

Example: Let not Ambition mock their useful toil, Their homely joys, and destiny obscure; Nor Grandeur hear with a disdainful smile The short and simple annals of the poor.

Rule IX. The names of the days of the week and the months of the year, but not the names of the seasons, although this is not unusual in verse.

Example: His boat will arrive on Saturday, the 18th March, and he will be returning in the late autumn.

Rule X. The pronoun I, and the letter O, when used before words of address.

Example: It is I, O King, who will save thee.

Rule XI. Words denoting important historical events.

Example: The. Flood, the Conquest, the Reformation, the Restoration.

Rule XII. The most important words in: a) official titles, b) descriptive titles, c) the titles of books, plays, films, etc.

Examples:

1. Mr. Gladstone was at that time Secretary of State for Foreign Affairs.

2. I am convinced that in a previous state of existence I must have been William the Conqueror: the date 1066 is so firmly imprinted on my memory.
3. Some of the works he had recently read were: The Cloister and the Hearth, the Comedy of Errors, Ode on the Popular Superstitions of the Highlands, and the Return of the Native.

Explanation of the Grammatical Terms Used

Sentence and Phrase: A Sentence is a group of words that makes complete sense; as, 'This was the noblest Roman of them all. '

A Phrase is a group of words that makes sense but not complete sense; as, 'At that time he was a man of little consequence.' Here, 'At that time' and 'of little consequence' are, phrases.

Subject and Predicate: Every sentence can be divided into two parts:

1. The part that names the person or thing of which something is said. This part is called the Subject.
2. The part which says something about the person or thing named. This part is called the Predicate.

Take; for example, the sentence, 'A good King is a public servant'. Here, `A good king' names the person of which something is said, and is therefore the subject: is a public servant' says something about the person named, and is therefore the predicate.

Clause: A Clause is a group of words forming part of a larger sentence and having subject and predicate of its own; as, 'A statesman makes the occasion, but the occasion makes the politician. ' Here, 'A statesman makes the occasion' and 'the occasion makes the politician' are clauses.

The Parts of Speech: The parts of Speech are the classes into which the words of a language fall according to the kind of work they do in a sentence. There are eight Parts of Speech: Noun, Pronoun, Verb, Adjective, Adverb, Preposition, Conjunction, and Interjection.

A noun is the name of a thing; as, table, clock, dog.

(A Proper Noun is one that names a particular person or thing: as Johnson, Thomas, St. Paul's.)

A Pronoun is a word used instead of a noun; as, he, she, they, her, them.

A Verb is a word that enables us to say something about a thing; as, 'Water *freezes*', 'Lions *roar*'.

(A Finite Verb is one that has a subject).

An Adjective is a word that limits the application of a noun; as, 'the green field', 'a round table', 'a square peg'.

An adverb is a word that modifies the meaning of a verb, an adjective, or another adverb; as, 'The procession slowly, moved along". 'He *seldom* goes to the club now', 'It doesn't happen *very often*', The girl had an *extremely* white face'.

A Preposition is a word that is placed before a noun or pronoun to show in what relation the person or thing named stands to something else; as, 'The dog was lying under the table', 'The lamp was on the desk'.

A Conjunction is a word that joins words or sentences; as, 'The point is well chosen, and it deserves to be met'. Some of the commonest conjunctions are and, or, but, for, yet.

An Interjection is a word that expresses some sudden emotion; as, Ah! Oh! Hurrah!

Simple, Double, and Complex Sentences: A simple Sentence is one that contains only one subject and one predicate; as, 'True obedience is true liberty'.

A Double Simple Sentence is one that is made up of two simple sentences; as, 'Genius begins great works, but labour alone finishes them'. Each of the simple sentences is called a coordinate clause, 'coordinate' meaning of equal rank or importance. Coordinate clauses are usually joined by a conjunction such as and, but, or.

A Complex Sentence is one that is made up of a Main Clause and one or more Subordinate Clauses; as, 'Kings will be tyrants from policy, when subjects are rebels from principle'. Here, 'Kings will be tyrants from policy' is the main clause, and 'when subjects are rebels from principle' the subordinate clause.

A Main Clause is the clause on which the complete construction of a complex sentence depends, and which is not equivalent to any part of speech.

A Subordinate Clause is that part of a complex sentence that is equivalent to a noun, an adjective, or an adverb, and that has a subject and predicate of its own. For instance, 'when subjects are rebels from principle' is a subordinate clause, because it is doing the work of an adverb, in that it modifies 'will be', and has a subject and predicate of its own.

Kinds of Subordinate Clauses: There are three kinds of Subordinate Clauses: Noun, Adjective, and Adverb.

A Noun Clause is one that does the work of a noun; it is, for instance, often either the subject or the object of a verb; as, 'That he will come is beyond doubt', where 'That he will come' is the subject of the verb is.

An Adjective Clause is one that does the work of an adjective; that is, it limits the application of a noun or its equivalent; as, 'it was not the kind of treatment that he was accustomed to', where 'that he was accustomed to' is an adjective clause limiting treatment.

An Adverb Clause is one that does the work of an adverb; that is, it limits a verb, an adjective, or another adverb, in some other clause of a complex sentence; as, 'Do you mind posting this letter, when you get to the post office?' where 'when you get to the post office' is an adverb clause limiting the verb 'do mind'.

Noun Phrase, Adjective Phrase, Adverb Phrase: A Phrase is a group of words making sense but not complete sense. The work done by a Noun Phrase, an Adjective Phrase, and an Adverb Phrase is similar in all respects to that done by the corresponding clauses.

Apposition: When two nouns stand side by side, and both refer to the same person or thing, the nouns are said to be in apposition; as, 'Brown the butcher', 'Edward the Peace-maker', 'Jack the Giant-killer'.

Parenthesis: A Parenthesis is a word, phrase, or clause inserted into a sentence as a kind of 'aside', and not forming part of its normal construction; as, 'It was, I may say, partly my own fault'.

The Absolute Construction: The Absolute Construction is one in which a word or phrase is used in such a way that it has no grammatical connection with the rest of the sentence; as, 'I'm not quite sure how many people will be there, but, say, a hundred'.

The Relative Pronoun: Study the following Sentences:

1. I gave the luggage to the man *who* called last Tuesday.
2. Are you reading the book *that I* recommended?
3. We have just seen a house *which* we are thinking of buying.

Each of the words printed in italics performs a double function. It relates to some preceding noun, and is therefore a pronoun; and it joins one clause to another, and is therefore a conjunction.

In the first sentence, for example, who is used instead of the noun man, and joins together the two clauses, 'I gave the luggage to the man', and 'The man called last Tuesday'. A word that performs this double function is called a Relative Pronoun, and the preceding noun or pronoun to which the relative refers is called its Antecedent.

There are three relative pronouns: who, which, and that. Who is used of persons only, which of things only, and that of both persons and things.

Defining and Non-defining Relative Clause: Consider these two sentences:

1. The hotel which was badly damaged is now wholly uninhabitable.
2. The hotel, which was badly damaged, is now wholly uninhabitable.

In the first of these sentences, the clause, 'which was badly damaged', is defining or restrictive; that is to say, it limits the application of the noun, hotel. It is not any hotel but 'the-hotel which-was-badly-damaged'. In the second sentence, the clause is coordinating or non-defining, and does not limit the application of the noun. It really forms a parenthesis, and might be enclosed in brackets. Here are some additional examples:

Defining:

1. These are the people who will help us with the work.
2. It is just like the car that Tom bought.
3. There is a garage next door which is a great nuisance.

Non-defining:

1. Macaulay, who was a poet as well as an essayist and historian, was born in 1800.
2. The battle, which was fought in a thick mist, proved indecisive.
3. There is a garage next door, which is a great nuisance.

Rectification in Style

Conventional usages in punctuation are to be followed, with some exceptions. The modern trend in news-writing is towards omitting unnecessary punctuation.

Managing the Text

Use comma before "and" in series: *"Cats, kittens, and dogs were playing in the yard."*

Use comma in geographical name identifying preceding geographical name: *"He was seen in Peru, Ind., last June."*

Use comma to set off year in date: *"He was born Oct. 10,1862, in New York." "He was born in October, 1862."*

Use comma in interjection: *"No, you must stay here. Oh, I don't care."*

Use commas and semicolons in lists of names and identifying phrases, such as offices: *"The committee consists of John Smith, chairman; Richard Jones, vice-chairman; Peter Roe, secretary, and Harold White, treasurer."* (Note: use of comma instead of semicolon before "and" in such construction).

Use comma to distinguish between restrictive clause or phrase and non-restrictive clause or phrase, depending upon the meaning you wish to convey.

Restrictive: *"He makes good grades in the studies which he likes."* Non-restrictive: *"He makes good grades in the studies, which he likes."* The restrictive sentence is NOT punctuated.

Use comma to set off two independent clauses joined by a coordinating conjunction: *"It is essential to isolate the patient, and his clothes and eating utensils should be washed separately."*

Use comma to set off two dependent clause: *"John Jones, though he was only a freshman, was given the lead in the play."*

Use commas to set off words or phrases in apposition. "His *wife, Mary, was there." "John Jones, the manager, is in the office." "My stylebook, the latest edition, never has been used."*

Use commas to point off general numbers of four or more digits: $1,000; attendance was estimated at 5,000.

Omit commas in phone, serial, and street numbers: *University 4-4757; dog licence 168431; 3000 N. Sacramento ave.*

Omit commas in such form as: *5 feet 11 inches tall; 7 hours 13 minutes overdue; Detective Henry White of the homicide detail; Peter Jones. Jr.*

Following are miscellaneous examples of correct use and omission of commas:

> *Commander Paul Griffith of the American Legion.*
>
> *Paul Griffith, commander of the American Legion.*
>
> *Paul Griffith, Indianapolis.*
>
> *Paul Griffith, Indianapolis, Ind., commander of the American Legion.*
>
> *Paul Griffith, 42 Indianapolis, Ind.*
>
> *Paul Griffith, 42 of 1622 S. Carter St.. Indianapolis, Ind.*

Use of Quotation Marks: Use quote marks for titles of books, plays, songs, operas, paintings, magazine articles, subjects of lectures, and sermons.

Omit quote mark from names of characters, newspapers, ships, trains, and animals and from nicknames and diminutives.

Use quotes (and colon, nothing that first word after colon is capitalised) in subjects of debates: *"Resolved: That the United States should recognise the government of Upsylvania."*

Use quotes At the beginning of each paragraph of continuous quotation of more than one paragraph but at end of last paragraph only.

A quote within a quote requires single quote marks; a quote within a quote reverts to double quote marks.

Terminal punctuation belongs inside the quote marks: *"We are met on a great battlefield of that war,"* And: *" 'We are met on a great battlefield of that war,' Lincolon said."*

Use ellipses (...) to indicate omissions in quotes: *"Now we are engaged in a great Civil war, testing whether that nation... can long endure."*

Use of Dash: Use dash (omitting quote marks) in question and answer matter:

Q. – Where did you get the gun? *A. – -1 bought it in a pawn shop.*

(Note that a period and a dash follow the "Q" and the "A" and that each question and its answer are in one paragraph.)

Use dash (omitting quote marks) in symposiums or blocks of interviews:

Sen. White – It's a good bill, and I'll vote for it.

Sen. Black – It's a fiendish scheme, and I'll fight it to my death.

(Note that each person's remark forms a separate paragraph. This form is used when each block is relatively short. If the blocks are so long as to be typographically unattractive in one-paragraph form, use quote marks. Be consistent, however, and do not use dashes in part of the symposium and quotes in other parts.)

Use of Colon

Use colon in *"The Homeric sailed at 10:50 am." "The winner made the first lap in 0:6:12."*

Omit colon in the flat hour: *"The Homeric sailed at 10 am"* (Not 10:00 am).

Omit colon in lists of names run into a single paragraph. "The *dead were John Smith, Peter White, and Herman Doe."*

(Note, however, that if name are set in tabular form, *as* sometimes is done with longer lists of dead and injured, with each name forming a separate paragraph, the form is:) *The dead were:*

John Smith, 30, of 1628 Sherzvin ave. Peter White, 21, of 747 N. Wabash nve. The injured are:

Nancy Green, 28, of 736 Wesley are, broken right arm. Janet Blue, 19, of U W. Elm St., broken left arm.

Brief Expressions

States and Territories: Abbreviate names of States, territories and possessions of the United States or Canadian provinces when they follow name of cities with the exception of Idaho, Utah, Alaska, and Hawaii. Thus: *"He lived in Little Rock, Ark." "He lived in Arkansas."*

Spell out name of state when it follows name of county: *"He lived in Tazewell county, Illinois."*

Observe following style in abbreviating name of state and provinces:

Albama	Ala	Georgia	Ga.
Alaska	Alaska	Hawaii	Hawaii
Alberta	Alta	Idaho	Idaho
Arizona	Ariz	Illinois	Ill
Arkansas	Ark.	Indiana	Ind.
British Columbia	B.C.	Iowa	la.
California	Cal.	Kansas	Kan.
Canal Zone	C.Z.	Kentucky	Ky.
Colorado	Colo.	Louisiana	La.
Connecticut	Conn.	Maine	Me.
Delaware	Del.	Manitoba	Man.
District of Columbia	D.C.	Maryland	Md.
Florida	Fla.	Massachusetts	Mass.
Michigan	Mich.	Ontario	Ont.
Minnesota	Minn.	Pennsylvania	Pa.
Mississippi	Miss.	Philippine Islands	P.I.
Missouri	Mo.	Puerto Rico	P.R.
Montana	Mont.	Quebec	Que.
Nebraska	Neb.	Rhode Island	R.I.
Navada	Nev.	Saskatchewan	Sask.
New Bruswick	N.B.	South Carolina	S.C.
Newfoundland	N.F.	South Dakota	S.D.
New Hampshire	N.H.	Tennessee	Term.
New Jersey	N.J.	Texas	Tex.

Contd.....

New Mexico	N.M.	Utah	Utah
New York	N.Y.	Vermont	Vt.
North Carolina	N.C.	Virginia	Va.
North Dakota	N.D.	Washington	Wash.
Nova Scotia	N.S.	West Virgina	W.Va.
Ohio	Oh.	Wisconsin	Wis.
Oklahama	Okla.	Wyoming	Wyo.
Oregon	Ore.		

Abbreviation of Titles: Do not abbreviate a title which stands alone. Abbreviate titles which precedes either the full name or the surname.

Political Abbreviations: Abbreviate political parties (and states) when they follow the names of legislators, in this form:

Sen. Dirksen (R; III.) introduced the bill.

(Note that a period and a comma follow the "R" that a period follows the abbreviation of the state, and that both the political designation and the state identification are in fingernails.)

Use the following abbreviations for political parties: *Rep. Dev. Soc. (Socialist), Prog. (Progressive), F.-L. (Farmer-Labour), and A.-L. (America n-Labour).*

Addresses: Abbreviate (but do not capitalise) specific address designations such as *ave., blvd., ct., dr., pi, pkwy., rd., sq., St., and ten.* (But do not abbreviate *lane, way or highway.*)

Abbreviate (and capitalise) compass designation when used in street addresses: *N. Main St..*

Spell out numbered streets through nine and use figures for streets numbered 10 or more: *N. Ninth St.., N. 10th St..* (This one-through-nine rule also governs ordinals: first, 10th.)

Avoid confusion in contiguous figures by using *"of* when age is interposed between name and street number: *"Herbert L White, 38, of 1740 N. 38th St.."* When the age is not used, however, omit the word "of" before addresses: *"Herbert L White, 1740 N. 38th St., Philadelphia," "Herbert L. White, Philadelphia."*

Other Abbreviations: Abbreviate names of months containing more than four letters when date follows: Jan 1. (Not Jan. 1st). Do not abbreviate name of month when it is followed only by the year; *January, 1948.*

Abbreviate *Saint, Fort,* and Mount in geographical names: *St. Louis. Ft. Atkinson, Mt. Vernon.*

Abbreviate (and capitalise) organisation name which through usage have become widely known: GOP, CIO, AFL, YMCA, WCTU, VFW, NLRB, OPA, and others. Note that periods are omitted in these forms. Do not, however, omit periods in US and , U.N. where such abbreviations are permitted (which is in headlines only).

In using names of federal alphabetical agencies spell out , (without capitalisation) the full name of the agency the first time: it is used in a story and abbreviate it in succeeding references: "The war production board today authorised limited production of new automobiles. Full production will be under way in two years, WPB officials said."

Abbreviate using periods, military designations when used after names: *USA, USN, USNR, USMD, and ROTC.*

Abbreviate (without capitalisation) time designations: am, pm (Do not let the hour stand alone). Make it "Breakfast was served at 8 o'clock," not "Breakfast was served at 8." Don't make it "at 8:00 o'clock." Make it *"7.30 pm Monday," not* "7.30 o'clock Monday night," Spot the hour before the day: "at 7.30. *pm Monday," not'Monday at 7:30 pm."*

Abbreviate (and capitalise) the word "junior" when it is used with a name: *("Albert Jones Jr. spoke."* Note use of the period and omission of commas.)

Abbreviate "number" when followed by a numeral: "No. I," "No. *10", "rescue squad No. 3."*

Make it "Chicago *ave. police station;" "... at Wabash and Grand aves."*

Not to Abbreviate

President. Vice President.

Points of compass, except in street addresses. Days of week.

United States (US), except in headlines and designation of highway numbers.

United Nations (U.N.), except in headlines.

Chaplain.

Christmas. (Xmas. A tip to copy readers: Use "Yule" in heads; it's half a unit shorter, too.)

Plural titles.

Auxiliary nouns when used as part of names: *Rollins College, North-Western Alumni association, Ford Motor Company, General Motors Corporation.*

(Note: The form for "incorporated" and for "limited," used with a corporate name, is abbreviated and capitalised: General Motor Inc., General Motor Ltd. Note use of comma before "Inc." and "Ltd.")

Capitalisation: Capitalise proper names, names of months, and days of week.

Capitalise titles preceding names: *Prof. Charles L. Allen of Northwestern university: Sen. Paul Douglas (D. III.).*

An occupational identification becomes a title when it precedes a name: Actress Arline Judge; Ash Hauler John Smith. In general, the preferred form is "Arline Judge, the actress" and "John Smith, an ash hauler."

A long title "reads" better when placed after a name instead of before it. "Peter White, acting assistant corporation counsel," is better than "Acting Assistant Corporation Counsel Peter White."

Capitalise names of sections of the country and special localities: *the East, the Middle-west, the North the West, and the South* (but not when used as compass points)", *North Shore, South Side, the Loop.*

Capitalise international groups which are working in concert, such as *Western powers* ("power" down), *the Big Four.*

Capitalise names of races and nationalities: Japanese, *Negro* (but not white).

Capitalise epithets standing alone or affixed to proper names: *Alexander the Great; Yankee; Wildcats.*

Capitalise abbreviations of college degrees: *B.A.; M.S.; Ph.D.* (But do not capitalise when degrees are spelled out).

Capitalise schools and colleges: *School of Journalism; College of liberal Arts; Law school.*

Capitalise figure, number, chapter, room, and similar forms, when followed by a number or by a letter: *Figure 30; No. 10, Chapter 111, Room 18, Room A.*

Capitalise (and abbreviate, using periods) *R.F.D.* ("rural free delivery") in referring to rural mail routes when the route number is used: *John Jones, R.F.D. 2.,.Elgin, III.*

Capitalise names of political parties and organisations: *Republican, Democrat, Progressive, Farmer-Labour, American-Labour, Communist, Fascist.* (But do not capitalise the adjectival forms: A republican form of government; a democratic form of government.) Capitalise principal words in titles of books, play, articles, poems, songs, and lectures, including the initial "A" *or* "The." Make it: The audience sang *"The Star Spangled Banner."* Not: The audience sang the "Star Spangled Banner."

Capitalise nicknames of cities, states, athletic organisations, and persons.

Use parentheses but not quote marks when nickname is used with a person's name: Charles (Butch) Jones. If nickname is used in subsequent references, make it Butch, not (Butch). Capitalise names of religious denominations and pronouns referring to a deity: *the New Testament; the Bible; the Koran; the Book of Genesis; God; Christ; Catholic; Protestant.*

Capitalise the distinguishing names of holidays and festivals: Labour day ("day" is *lower case); Thanksgiving day; Christmas eve; Christmas day; New Year's eve* (note apostrophe); *the Fourth of Inly.*

Capitalise *President,* when referring to President of the United States, even when the title is standing alone. (This is the only title capitalised when standing alone.)

Capitalise *World War I, World War II, Revolutionary war,* and *Civil war.* (Note that "war" is lower case in the latter two) Capitalise *War of 1812.* Capitalise *Mexican war* and *Spanish-American war.*

To Capitalise

United Nations: Capitalise the distinguishing words, but not the general terms, in names of streets, schools, buildings, rivers, islands, canals, parks, churches, clubs and societies, courts, and business organisations. The following examples illustrate the style:

American Legion.
American Red Cross.
American Veterans of World War II. (This is the AMVESTS organisation.)
Boys' court.
Chicago river.
Circuit court.
Cook county Circuit court.
Com Exchange National bank.
District court.
Evanston Municipal court.
Evanston Township High School.
Ellis island.
Export-Import bank.
Federal District court.
Felony court.
First Baptist church.
Illinois highway 12.
Veterans of Foreign Wars.
Illinois Supreme court.
Kiwanis club.
Lincoln park.
New York Central lines.
North Shore Country Day school
Northwestern university.
Panama canal.
Pattern gymnasium.
Pure Oil building.
Reconstruction Finance corporation.
Red Cross.
Renter's court.
Sherman ave.
State St..
Traffic
Union padfic railway
Union station
United States Supreme Court.
US- highway 12.

Not to Capitalise: Do not capitalise titles used after names, except President when referring to the President of the United States. (Make it *"the King of England"; "the Prince of Wales"; "the Royal Princess" but "King George," "Princess Elizabeth.")*

Do not capitalise a title which stands alone (except President, referring to President of the United States).

Do not capitalise address designations: *St.., ave., blvd., pi, rd.,* and so on.

Do not capitalise seasons: *spring, summer, autumn, winter.*

Do not capitalise compass points: *east, west, south, north.*

Do not capitalise studies or departments in a school, except when proper nouns are used: *geology department; French department; English department.*

Do not capitalise college degrees when spelled out: *bachelor of science, doctor of philosophy.*

Do not capitalise scientific names of plants, animals, and birds, and common nouns that originally were proper nouns: *India rubber, bessemer steel, paris green.*

Do not capitalise breed names of animals: *collie doS, Shetland pony, poland china has, Shropshire Sheep, belgiam hare.*

Do not capitalise names of school classes: *freshman, sophomore.*

Do not capitalise common religious terms: *heaven, hell, devil, scriptures, biblical.*

Do not capitalise *am* or *pm.*

Do not capitalise names of boards, departments, political and legislative bodies, federal alphabetical agencies and bureaus, state agencies and committees.

The following examples illustrate the style:

army. (But Third Army, 10th	hook and ladder company No.2.
Army, when referring to specific	house of commons.
committee. *(When in doubt, lower case.)*	house of representative
Figures unit of the Army.)	(state and national).
boy scouts	house ways and means committee.
campfire girls.	Illinois national guard, marine corps.
chamber of deputies.	(But marine Raiders, Seabees.)
Chicago board of health.	municipal board, national labour
coast guard.	relations board, naval air corps,
congress.	navy. (But Sixth Naval district,
department of agriculture.	when referring to specific naval
department of the air force.	unit.) Parliament. rescue squad
department of the army.	No. 9. security council (of United
department of defence.	Nations). senate (state and
department of the navy.	national), senate foreign relations
engine company No. 4.	committee,
Evanston city council.	
federal bureau of investigation.	
federal communications	
commission.	
general assembly	
(a unit of United Nations).	(when in doubt, lower case,)

Figures: Numbers above nine are to be put in figures and those from one through nine are to be spelled out, with some exceptions. Use

figures for the following at all times:

Dates: *Jan.* 4

Temperature: *It was 7 below zero.*

Money: *A stick of gum costs 1 cent. A pencil costs* 5 *cents. A pen costs $5.*

Percentage: 6 *per cent.* ("Per cent" is two words, but "percentage" is one word. Do not use the per cent symbol in a news story, except in tabular form.)

Telephone numbers: *University 4-4757.* (Note omission of comma.)

Time of day. 1 *am*

Time in races: *5:07*

Longitude and latitude: He *reported reaching 7 degrees east longitude.*

Votes: *Davis,* 2; *Martin, 15.* (Note comma-semicolon construction.)

Betting odds: *The odds are* 3 to 1. Score; *The Wildcats won, 7 to 6.*

Ages: *John Smith, 5.* (Omit "year old" or "of age." In general, make it "John Smith, 5," not "5-year-old John Smith,")

Height of persons: *He is 6 feet 1 inch toll-* (Note omission of Dimensions: *The box was* 27 *feet by 14 feet. The box was 8 A feet by 10 feet by 4 feet. It was a 6-foot wall. The fish was 6 inches long.* Split out fractions/except after numerals; He *holds one-fourth share.* (Note use of hyphen.) He *holds nine and one-fourth shares. He holds 101/4 shares.*

Spell out round numbers (note exception to the one-through nine rule) when the numbers are millions or billions or are so great as to cause possible confusion when expressed in ciphers.

Make it *"6 million,'"* not'6,000,000" and not *"six million,"* Make "it "5 *million dollars,"* not "$5,000;00b./and not *"$5 million."* Make it "6½ *million dollars."* Make it *"10 million dollars/* not *"$10,000,000."*

Make it *"16 billion 400 million dollars,"* not *"$16,400,000,000."* But make it *"6,384,584,"* not "six million three hundred eighty-four thousand five hundred eighty-four."

Never begin a sentence with numerals; spell out the number. Make it *"Twelve persons were killed today...,"* not "12 persons were killed today..." If spelling out the numeral will result in an awkward sentence, recast the sentence so that it does not begin with a number.

Use the one-through-nine rule of ordinals: *First, second, ninth, 10th.* Make it *"22d,"* not "22nd" and *"33d,"* not "33rd". Make it *"31st"* and *"34th"*

Titles: Use a person's full name (preferably including the middle initial) the first time he is mentioned in a story: *"Herbert L Pitts. "Herbert Pitts"* is acceptable only if you cannot get the middle initial or if Pitts does not use a middle initial. *"H. L Pitts"* is acceptable if you can get the middle initial and not the first name. Shun the bobtail form "H. Pitts."

Omit "Mr." before last name when last name stands alone except in: 1) *obits,* or in 2) *reference to the President of the United States,* or in 3) *reference to a minister of the gospel.*

In referring to an unmarried woman, make it *"Miss Myrtle A. Ritts"* or "Miss *Myrtle Ritts,"* not *"Miss M.A. Ritts."*

Write it *"Mr. and Mrs. Herbert L. Pitts,"* not "Herbert L. Pitts and wife" or "Herbert and Myrtle Pitts."

Do not write it "Mrs. Dr. Herbert Pitts." The title belongs to the man.

In general, precede the full name of a woman with either the word "Miss" or the word *"Mrs."* Common sense will dictate some exceptions, however. For example, you could not identify Jane Russell, the actress, as "Miss Jane Russel, the film actress." Subsequent reference to her, however, would require her identification as "Miss Russell."

Rectification of Mistakes

This pretence of infallibility was absurd. Inaccurate reporting produced (and is producing) millions of wrong details, false accounts and not a few spectacularly duff stories. On the 15 April 1912, for instance, the *Baltimore Evening Sun* ran a story headlined 'All Titanic Passengers Safe'. On 3 November 1948, the *Chicago Daily Tribune* proclaimed 'Dewey defeats Truman' and on May 1983, *The Times* declared all over its front page 'Hitler's Secret Diaries to be published'.

As contemporaries knew very soon after each of these stories appeared, 1, 500 died on the Titanic, Harry Truman beat Dewey and the diaries were not written by Hitler but by a little German crook called Konny Fischer.

These days, newspapers of quality do admit mistakes and they put them right as soon as they can. They recognise that stories are written by fallible human beings under great pressure and without access to all the sources. Inevitably, some errors will creep in. They fall into one of six categories:

- Errors of detail-names, ages, addresses, etc.
- Errors of narrative - false part of an otherwise true account.
- Hoaxes and inventions - where the entire story is fiction.
- Errors of context-incorrect or missing background causing a false account.
- Errors of omission - an account made misleading by a missing part.
- Errors of interpretation - adding two and two and coming up with five.

The better papers such as the *Chicago Tribune* also have a system for recording and tracking mistakes, and attempting to put right any part of their processes that caused the error. Such papers have learnt a great deal about how mistakes arise, and who makes them. And the truth is that no group of journalists produce more errors than reporters. According to surveys carried out at The *Guardian* and the *Fort Worth Star-Telegram* in Texas, reporters made half the errors that were published. (Copy editors were responsible for about one mistake in five.) This is an important insight for the papers and even more for individual writers; for nothing destroys a reporter's reputation faster (or more comprehensively) than a record of generating errors.

Reporters serious about not falling into this category should realise two things. First that the accuracy of their stories is their responsibility and is not something that can be passed up the production chain to a news editor or copy editor. Second, train yourself to be so aware of how errors creep in that checking for these potential ambushes becomes second nature. Learn not just from your mistakes but also from those of others. When you see a correction in a paper, think of how it might have occurred.

There are eight main causes of errors in stories:

False Information from Sources: With simple facts like names, dates and ages there is said to be not a lot you can do about wrong information. I disagree. You can double-check, ask yourself if the source is in a position to know what they are telling, listen out for the tell-tale clues to uncertainty ('I think...', '...probably...', ,...or so I was told...', etc.) and ask if the information sounds plausible. Often a little reflection will tell you that it does not. A related source of error is to take information given to you (perhaps in the midst of an as yet unclear situation) and present it as unattributed fact, rather than a sourced contention. This was where the *Titanic* error was made, because the papers took on trust assurances from the ship's owners, the White Star Line, and did not attribute them when reporting the passengers were all saved.

Poor Note-taking: Shaky notes – from an uncertain shorthand outline to a long-hand word that could be this or could be that – often make shaky stories. Time to brush up on the shorthand or handwriting. And don't guess what sources meant – ask them again. Few will mind as much as you imagine, if at all. And learn to ask them to spell out, or write down, names.

Failure to Double-check Facts with Sources: Often one source tells you something that contradicts an earlier source. Check it, double check it and triple check it, if necessary. The same applies to working from documents. A few seconds checking that you have copied figures and names correctly will save untold grief.

Reluctance to Check 'Sensational' Facts or Developments: There is a smirking part of the culture of journalism which discourages reporters from checking too closely the more outrageous parts of stories, lest someone deny them or water them down. Such perilous idiocy flies in the face of generations of experience, which is that few stories are as straightforward, black and white, or outrageous as they first appear. If you were not born with healthy scepticism, acquire some.

Failure to Read a Story Once Written: We all make typing errors when working quickly, and we also have 'facts' in our heads that are not borne out by our notes. A read for accuracy (apart from one for style and possible cuts) stops a lot of these errors.

Failure to Listen to your Own Anxieties about a Story: Any experienced reporter knows the feeling of having a 'sensational' story, which will make big headlines, but about which they have some anxieties. It does not quite ring true, it does not fit with what you know of the world, etc. The mistake is to charge ahead, afraid that caution will rob you of front page glory. Instead, listen to those doubts. Most of the time they will prove correct. Many of the errors I have made were when my show-off ego would not heed the wise doubts of the sensible little journalist in my head.

Omission of Facts not Fitting with a Pre-conceived Theory: Making your mind up about a situation before knowing all the facts (although you can never know all the facts) is one of the great traps a journalist must perpetually fight to avoid. It is an ever-present danger on major incident stories, for there is then great pressure to deliver both a seemingly all-knowing account and a pat explanation for the incident.

Rushing into Print too Early: This was the mistake with the Hitler Diaries. The anxiety to protect an exclusive property (exacerbated by the belief within News International that, ultimately, entertainment and not truth was the object of journalism) meant that the story was published before all the scientific checks were made. This fear of being scooped rushed Murdoch into sanctioning publication, despite strongly expressed misgivings by some of his most senior *Sunday Times* journalists. The pitfalls of dashing into print with a story that is far more emphatic than the evidence warrants is a frequent cause of major errors on stories large and small. The moral is obvious - publish only that of which you are certain.

(Note the absence of fatigue and inexperience from this list. They are not causes of errors, but excuses for them.)

Finally, for reporters who think the importance of accuracy is not quite all it's cracked up to be, a sobering story. It appeared in the *C-Ville Weekly,* a tabloid circulating in Charlottesville, Virginia. It told of the discovery by a female health club client of a two-way mirror that had been installed in the women's changing room. The paper also carried pictures and detailed graphics. The story went on to speculate freely (via quotes from a psychologist) about the motives of the person who had set up such a peephole. The story proved true in every detail, which was just as well because five days after it appeared, the owner of the health club was found dead in a local park. He had committed suicide. The repercussions for the reporter, had the story proved inaccurate in any way, hardly bear thinking about. The tale is a reminder that, since you never know the effects your stories can have, they had better be correct.

'Quickly and with candour' is the answer. This applies in spades if, as is often the case, you realise your mistake before anyone else does. Move speedily - there may be time to correct the mistake before the story is published, or, on larger papers, to correct between editions. Even if it is too late, a prompt confession (and, if the mistake is bad enough, contacting the source affected) will help to mitigate the consequences for the paper legally and for you personally. My experience is that, providing the error is not too crass, journalists who speedily hold their hands up and take responsibility emerge with reputations far less damaged than those who lurk in the shadows waiting to be unmasked. Those are the ones who are sacked.

With complaints from outside the paper, the first thing is to establish that the 'mistake' definitely is one. Sources often try it on, especially those whose openness with you may have caused them trouble within their own organisation. Many claims, especially of misquotation, prove to be nothing more than sources trying to cover their tracks.

Once an error has been established, a speedy correction should be published, preferably in a regular place. Some papers, such as the *Mobile Register* in Alabama, run all corrections on page one. At the Cleveland *Plain Dealer*, the correction goes as close as it can to where the original mistake was published and is indexed on page 2. The *Augusta Chronicle* does the same and, if the mistake occurs on page 1, then that's where the correction goes. Such policies are not an admission of weakness, but a simple matter of honesty and better informing the reader.

(Promptness is another virtue in corrections, but on a few occasions newspapers have not been deterred by the passage of time. In 1920 the *New York Times* publicly ridiculed Professor Robert Goddard, the father of space exploration, for his claim that rockets could operate in a vacuum. Some 49 years later, when Apollo 1.1 carried the first men to the moon, the *Times* published the following: 'It is now definitely established that a rocket can function in a vacuum. The *Times* regrets its error.' The record, however, is the 199 years that elapsed between the *Observer* of London reporting the death of Mozart as having happened on 5 December 1791 and it correcting this date to 3 December in early 1991.)

Honesty is not the only motive in correcting errors. Avoiding a law suit is also a pretty powerful reason for prompt correction. Some years ago, the following appeared in an Irish newspaper: 'In the edition of the *Sunday Press* dated March 18, 1990 a photograph of Proinsias De Rossa TD was published with the caption "prospective monster". This should have read "prospective minister".' Similarly an English local paper ran this correction to a court report: '"Father head butts his son" should have read, "Father head butts his son's attacker".'

You can almost hear the rustle of potential legal proceedings in the distance as you read these corrections. No doubt the editors who ordered them into print were well aware that speedy correction can help stave off a defamation lawsuit, or at least form part of the subsequent defence.

Gilbert Cranberg, the former editorial page editor of the *Des Moines Register*, who surveyed 164 libel plaintiffs in 1987, found that most people who sued for libel did not originally want money.

They wanted a correction. Only after they were brushed off by the paper did they then go to law.

However, unless corrections are being carried at the point of a lawyer's writ, they merely have to recall the mistake and amend it. There is no need to grovel, promise you won't do it again, apologise or launch into an explanation of how it was the regular editor's night off and his assistant was feeling under the weather. A few publications, like *American Lawyer,* actually name the reporter and editor who made the mistake. Others, like the *San Jose Mercury News,* go the other way and have eliminated any words of blame such as 'due to an editing error', etc. And there is, somewhere, a limit to what can be sensibly corrected. For instance, on the day after it carried a review of a new cartoon film, the *Boston Globe* carried the following: 'In our film review yesterday, statements made by Sylvester the Cat were erroneously attributed to Daffy Duck.'

Finally, factual errors are easy to correct; other types less so. Many complaints to newspapers centre on inappropriate or missing context, or a missing element which alters the overall story or the impression it gives. For these, papers can offer space in the letters page, or, more rarely, comment columns. To deal with such cases, the *New York Times* runs an Editors' Note to 'amplify articles or rectify what the editors consider significant lapses of fairness, balance or perspective.' It publishes about 2 5 of them annually. It is a useful device that deserves to be more widely copied.

Bibliography

Adams, Kenneth A.: *A Manual of Style for Contract Drafting*, ABA, Section of Business Law, Chicago, 2004.

Alexandre, Pierre: *Languages and Language in Black Africa*, Northwestern University Press, Evanston, 1972.

Alfred, Fairbank: *The Story of Handwriting: Origins and Development*, Watson-Guptill, New York, 1970.

Armstrong, Stephen V. and Timothy P. Terrell: *Thinking Like a Writer: A Lawyer's Guide to Effective Writing and Editing*, Practising Law Institute, New York, 2003.

Astle, T.: *The Origin and Progress of Writing*, AMS Press, New York, 1973.

Bahrych, Lynn and Marjorie Dick Rombauer: *Legal Writing in a Nutshell*, Thomson, St. Paul, 2003.

Ballhorn, F.: *Grammatography: A Manual of Reference to the Alphabets of Ancient and Modern Languages*, Trubner & Co., London, 1861.

Bazerman, Charles: *Handbook of Research on Writing: History, Society, School, Individual, Text*, Lawrence Erlbaum Associates, New York, 2008.

Berlitz, Charles: *Native Tongues*, Grosset & Dunlap, New York, 1982.

Bernal, Martin: *Cadmean Letters*, Eisenbrauns, Winona Lake, 1990.

Berring, Robert C.: *The Bluebook: A Uniform System of Citation*, Harvard Law Review Association, Cambridge, 2005.

Bliss, C.K.: *Semantography (Blissymbolics): A Logical Writing for an Illogical World*, Semantography Publications, Australia, 1965.

Bodmer, Frederick: *The Loom of Language*, W.W. Norton & Co., New York, 1944.

Brown, Michelle P.: *The British Library Guide to Writing and Scripts: History and Technique*, University of Toronto Press, Toronto, 1998.

Buhler-Oppenheim, Kristin: *Signs, Brands, Marks*, Communication Arts Books, New York, 1971.

Burns, Alfred: *The Power of the Written Word: The Role of Literacy in the History of Western Civilization*, Peter Lang, New York, 1989.

Canepari, Luciano: *Phonetic Notation*, Libreria Editrice Cafoscarina, Italy, 1983.

Carter, M. L. and Schoville K. N.: *Sign, Symbol, Script: An Exhibition on the Origins of Writing and the Alphabet*, University of Wisconsin Press, Madison, 1984.

Chadwick, John: *Linear B and Related Scripts*, University of California Press, Berkeley, 1990.

_______________: *The Decipherment of Linear B.*, Cambridge University Press, Cambridge, 1990.

Chappell, Warren: *The Living Alphabet*, University Press of Virginia, Charlottesville, 1975.

Chiera, Edward: *They Wrote on Clay*, University of Chicago Press, Chicago, 1938.

Christin, Anne-Marie: *A History of Writing: From Hieroglyph to Multi-media*, Flammarion, Paris, 2002.

Claiborne, Robert: *The Birth of Writing*, Time-Life Books, Alexandria, 1974.

Cleator, P.E.: *Lost Languages*, John Day, New York, 1961.

Clodd, Edward: *The Story of the Alphabet*, Phillips & Co., New York, 1904.

Coulmas, Florian: *The Writing Systems of the World*, Basil Blackwell, New York, 1989.

_______________: *Writing Systems: An Introduction to their Linguistic Analysis*, Cambridge University Press, Cambridge, 2003.

Cutts, Martin: *Plain English Guide*, Oxford University Press, New York, 1996.

Daniels, Peter T. and Bright William: *The World's Writing Systems*, Oxford University Press, New York, 1996.

DeFrancis, John: *Visible Speech: The Diverse Oneness of Writing Systems*, University of Hawaii Press, Honolulu, 1989.

DeKerckhove, Derrick and Lumsden Charles J.: *The Alphabet and the Brain: The Lateralization of Writing*, Springer-Verlag, Berlin, 1988.

Diringer, David: *A History of the Alphabet*, Unwin Brothers Ltd., England, 1977.

————————: *The Alphabet: A Key to the History of Mankind*, Funk & Wagnalls, New York, 1998.

Doblehofer, Ernst: *Voices in Stone: The Decipherment of Ancient Scripts and Writings*, Viking, New York, 1961.

Driver, Godfrey Rolles: *Semitic Writing: From Pictograph to Alphabet*, Oxford University Press, London, 1976.

Drucker, Johanna: *Figuring the Word: Essays on Books, Writing and Visual Poetics*, Granary Books, New York, 1998.

————————: *The Alphabetic Labyrinth: The Letters in History and Imagination*, Thames & Hudson, London, 1995.

Fabre, Maurice: *A History of Communication*, Hawthorne, New York, 1963.

Firmage, Richard A.: *The Alphabet Abecedarium: Some notes on Letters*, David R. Godine, Boston, 1993.

Fischer, Judith D.: *Pleasing the Court: Writing Ethical and Effective Briefs*, Carolina Academic Press, Durham, 2005.

Fischer, Steven Roger: *A History of Writing*, Reaktion Books, London, 2001.

Fisher, Leonard E.: *Letter Art*, Four Winds Press, New York, 1977.

————————: *Number Art*, Four Winds Press, New York, 1982.

————————: *Symbol Art*, Four Winds Press, New York, 1985.

Fishman, Joshua: *Advances in the Creation and Revision of Writing Systems*, Mouton & Co., Netherlands, 1977.

Foreman, Grant: *Sequoyah*, University of Oklahoma Press, Norman, 1938.

——————: *Writing Systems*, Ginn & Co., Boston, 1965.

Friedrich, Johannes: *Geschichte der Schrift*, Carl Winter / Universitats Verlag, Germany, 1966.

Frutiger, Adrian: *Signs and Symbols: Their Design and Meaning*, Van Nostrand Reinhold, New York, 1989.

Fry, Edmund: *Pantographia*, Sherwin & Freutel, Los Angeles, 1970.

Ganguly, Subrata: *Symbol, Script and Writing: From Petrogram to Printing and Further*, Sharada, Dehli, 2004.

Garner, Bryan A.: *A Dictionary of Modern Legal Usage*, Oxford University Press, New York, 1995.

——————: *Elements of Legal Style*, Oxford University Press, New York, 1991.

——————: *Legal Writing in Plain English: A Text with Exercises*, University of Chicago Press, Chicago, 2001.

——————: *The Winning Brief: 100 Tips for Persuasive Briefing in Trial and Appellate Courts*, The American Law Institute, Philadelphia, 2004.

Gaur, Alberine: *Literacy and the Politics of Writing*, Intellect Books, Bristol, 2000.

——————: *A History of Writing*, Charles Scribner's Sons, New York, 1984.

Gelb, I.J.: *A Study of Writing*, University of Chicago Press, Chicago, 1974.

George, Joyce J.: *Judicial Opinion Writing Handbook*, William S. Hein, Buffalo, 2000.

Gerstner, Karl: *Compendium for Literates*, Massachusetts Institute of Technology Press, Cambridge, 1974.

Gilyarevsky, R.S. and Grivnin V.S.: *Languages Identification Guide*, Nauka Publishing, Moscow, 1970.

Godin, Seth: *The Smiley Dictionary: Cool Things to do with your Keyboard*, Peachpit Press, Berkeley, 1993.

Gordon, Cyrus H.: *Forgotten Scripts: Their Ongoing Discovery and Decipherment*, Basic Books, New York, 1982.

Haas, W.: *Alphabets for English*, Manchester University Press, Manchester, 1969.

————————: *Writing without Letters*, Rowman & Littlefield, New Jersey, 1976.

Haggard, Thomas R.: *Legal Drafting in a Nutshell*, Thomson, St. Paul, 2003.

————————: *Good Writing as a Professional Responsibility*, Scribes Journal of Legal Writing, 2002.

Harris, Roy: *The Origin of Writing*, Gerald Duckworth & Co., Ltd, London, 1986.

Havelock, Eric A.: *Origins of Western Literacy*, Ontario Institute for Studies in Education, Toronto, 1976.

Healy, John F.: *The Early Alphabet*, University of California Press, Berkeley, 1991.

Helfman, Elizabeth S.: *Blissymbolics: Speaking without Speech*, Elsevier/Nelson Books, New York, 1981.

Hofsinde, Robert: *Indian Picture Writing*, William Morrow & Co, New York, 196?.

Hofstadter, Douglas R.: *Doughalese & the Semiotic Mystery*, Cambridge University Mathematical Society, Cambridge, 1988.

————————: *Metamagical Themas: Questing for the Essence of Mind and Pattern*, Basic Books, New York, 1985.

————————: *Letter Spirit in Fluid Concepts and Creative Analogies: Computer Models of the Fundamental Mechanisms of Thought*, Basic Books/HarperCollins, New York, 1995.

Holmes, Ruth B. and Smith Betty S.: *Beginning Cherokee*, University of Oklahoma Press, Norman, 1978.

Hooker, J.T.: *Reading the Past: Ancient writing from Cuneiform to the Alphabet*, University of California Press, Berkeley, 1990.

Hoskins, R.F. and Meredith-Owens, G.M.: *A Handbook of Asian Scripts*, The Trustees of the British Museum, London, 1966.

Houston, Stephen D.: *The First Writing: Script Invention as History and Process*, Cambridge University Press, Cambridge, 2004.

Humez, Alexander and Nicholas: *A B C et Cetera: The Life and Times of the Roman Alphabet*, David R. Godine, Boston, 1985.

——————: *Alpha to Omega: The Life and Times of the Greek Alphabet*, David R. Godine, Boston, 1981.

Illich, Ivan and Sanders Barry: *The Alphabetization of the Popular Mind*, North Point Press, San Francisco, 2002.

Irwin, Keith Gordon: *The Romance of Writing*, Viking, New York, 1961.

Jackson, Donald: *The Story of Writing*, Taplinger Publishing Co., New York, 1981.

Jensen, Hans: *Sign, Symbol and Script: An Account of Man's Efforts to Write*, G.P. Putnam's Sons, New York, 1969.

Kannaiyan, I.: *Scripts in and Around India*, Madras Government Museum, Madras, 1956.

Katzner, Kenneth: *The Languages of the World*, Routledge & Kegan Paul, London, 1986.

Kellogg, Rhoda: *Analyzing Children's Art*, National Press Books, Palo Alto, 1970.

Klausner, Janet: *Sequoyah's Gift: A Portrait of the Cherokee Leader*, HarperCollins, New York, 1993.

Kluh, J.M.: *The Etymologic Cipher Alphabet*, J.M. Kluh, Chicago, 1922.

Lee, Debra S. and Marsha Hurley: *American Legal English: Using Language in Legal Contexts*, University of Michigan Press, Ann Arbor, 1999.

LeGuin, Ursula: *Always Coming Home*, Harper & Row, New York, 1985.

Logan, Robert K.: *The Alphabet Effect*, William Morrow & Co., New York, 1986.

Machet, Anne: *Ecriture, Typographie, Pedagogie: Proceedings of the International Center for Applied Linguistics*, L'Ecole des Beaux-Arts de Besancon, Besancon, 1982.

Man, John: *Alpha Beta: How 26 Letters Shaped the Western World*, John Wiley & Sons, New York, 2000.

Manguel, Alberto: *A History of Reading*, Viking/Penguin, New York, 1996.

Martin, Henri-Jean: *The History and Power of Writing*, Univ. of Chicago Press, Chicago, 1999.

Martlew, Margaret: *The Psychology of Written Language: Developmental and Educational Perspectives*, John Wiley & Sons, New York, 1983.

Mason, William: *History of the Art of Writing*, The McMillan Co., New York, 1920.

McGrath, Alister: *In the Beginning: The Story of the King James Bible*, Doubleday/Random House, New York, 2001.

Mercer, Samuel A.: *Assyrian Grammar*, Frederick Ungar, New York, 1961.

————: *The Origin of Writing and our Alphabet*, Luzac & Co., London, 1951.

Miller, Jonathan: *Marshall McLuhan*, Viking, New York, 1971.

Moore, Hyatt: *The Alphabet Makers*, Summer Institute of Linguistics, Huntington Beach, 1991.

Moorhouse, A.C.: *The Triumph of the Alphabet: A History of Writing*, Henry Schuman, New York, 1953.

Moran, Hugh A. and Kelley, David H.: *The Alphabet and the Ancient Calendar Signs*, Daily Press, Palo Alto, 1969.

Morison, Stanley: *Politics and Script: Aspects of Authority and Freedom*, Clarendon Press, Oxford, 1972.

Moss, Miriam: *Language and Writing*, The Bookwright Press, New York, 1988.

Myller, Rolf: *Symbols and their Meaning*, Atheneum, New York, 1980.

Nakanishi, Akira: *Writing Systems of the World: Alphabets, Syllabaries, Pictograms*, Chas. E. Tuttle, Rutland, 1980.

Nasr, Seyyed H.: *The Spritual Message of Islamic Calligraphy*, SUNY Press, Albany, 1987.

Naveh, Joseph: *Early History of the Alphabet*, The Magnes Press/ Hebrew University, Jerusalem, 1982.

Nilsen, Don L.: *Language Play*, Newbury House, Rowley, 1987.

Noel, Ruth S.: *The Languages of Tolkien's Middle-Earth*, Houghton Mifflin, Boston, 1980.

Norman, James: *Ancestral Voices: Decoding Ancient Languages*, Four Winds Press, New York, 1975.

Ogg, Oscar: *An Alphabet Sourcebook*, Harper & Brothers, New York, 1940.

Olson, David R.: *The World on Paper: The Conceptual and Cognitive Implications ofWriting and Reading*, Cambridge University Press, England, 1994.

Oppenheim, Joanne: *Sequoyah: Cherokee Hero*, Troll Associates, Mahwah, 1979.

Ouaknin, Marc-Alain: *Mysteries of the Alphabet: The Origins of Writing*, Abbeville Press, New York, 1999.

Page, R.I.: *Runes: Reading the Past*, University of California Press, Berkeley, 1987.

Petrucci, Armand: *Public Lettering: Script, Power and Culture*, University of Chicago Press, Chicago, 1993.

Prince, Mary Miles: *Prince's Dictionary of Legal Citations: A Reference Guide for Attorneys, Legal Secretaries, Paralegals and Law Students*, Williams S. Hein, Buffalo, 2006.

Pullum, Geoffrey K. and Ladusaw, William A.: *Phonetic Symbol Guide*, University of Chicago Press, Chicago, 1986.

Rahi, Ishwar Chandra: *World Slphabets: Their Origin And Development*, Bharagava Printing, India, 1977.

Rambo, Teresa J. Reid and Leanne J. Pflaum: *Legal Writing by Design: A Guide to Great Briefs and Memos*, Carolina Academic Press, Durham, 2001.

Rees, Ennis: *The Little Greek Alphabet Book*, Prentice-Hall, Englewood Cliffs, 1968.

Reisner, R.: *Graffiti: Two Thousand Years of Wall Writing*, Cowles Books, New York, 1971.

Reynolds, Henry J.: *The World's Oldest Writings*, The Antiquitas Corp, Chicago, 1938.

Reynolds, Lloyd J.: *Straight Impressions*, TBW Books, Woolwich, 1979.

Robinson, Andrew: *Lost Languages: The Enigma of the World's Undeciphered Scripts*, Nevraumont/McGraw-Hill, New York, 2002.

————: *The Story of Writing*, Thames & Hudson, London, 1995.

Rogers, Henry: *Writing Systems: A Linguistic Approach*, Blackwell, Oxford, 1965.

Rohr, Heinz Markus: *Writing: Its Evolution and Relation to Speech*, Universitätsverlag, Germany, 1994.

Rovin, Jeff: *Transgalactic Guide to Solar System M-17*, Perigee/G.P. Putnam's., New York, 1981.

Sacks, David: *Language Visible: Unraveling the Mystery of the Alphabet from A to Z*, New York: Broadway Books, 2003.

Saljo, Roger: *The Written Word: Studies in Literate Thought and Action*, Springer-Verlag, Berlin, 1988.

Samoyault, Tiphaine: *Alphabetical Order: How the Alphabet Began?*, Viking/Penguin, New York, 1998.

Sampson, Geoffrey: *Writing Systems: A Linguistic Introduction*, Stanford University Press, Stanford, 1985.

Scheiss, Wayne: *Better Legal Writing: 15 Topics for Advanced Legal Writers*, W.S. Hein, Buffalo, 2005.

————: *Writing for the Legal Audience*, Carolina Academic Press, Durham, 2003.

Schmandt-Besserat, Denise: *Before Writing*, University of Texas Press, Austin, 1992.

Scinto, Leonard F.M.: *Written Language and Psychological Development*, Academic Press, Orlando, 1986.

Scott, Kim: *Inversions: A Catalog of Calligraphic Cartwheels*, BYTE Books (McGraw Hill), Peterborough, 1981.

Scribner, S. and Cole M.: *The Psychology of Literacy*, Harvard University Press, Cambridge, 1981.

Sears, Peter: *Secret Writing: Keys to the Mysteries of Reading and Writing*, Teachers & Writers Collaborative, New York, 1986.

Senner, Wayne M.: *The Origins of Writing*, University of Nebraska Press, Lincoln, 1989.

Siviglia, Peter: *Writing Contracts: A Distinct Discipline*, Carolina Academic Press, Durham, 1996.

Small, Daniel and Robin Page West: *Letters for Litigators: Essential Communications for Opposing Counsel, Witnesses, Clients and Others*, GP/Solo, ABA General Practice, Chicago, 2004.

Smalley, William A.: *Orthography Studies*, United Bible Society, London, 1964.

Sommer, F.E.: *The Arabic Writing in Five Lessons*, Frederick Ungar, New York, 1942.

Southerland, H.P.: *English as a Second Language – Or Why Lawyers Can't Write*, Thomas Law Review, 2005.

Spencer, Herbert: *Pioneers of Modern Typography*, Hastings House/ Visual Communications Books, New York, 1969.

——————: *The Visible Word*, Visual Communications Books/ Hastings House, New York, 1968.

Stark, Tina L.: *Negotiating and Drafting Contract Boilerplate*, ALM Pub., New York, 2003.

Sterba, M. John: *Drafting Legal Opinion Letters*, Wiley Law Publications, New York, 2001.

Stevens, John: *Sacred Calligraphy of the East*, Shambhala, Boulder, 1981.

Stryker-Rodda, Harriet: *Understanding Colonial Handwriting*, Geneological Publishing, Baltimore, 1986.

Swann, Donald and Tolkien, J.R.R.: *The Road Goes Ever on: A Song Cycle*, Houghton-Mifflin, New York, 1978.

Thornton, Tamara Plakins: *Handwriting in America: A Cultural History*, Yale University Press, New Haven, 1996.

Top, Alsexander: *The Olive Leaf*, The Scolar Press, Ltd, England, 1971.

Tschichold, Jan: *An Illustrated History of Writing and Lettering*, Columbia University Press, New York, 1948.

Tsuen-Hsuin, Tsien: *Written on Bamboo and Silk: The Beginnings of Chinese Books and Inscriptions,* University of Chicago Press, Chicago, 1962.

Ullman, B.L.: *Ancient Writing and its Influence,* Cooper Square Publishers, New York, 1963.

Vachek, Josef: *Written Language,* John Benjamins, Amsterdam, 1989.

Vinson, Kathleen Elliott: *Improving Legal Writing: A Life-Long Learning Process and Continuing Professional Challenge,* Touro Law Review, 2005.

Walker, C.B.F.: *Cuneiform: Reading the Past,* University of California Press, Berkeley, 1987.

Walsh, Michael G.: *Legal Consequences of Poor or Ungrammatical Writing,* The Practical Lawyer, 2006.

Watt, W.C.: *Writing Systems and Cognition: Perspectives from Psychology, Physiology, Linguistics and Semiotics,* Kluwer Academic Publishers, Boston, 1994.

Welman, William S.: *African Language Structure,* University of California Press, Berkeley, 1973.

Wemyss, Stanley: *The Languages of the World,* Author, Philadelphia, 1950.

Whiteman, M.F.: *Writing: The Nature, Development and Teaching of Written Communication,* L. Erlbaum, Hillsdale, 1981.

Wydick, Richard S.: *Plain English for Lawyers,* Carolina Academic Press, Durham, 1998.

Zapf, Hermann: *About Alphabets: Some Marginal notes on Type Design,* MIT Press, Cambridge, 1970.

Index

F

G

H

I

J

K

L

M

❑❑❑